Seventh Workshop on Computational Models of Reference, Anaphora and Coreference (CRAC 2024)

Miami, Florida, USA
15 November 2024

ISBN: 979-8-3313-0843-8

Printed from e-media with permission by:

Curran Associates, Inc.
57 Morehouse Lane
Red Hook, NY 12571

Printed with permission by Curran Associates, Inc. (2025)

Association for Computational Linguistics
209 N. Eighth Street
Stroudsburg, Pennsylvania 18360

Phone: 1-570-476-8006
Fax: 1-570-476-0860

acl@aclweb.org

Additional copies of this publication are available from:

Curran Associates, Inc.
57 Morehouse Lane
Red Hook, NY 12571 USA
Phone: 845-758-0400
Fax: 845-758-2633
Email: curran@proceedings.com
Web: www.proceedings.com

CRAC 2024

The Seventh Workshop on Computational Models of Reference, Anaphora and Coreference

Proceedings of the Workshop

November 15, 2024

Order copies of this and other ACL proceedings from:

Association for Computational Linguistics (ACL)
209 N. Eighth Street
Stroudsburg, PA 18360
USA
Tel: +1-570-476-8006
Fax: +1-570-476-0860
acl@aclweb.org

Message from the Program Chairs

Time flies. This is already the seventh edition of the Workshop on Computational Models of Reference, Anaphora and Coreference (CRAC). After two consecutive years in Asia, CRAC returned to North America this year.

Here is a bit of history for those of you who are participating in the workshop for the first time. CRAC was first held in New Orleans six years ago in conjunction with NAACL HLT 2018. The workshop series, however, dates back to its predecessor, Coreference Resolution Beyond OntoNotes (CORBON), which started in 2016 and has arguably become the primary forum for coreference researchers to present their latest results since the demise of the Discourse Anaphora and Anaphor Resolution Colloquium series in 2011. While CORBON focused on under-investigated coreference phenomena, CRAC has a broader scope, covering all cases of computational modeling of reference, anaphora, and coreference.

To facilitate the planning of the workshop, we decided in late 2019 that starting in 2020, CRAC would be held towards the end of each calendar year. Since then, we have received a healthy number of submissions every year, until this year when the number of submissions was lower than expected. Specifically, we received eight submissions, all of which were rigorously reviewed by three to four program committee members. Based on their recommendations, we accepted six papers and conditionally accepted one paper. The one conditionally accepted paper was eventually accepted to the workshop after we made sure that the authors adequately addressed the reviewers' comments in the final camera-ready version. While we are still investigating the reasons for the decline in the number of submissions, we speculate that the proximity of the CRAC submission deadline to the COLING 2025 submission deadline might have played a role.

This year we continued to partner with our colleagues at Charles University, Prague and hosted the shared task on *Multilingual Coreference Resolution* for the third time at CRAC. The shared task allowed researchers who did not participate in the workshop to disseminate their work to a smaller and more focused audience which should promote interesting discussions. In a departure from last year, we decided to merge the shared task proceedings with the CRAC workshop proceedings this year. In other words, you can enjoy both the workshop papers and the shared task papers in this proceedings.

We are grateful to the following people, without whom we could not have assembled an interesting program for the workshop. First, we are indebted to our program committee members. This year the average reviewing load was three papers per reviewer. All of our program committee members did the incredible job of completing their reviews in a short reviewing period. Second, we thank Jackie Chi-Kit Cheung, an established researcher in Discourse and Coreference, for accepting our invitation to be this year's invited speaker. Those of us who care about the future of coreference would not want to miss our panel discussion on "Coreference resolution in the era of LLMs," which will be led by our colleagues from Prague. Finally, we would like to thank the workshop participants for joining us in this event.

We hope you will enjoy the workshop and sunny Miami as much as we do!

— Sameer Pradhan, Maciej Ogrodniczuk, Michal Novák, Massimo Poesio, and Vincent Ng

Organizers

Organizing Committee:

Maciej Ogrodniczuk, Institute of Computer Science, Polish Academy of Sciences, Poland
Anna Nedoluzhko, Charles University in Prague, Czechia
Massimo Poesio, Queen Mary University of London, UK
Sameer Pradhan, `cemantix.org`, USA
Vincent Ng, University of Texas at Dallas, USA

Program Committee:

Arie Cattan, Bar-Ilan University, Israel
Sobha Lalitha Devi, Anna University of Chennai, India
Elisa Ferracane, Abridge
Yulia Grishina, Amazon, USA
Christian Hardmeier, IT University of Copenhagen, Denmark
Lars Hellan, Norwegian University of Science and Technology, Norway
Veronique Hoste, Ghent University, Belgium
Ekaterina Lapshinova-Koltunski, University of Hildesheim, Germany
Sharid Loáiciga, University of Gothenburg, Sweden.
Costanza Navaretta, University of Copenhagen, Denmark
Michal Novák, Charles University in Prague, Czechia
Massimo Poesio, Queen Mary University of London, UK
Ian Porada, Mila–Quebec Artificial Intelligence Institute, Canada
Carolyn Rosé, Carnegie Mellon University, USA
Juntao Yu, University of Essex, UK
Amir Zeldes, Georgetown University, USA
Yilun Zhu, Georgetown University, USA

Invited Talk

Reference at the Heart of Natural Language Processing

Jackie Chi Kit Cheung, McGill University, Montreal, Canada

Abstract

Natural language is traditionally framed as a mapping from form to content, with reference being the connection between the two. Yet curiously, large language models have achieved impressive levels of performance and adoption through training on distributional signals, which concerns form alone. In this talk, I argue for the importance of reference and coreference in NLP, and discuss topics in NLP which are touched by these phenomena, including model "hallucinations" and factual errors, knowledge updating, common sense reasoning, and conversational agents. I discuss how existing evaluation practices based on large-scale benchmarking often masks the importance of reference-related phenomena, and present work from my lab that reflects on current evaluation practices and their validity. I call for more serious consideration of reference including targeted evaluation of reference-related phenomena as a necessary step towards achieving robust NLP systems.

Speaker Bio

Jackie Chi Kit Cheung is an associate professor at McGill University's School of Computer Science, where he co-directs the Reasoning and Learning Lab. He is a Canada CIFAR AI Chair and an Associate Scientific Co-Director at the Mila Quebec AI Institute. His research focuses on topics in natural language generation such as automatic summarization, and on integrating diverse knowledge sources into NLP systems for pragmatic and common-sense reasoning. He also works on applications of NLP to domains such as education, health, and language revitalization. He is motivated by how the structure of the world can be reflected in the structure of language processing systems. He is a consulting researcher at Microsoft Research Montreal.

Table of Contents

Workshop Program

Friday, November 15, 2024

Opening Remarks

09:00–09:15 *Opening and Welcome*
Vincent Ng, Maciej Ogrodniczuk

Invited Talk

09:15–10:30 *Reference at the Heart of Natural Language Processing*
Jackie Chi Kit Cheung

Short Break

10:30–11:00 *Coffee Break*

Findings Paper Session

11:00–11:20 *Challenges to Evaluating the Generalization of Coreference Resolution Models: A Measurement Modeling Perspective*
Ian Porada, Alexandra Olteanu, Kaheer Suleman, Adam Trischler and Jackie Chi Kit Cheung

11:20–11:40 *Any Other Thoughts, Hedgehog? Linking Deliberation Chains in Collaborative Dialogues*
Abhijnan Nath, Videep Venkatesha, Mariah Bradford, Avyakta Chelle, Austin Collin Youngren, Carlos Mabrey, Nathaniel Blanchard and Nikhil Krishnaswamy

11:40–11:50 *MMAR: Multilingual and Multimodal Anaphora Resolution in Instructional Videos*
Cennet Oguz, Pascal Denis, Simon Ostermann, Emmanuel Vincent, Natalia Skachkova and Josef van Genabith

Friday, November 15, 2024 (continued)

EMNLP Paper

11:50–12:10 *Major Entity Identification: A Generalizable Alternative to Coreference Resolution*
Kawshik S. Manikantan, Shubham Toshniwal, Makarand Tapaswi and Vineet Gandhi

Long Break

12:10–13:50 *Lunch Break*

Research Paper Session

13:50–14:00 *Enriching Conceptual Knowledge in Language Models through Metaphorical Reference Explanation*
Zixuan Zhang and Heng Ji

14:00–14:10 *Polish Coreference Corpus as an LLM Testbed: Evaluating Coreference Resolution within Instruction-Following Language Models by Instruction–Answer Alignment*
Karol Saputa, Angelika Peljak-Łapińska and Maciej Ogrodniczuk

14:10–14:30 *MSCAW-coref: Multilingual, Singleton and Conjunction-Aware Word-Level Coreference Resolution*
Houjun Liu, John Bauer, Karel D'Oosterlinck, Christopher Potts and Christopher D. Manning

14:30–14:50 *Unifying the Scope of Bridging Anaphora Types in English: Bridging Annotations in ARRAU and GUM*
Lauren Levine and Amir Zeldes

14:50–15:10 *WinoPron: Revisiting English Winogender Schemas for Consistency, Coverage, and Grammatical Case*
Vagrant Gautam, Julius Steuer, Eileen Bingert, Ray Johns, Anne Lauscher and Dietrich Klakow

15:10–15:30 *DeepHCoref: A Deep Neural Coreference Resolution for Hindi Text*
Kusum Lata, Pardeep Singh, Kamlesh Dutta and Abhishek Kanwar

Friday, November 15, 2024 (continued)

Short Break

15:30–16:00 *Coffee Break*

Shared Task Paper Session

16:00–16:30 *Findings of the Third Shared Task on Multilingual Coreference Resolution*
Michal Novák, Barbora Dohnalová, Miloslav Konopik, Anna Nedoluzhko, Martin Popel, Ondrej Prazak, Jakub Sido, Milan Straka, Zdeněk Žabokrtský and Daniel Zeman

16:30–16:50 *CorPipe at CRAC 2024: Predicting Zero Mentions from Raw Text*
Milan Straka

16:50–17:10 *End-to-end Multilingual Coreference Resolution with Headword Mention Representation*
Ondrej Prazak and Miloslav Konopík

17:10–17:20 *Multilingual coreference resolution as text generation*
Natalia Skachkova

Panel Discussion

17:20–17:50 *The future of coreference resolution in the era of LLMs*
Michal Novák, Ondřej Pražák and Martin Popel

Closing Remarks

17:50–18:00 *Closing of the workshop*
Maciej Ogrodniczuk

Major Entity Identification: A Generalizable Alternative to Coreference Resolution

Kawshik Manikantan[1], **Shubham Toshniwal**[2], **Makarand Tapaswi**[1], **Vineet Gandhi**[1]
[1]CVIT, IIIT Hyderabad [2]NVIDIA
kawshik.manikantan@research.iiit.ac.in, stoshniwal@nvidia.com, {makarand.tapaswi, vgandhi}@iiit.ac.in

Abstract

The limited generalization of coreference resolution (CR) models has been a major bottleneck in the task's broad application. Prior work has identified annotation differences, especially for mention detection, as one of the main reasons for the generalization gap and proposed using additional annotated target domain data. Rather than relying on this additional annotation, we propose an alternative referential task, **M**ajor **E**ntity **I**dentification (MEI), where we: (a) assume the target entities to be specified in the input, and (b) limit the task to only the frequent entities. Through extensive experiments, we demonstrate that MEI models generalize well across domains on multiple datasets with supervised models and LLM-based few-shot prompting. Additionally, MEI fits the classification framework, which enables the use of robust and intuitive classification-based metrics. Finally, MEI is also of practical use as it allows a user to search for all mentions of a particular entity or a group of entities of interest. [1]

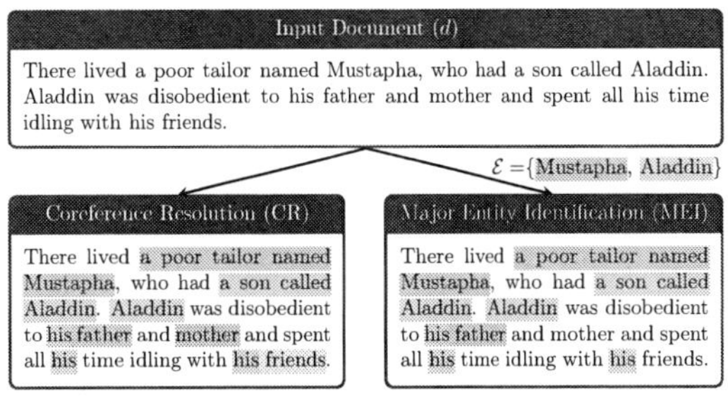

Figure 1: CR *vs.* MEI. The CR task aims to detect and cluster all mentions into different entities, shown in various colors. MEI takes major entities as additional input and aims to detect and classify the mentions that refer only to these entities.

1 Introduction

Coreference resolution (CR) is the task of finding text spans that refer to the same entity. CR is a fundamental language understanding task relevant to various downstream NLP applications, such as question-answering (Dhingra et al., 2018), building knowledge graphs (Koncel-Kedziorski et al., 2019), and summarization (Sharma et al., 2019). Despite the importance of CR and the progress made by neural coreference models (Dobrovolskii, 2021; Bohnet et al., 2023; Zhang et al., 2023), domain generalization remains an issue even with the best-performing supervised models (Xia and Van Durme, 2021; Toshniwal et al., 2021).

The lack of domain generalization in CR models can largely be attributed to differences in annotation guidelines of popular CR benchmarks, specifically annotation guidelines about what constitutes a mention (Porada et al., 2023). For example, OntoNotes (Pradhan et al., 2013) does not annotate singletons, confounding mention identity with being referential. Thus, models trained on OntoNotes generalize poorly (Toshniwal et al., 2021). The importance of mention detection for CR generalization is further highlighted by Gandhi et al. (2023), showing that solely annotating mentions is sufficient and more efficient for adapting pre-trained CR models to new domains (in comparison to annotating coreference chains). Similarly, GPT-4 struggles with zero-/few-shot mention prediction, but with ground-truth mentions, its CR performance (Le and Ritter, 2023) is competitive with that of supervised models (Toshniwal et al., 2021).

Given these observations, we hypothesize that current CR models, including large language models, generalize well at *mention clustering* but struggle to generalize on *mention detection* due to idiosyncrasies of different domains/benchmarks. We put forth an alternative referential task where the entities of interest are known and provided as additional input. Assuming entities to be part of the input offloads the required domain adaptation from training to inference. Specifically, we propose the

[1]Code for the paper is available at `https://github.com/KawshikManikantan/MEI`

Proceedings of the Seventh Workshop on Computational Models of Reference, Anaphora and Coreference (CRAC 2024), pages 1–17
November 15, 2024.

Statistics	LitBank CR	LitBank MEI	FantasyCoref CR	FantasyCoref MEI
# of Mentions	29103	16985	56968	35938
# of Non singletons	23340	16985	56968	35938
Mean ant. dist.	55.31	36.95	57.58	30.24
# of Clusters	7927	490	5829	942
Avg. cluster size	3.67	34.66	9.77	38.15

Table 1: Comparing CR and MEI. MEI has fewer but larger clusters, and a smaller mean antecedent distance (Mean ant. dist.). Our formulation's frequency-based criterion for deciding major entities means that singleton mentions are typically not a part of MEI.

task of Major Entity Identification (MEI), where we assume the major entities of the narrative, to be provided as input along with the text (see Fig. 1). We focus on major entities for the following reasons: (a) Specifying major entities of a narrative is intuitively easier. (b) A handful of major entities often dominate any discourse. Table 1 shows that in FantasyCoref roughly 16% of entities (942 of 5829) contribute to 63% of the mentions (35938 of 56968).

In this work, we adapt two literary CR benchmarks, namely LitBank (Bamman et al., 2020) and FantasyCoref (Han et al., 2021) by identifying frequently occurring entities as major entities and customizing a state-of-the-art coreference model (Toshniwal et al., 2021) to MEI. Our tests for generalizability reveal that while there is a big gap in CR performance between in- and out-of-domain models (Toshniwal et al., 2021), this performance gap is much smaller for MEI (Section 5.1). To test this hypothesis further, we evaluate large language models (LLMs) for MEI in a few-shot learning setup. On CR, LLMs are shown to struggle with mention detection and perform worse than supervised models (Le and Ritter, 2023). Contrary to this, on MEI, top LLMs (*e.g.* GPT-4) are only slightly behind supervised models (Section 5.2). These experiments in the supervised setting and the few-shot setting demonstrate that the MEI task is more generalizable than CR.

Additionally, we argue that MEI is easier to evaluate than CR. The MEI task can be viewed as a classification task in which any text span either refers to one of the input entities or the null class (*minor* entities and other non-mention spans). The classification metrics maintain consistent granularity, proportionally penalize perturbations, and exhibit high discriminatory power while intuitively meeting multiple desired specifications (Moosavi and Strube, 2016; Recasens and Hovy, 2011).

Furthermore, MEI, by its definition, disregards insignificant and smaller clusters known to inflate the CR metrics (Moosavi and Strube, 2016; Lu and Ng, 2020; Kummerfeld and Klein, 2013). As an aside, formulating MEI as a classification task allows for a trivial parallelization across candidate spans (Appendix A.1).

Finally, MEI's explicit mapping of mentions to predefined entities improves its usability over CR in downstream applications that focus on mentions of specific entities. MEI effectively replaces tailored heuristics employed to extract CR cluster(s) referring to entities of choice in such applications (entity understanding (Inoue et al., 2022), sentiment and social dynamics analysis (Zahiri and Choi, 2017; Antoniak et al., 2023)).

2 Task Formulation

Notation. For a document d, let $\mathcal{E} = \{e_j\}_{j=1}^{L}$ be the set of L major entities that we wish to identify. We define $\mathcal{M}_{\text{all}}$ as the set of all mentions that could refer to any entity and subsequently $\mathcal{M}_j \subseteq \mathcal{M}_{\text{all}}$ as the set of mentions that refer to a major entity e_j. Furthermore, we denote $\mathcal{M} = \bigcup_j \mathcal{M}_j$ as the set of mentions that refer to one of the major entities while mentions that do not correspond to any major entity are designated as $\mathcal{M}_{\text{other}} = \mathcal{M}_{\text{all}} \setminus \mathcal{M}$.

Task formulation. In MEI, the input consists of the document d and designative phrases $\mathcal{P} = \{p(e_j)\}_{j=1}^{L}$ where $p(e_j)$ succinctly represents the entity e_j. For example, in Fig. 1, the phrases *"Aladdin"* and *"Mustapha"* uniquely represent Aladdin and his father who appear in *"Aladdin And The Wonderful Lamp"*. Note that in CR, the designative phrases $\mathcal{P}$ are not part of the input.

In contrast to CR's clustering foundations, MEI starts with a prior for each entity (the designative phrase) and can be formulated as an open set classification, where every mention is either classified as one of the major entities or ignored. Formally, MEI aims to assign each mention $m \in \mathcal{M}_j$ to e_j and mentions $m \in \mathcal{M}_{\text{other}}$ to $\varnothing$, a null entity.

3 Supervised MEI models

We propose MEIRa, **M**ajor **E**ntity **I**dentification via **Ra**nking, which draws inspiration from the entity ranking formulation (Xia et al., 2021; Toshniwal et al., 2020) and maintains an explicit representation for entities. The MEIRa models consist of 3 steps: encoding the document, proposing candidate mentions, and an identification (id) module that tags mentions with major entities or the null entity.

Document encoding is performed using a Longformer-Large (Beltagy et al., 2020), ϕ, that we finetune for the task. Mentions (or spans) are encoded as $\mathbf{m}_i = \phi(m_i, d)$ by concatenating the first, last, and an attention-weighted average of the token representations within the mention span. In MEI, an additional input is the set of designative phrases $\mathcal{P}$ for the major entities. Since each phrase is derived from the document itself, we also obtain its encoding using the backbone: $\mathbf{e}_j = \phi(p(e_j), d)$.

Mention detection. Similar to prior efforts (Toshniwal et al., 2021), we use a mention proposal network that predicts high-scoring candidate mentions. This step finds all mentions $\mathcal{M}_{\text{all}}$ and not just the ones corresponding to the major entities $\mathcal{M}$.Training a model to only detect mentions of major entities would confuse it leading to poor performance.

Identification module. As illustrated in Fig. 2, we initialize a working memory $\mathcal{E}^W = [\mathbf{e}_j]_{j=1}^{L}$ as a list of L major entities based on their designative phrase representations. Given a mention m_i, the id module computes the most likely entity as:

$$[s_i^*, e_i^*] = \max_{j=1...L} f([\mathbf{m}_i, \mathbf{e}_j, \chi(m_i, e_j)]) , \quad (1)$$

where $f()$ is an MLP that predicts the score of tagging mention m_i with the entity e_j, and $\chi(m_i, e_j)$ encodes metadata. The output s_i^* corresponds to the highest score and e_i^* is the top-scoring entity. Based on the score, m_i is assigned to:

$$y(m_i) = \begin{cases} e_i^* & \text{if } s_i^* > \tau , \\ \varnothing & \text{otherwise} , \end{cases} \quad (2)$$

where τ is a threshold (set to 0 in practice).

The metadata $\chi(m_i, e_j)$ contains a distance (position) embedding representing the log distance between the mention m_i and the last tagged instance of the entity e_j. If no mention is yet associated with the entity, we use a special learnable embedding.

Updates to the working memory. We investigate two approaches:

(i) **MEIRa-S**tatic: As the name suggests, the working memory $\mathcal{E}^W$ of the entity representations remains constant ($\mathcal{E}^{W(0)}$) and is not updated with new mention associations. This makes the approach highly parallelizable.

(ii) **MEIRa-H**ybrid: Similar to traditional CR, this variation maintains a dynamic working memory $\mathcal{E}^W$, which is updated with every new mention-id association. Specifically, assuming m_i is assigned to e_j^*, the working memory would be updated using a weighted mean operator g as $\mathbf{e}_j \leftarrow g(\mathbf{e}_j, \mathbf{m}_i)$, similar to Toshniwal et al. (2020). To prevent error accumulation, we evaluate the mentions against $\mathcal{E}^W$ and the initial entity representations ($\mathcal{E}^{W(0)}$), then compute the average score. This hybrid approach reaps benefits from both, the initial clean designative phrases and the dynamic updates.

Following Toshniwal et al. (2020), the mention detection and identification modules are trained end-to-end using separate cross-entropy loss functions.

4 Few-shot MEI with LLMs

We propose a prompting strategy to leverage LLMs for MEI, addressing their challenges in CR.

Mention detection challenges. CR or MEI can be addressed using separate few-shot prompting strategies for mention detection and mention clustering/identification. However, Le and Ritter (2023) found that this strategy faced significant challenges with mention detection, performing worse than a deterministic mention detector. Thus, they assume access to an oracle mention detector and focus on evaluating LLMs' linking capabilities.

An alternative is to use an external supervised mention detector instead of the oracle. However, this requires annotated training data and may not align with a true few-shot LLM prompt paradigm. Additionally, supervised mention detectors often fail to generalize across CR datasets due to annotation variability (Lu and Ng, 2020).

MEI with LLMs. We demonstrate that transitioning from CR to MEI addresses this gap in mention detection and proposes an end-to-end, few-shot prompting approach for MEI. Inspired by Dobrovolskii (2021), we develop a prompting strategy that first performs MEI at word-level (rather than span), followed by a prompt to retrieve the span corresponding to the word.

In addition to the document d and the set of phrases $\mathcal{P}$, we also provide entity identifiers (*e.g.* #1, #2) to the LLM. We will use the following example:

Document: *That lady in the BMW is Alice's mom.*
Major Entities: 1. *Alice*; 2. *Alice's mother.*

Prompt 1. Word-level MEI. Mention detection with LLMs is challenging due to the frequent occurrence of nested mentions. We overcome this by prompting the LLM to tag each word. Specifically, through few-shot examples, we ask the LLM

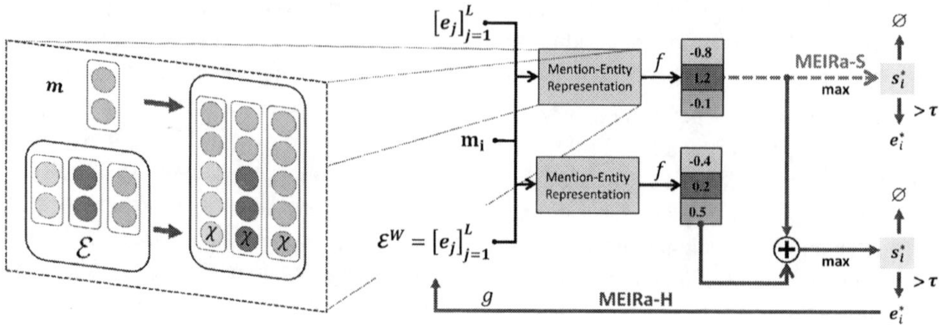

Figure 2: Identification module of MEIRa. A mention encoding $\mathbf{m}_i$ is concatenated with each entity's embedding in $\mathcal{E}^W$ and the metadata $\chi(m_i, e_j)$. Network f scores the likelihood of assigning m_i to each major entity. If the highest score s_i^* is above the threshold τ, m_i is associated with the highest scoring major entity e_i^* or discarded. In MEIRa-S, the entity memory $\mathcal{E}^W$ remains static. For MEIRa-H (blue path), the assigned entity's working memory is updated, and both the static (top half) and updated working memory (bottom half) are utilized to compute a final score.

to detect and tag the **syntactic heads**[2] (e.g., *lady*, *Alice*, *mom*) of mentions that refer to the major entities. Other words are left untagged (implicitly assigned to ∅, the null entity). To create the few-shot examples, a contiguous set of words annotated with the same entity is considered as a span and its syntactic head is extracted using `spaCy` (Honnibal et al., 2020).

The ideal output for the example above is:

"That lady#2 in the BMW is Alice#1's mom#2..".

Note that, even though the span *"BMW"* might be a valid mention, it is not annotated as it does not refer to one of the major entities. The exact prompt used for this is provided in the Appendix, Table 9.

Prompt 2. Head2Span retrieval. The entity tagged heads are passed to the Head2Span (H2S) module, along with the document to retrieve the span. The prompt consists of the document pre-annotated with the positions of the head, where each candidate head-word is followed by a "#" and is instructed to be replaced by the complete span (including any existent determiners and adjectives). For the input:

That lady# in the BMW is Alice#'s mom#.

the expected ideal output is

That lady (That lady in the BMW) in the BMW is Alice(Alice's)'s mom (Alice's mom).

Table 10 in the appendix shows the H2S prompt.

Preserving structure. We pose MEI as a structured generation task, prompting LLMs to reproduce documents and generate MEI tags at specific locations. Proprietary models like GPT-4 generally reproduce documents faithfully but for rare failures, we use the Needleman-Wunsch algorithm (Needleman and Wunsch, 1970) to align documents and extract tags In the case of open-source models, we employ regular expression-based constrained decoding with the `outlines` library (Willard and Louf, 2023)

5 Experiments

Datasets. We evaluate three literary datasets chosen for their longer length and identifiable major entities, particularly the key narrative elements such as characters or plot devices. Table 1 compares statistical aspects of MEI and CR, revealing that MEI features fewer clusters (entities) but larger cluster sizes (more mentions per cluster).

(i) *LitBank* (Bamman et al., 2020) annotates coreference in 100 literary texts, each averaging around 2000 words. Following prior work (Toshniwal et al., 2021), we utilize the initial cross-validation split, dividing the documents into training, validation, and test sets with an 80:10:10 ratio.

(ii) *FantasyCoref* (Han et al., 2021) provides OntoNotes (Pradhan et al., 2013)-style[3] coreference annotations for 211 documents from Grimm's Fairy Tales, with an average length of approximately 1700 words. The dataset includes 171 training, 20 validation, and 20 test documents.

(iii) *Additional Fantasy Text (AFT)* (Han et al., 2021) provides annotations for long narratives: (a) Aladdin (6976 words), (b) Ali Baba and the Forty Thieves (6911 words), and (c) Alice in Wonderland (13471 words).

Metrics. In contrast to CR, MEI facilitates the use of simple classification metrics. We define standard

[2] A syntactic head of a phrase is a word (*lady*) that is central to the characteristics of the phrase (*The lady in the BMW*).

[3] The exact guidelines are documented here

Model	FantasyCoref Macro-F1	FantasyCoref Micro-F1	LitBank Macro-F1	LitBank Micro-F1
Coref-ID	72.5±2.2	78.8±2.7	79.7±2.7	80.6±3.7
Coref-CM	77.7±1.8	82.4±2.2	74.1±2.5	76.0±3.0
Coref-FM	77.9±1.7	83.2±2.2	77.4±2.3	80.6±4.7
MEIRa-S	**80.7**±0.6	**84.9**±0.5	80.8±0.8	81.8±1.0
MEIRa-H	80.3±1.4	84.3±2.0	**82.3**±1.2	**83.2**±2.5

Table 2: Results for models trained jointly on FantasyCoref and LitBank.

Model	FantasyCoref Macro-F1	FantasyCoref Micro-F1	LitBank Macro-F1	LitBank Micro-F1
Coref-ID	63.4±1.8	69.5±3.6	58.0±2.4	57.7±1.0
Coref-CM	72.8±0.3	76.5±0.5	61.0±5.9	61.2±5.2
Coref-FM	71.2±1.5	75.2±1.3	66.1±2.1	67.1±3.9
MEIRa-S	**75.7**±1.5	78.5±1.2	74.6±1.1	74.7±1.6
MEIRa-H	74.7±1.0	**78.5**±0.8	**77.2**±1.9	**78.6**±2.7

Table 3: Results for models trained on OntoNotes.

precision and recall for each major entity considered as an individual class of its own.

For a dataset $\mathcal{D} = \{d_1, \ldots, d_{|\mathcal{D}|}\}$, the evaluation metrics are defined as follows:

$$\text{Macro-F1} = \frac{\sum_{d \in \mathcal{D}} \sum_{e_j \in \mathcal{E}_d} F1(e_j)}{\sum_{d \in \mathcal{D}} |\mathcal{E}_d|}, \text{ and} \quad (3)$$

$$\text{Micro-F1} = \frac{1}{|\mathcal{D}|} \sum_{d \in \mathcal{D}} \frac{\sum_{e \in \mathcal{E}} F1(e_j) \cdot |\mathcal{M}_j|}{\sum_{e \in \mathcal{E}} |\mathcal{M}_j|}. \quad (4)$$

Macro-F1 is the average F1-score of entities across the dataset, while Micro-F1 is the frequency-weighted F1-score of entities within a document, averaged across the dataset.

Major entity selection. We select as major entities, the top-k entities ranked as per the frequency of occurrences. We use k=5 for LitBank and FantasyCoref after visualizing the frequency plots of their training sets. For longer documents in AFT, we select up to 9 entities to ensure coverage of all key entities from the story. We also enforce that every entity $e_j \in \mathcal{E}$ has a mention count $|\mathcal{M}_j| \geq 5$. We derive the representative span for each selected e_j from the set of mentions $\mathcal{M}_j$ by selecting the most commonly occurring name or nominal mention.

Implementation details.
Supervised models: Model hyperparameters are derived from Toshniwal et al. (2021). To ensure consistent performance across different numbers of target entities, we randomly select a subset of major entities at each training iteration (more details in Appendix A.2). Supervised models were trained five times with random seeds, and we present aggregated results as the mean and standard deviation.
LLMs: We follow a few-shot prompting mechanism across the setups and experiments. Prompts that perform referential tasks consist of 3 examples of 6 sentences each. These 3 examples contain a mixture of narrative styles (narratives, dialogues), types of entities (major, non-major entities), categories of mentions (names, nominals, pronouns), and plurality. Additionally, before producing the MEI output, we ask the LLM to describe each major entity briefly. We find that this additional step improves performance. For the H2S prompt, we provide 9 sentences as examples, balancing the number of pre- and post-modifiers to the head. All examples were selected from LitBank's train set and kept constant throughout the experiments. We set the temperature to 0 for all the models to ensure consistent and reproducible outputs.

5.1 Experiments: Supervised Models

Baselines. We train the `longdoc` model (Toshniwal et al., 2021) for CR and perform the following three inference-time adaptations for MEI:

Coref-ID: `longdoc` uses active lists of entity representations, resolving coreference by associating mentions with existing clusters or generating new ones. During inference, we disable the cluster creation step and pre-fill the entity list with the encoded vector representations of the major entities. Hence, all the detected mentions either get mapped to one of the major entities or are discarded.

Coref-Cosine Map (Coref-CM): Since CR clusters obtained from `longdoc` lack explicit entity association, we employ the Kuhn-Munkres (KM) algorithm (Munkres, 1957) to find the optimal matching cluster for each major entity. The cost matrix uses the cosine similarity between the encoded representation of the major entities and the predicted cluster embeddings, both derived from `longdoc`.

Coref-Fuzzy Map (Coref-FM): This method uses the KM algorithm to derive optimal mappings by constructing a cost matrix from accumulated fuzzy-string matching scores between designative phrases and the predicted cluster's mention strings.

Supervised results. In this experiment, we train MEIRa and the baseline models on the joint training set of LitBank and FantasyCoref. Subsequently, we assess their performance on the individual test sets, with results summarized in Table 2. Overall, MEIRa models consistently outperform the baselines on both metrics while also exhibiting better

Model	AFT Macro-F1	AFT Micro-F1
Coref-ID	68.1±5.9	78.7±6.1
Coref-CM	71.1±2.8	82.4±4.2
Coref-FM	71.1±4.7	83.2±4.7
MEIRa-S	81.6±1.4	88.8±1.3
MEIRa-H	**82.8**±**1.1**	**89.5**±**1.0**

Table 4: Results on the AFT dataset.

stability with a lower variance. The considerable variance observed in the performance of baseline methods across all experiments underscores the non-trivial nature of identifying clusters corresponding to major entities within the output clusters provided by the CR algorithms. MEIRa-H and MEIRa-S exhibit competitive parity on FantasyCoref (children stories), while MEIRa-H edges out on LitBank dataset, showcasing its adaptability in elaborate sentence constructions.

Generalization across datasets. To evaluate the generalization capabilities of MEIRa and baseline models, we train them on the OntoNotes dataset and then test their performance on LitBank and FantasyCoref. The results are presented in Table 3. When compared with Table 2, we observe a significant performance drop across the baseline models (*e.g.* for Coref-ID, the average Micro-F1 scores drop from 80.6 to 57.7 on LitBank). The performance gap for the baseline models is more pronounced on LitBank than on FantasyCoref because LitBank's annotation strategies differ more significantly from those of OntoNotes. The observations aligns with previous work (Toshniwal et al., 2021), that showcase poor generalization of models trained for CR. In contrast, MEIRa models recover most of the underlying performance on both the datasets (MEIRa-H drops a little from 83.2 to 78.6 on LitBank Micro-F1), demonstrating MEI as a more adaptable task, bringing robustness over varying annotation strategies.

Long documents. Table 4 presents results on the AFT dataset of the models trained using a combined training set of LitBank and FantasyCoref. MEIRa models significantly outperform the baseline models, with MEIRa-H gaining 11.7% in Macro-F1 over the best baseline. The results demonstrate the efficacy of MEIRa models on resolving key entities in longer narratives.

Computational performance. MEIRa-S supports parallel batched processing since it does not update the working memory after associating mentions,

Model	FantasyCoref Macro-F1	FantasyCoref Micro-F1	LitBank Macro-F1	LitBank Micro-F1
MEIRa-H	88.5	91.0	86.1	85.4
GPT-4	**90.7**	**92.0**	**88.8**	**91.6**
GPT-3.5	69.2	74.2	74.3	75.8
Code Llama-34B	67.0	72.4	68.9	73.1
Llama3-8B	53.8	60.6	50.2	53.4
Mistral-7B	67.3	75.8	61.6	73.9

Table 5: Few-shot LLM prompting results assuming the availability of ground-truth mentions.

i.e. the mentions need not be processed sequentially from left to right. Hence, post-mention detection (common to all models), MEIRa-S is about 25× faster than `longdoc` when assessed across LitBank, FantasyCoref and AFT datasets on an NVIDIA RTX 4090 (see Fig. 3 in the appendix). Additionally, with the model's small memory footprint during inference, the entire process can also be parallelized across chunks of documents making it extremely efficient. Hence, we pose MEIRa-S as a faster while competitive alternative to MEIRa-H (that requires dynamic updates and has similar computational performance as `longdoc`).

5.2 Experiments: Few-shot prompting

Models. We experiment with GPT-4[4] (OpenAI, 2024), GPT-3.5[5], Code Llama-34B (Rozière et al., 2024), Mistral-7B (Jiang et al., 2023), and Llama3-8B.[6] Following Le and Ritter (2023), we use the instruction-tuned versions for open-source models. These models were chosen for their ability to handle the extended context required for our benchmarks.

5.2.1 Linking Performance w/ Gold Mentions

We first evaluate all the models assuming the availability of an oracle mention detector. The experimental configuration is aligned with that of Le and Ritter (2023), albeit with the distinction that we assess them for the MEI task rather than for CR. The prompt used in our setup is provided in Table 11 of Appendix. For comparison, we also perform inference on golden mentions with MEIRa-H.

The results in Table 5 show that GPT-4 surpasses the supervised MEIRa-H model in this setup. Among LLMs, GPT-4 is easily the best-performing model. Code Llama-34B performs the best among open-source models, closely followed by Mistral-

[4]Specifically, `gpt-4-1106-preview`

[5]Specifically, `gpt-3.5-turbo-0125`

[6]https://ai.meta.com/blog/meta-llama-3/

Model	FantasyCoref Macro-F1	FantasyCoref Micro-F1	LitBank Macro-F1	LitBank Micro-F1
MEIRa-H	**80.3**	**84.3**	82.3	83.2
GPT-4 w/ Ext det	80.1	82.2	78.7	83.9
GPT-4 with varying prompting strategies				
Single prompt	51.8	57.5	61.1	70.7
Two-stage prompt	70.5	74.9	76.5	81.3
Word-level MEI + spaCy H2S				
GPT-4	77.1	79.4	**82.5**	**85.5**
GPT-3.5	50.1	54.4	60.1	63.1
Code Llama-34B	30.0	31.4	22.7	23.2
Llama3-8B	29.2	32.1	20.5	26.0
Mistral-7B	19.4	21.9	12.9	14.0

Table 6: Results on LLMs with different mention detection and linking strategies.

Error Type	MEIRa-H	GPT-4
Missing Major	162	793
Major-Major	210	154
Major-Other	243	0
Other-Major	200	516
Extra-Major	461	896
Total	1276	2359

Table 7: Breakdown of errors by MEIRa-H and GPT-4 on the combined LitBank and FantasyCoref test set.

7B. While Code Llama-34B is tailored for the code domain, surprisingly, it outperforms strong LLMs suited for natural language. This result corroborates a similar finding by Le and Ritter (2023) for CR and related evidence regarding code pretraining aiding entity tracking (Kim et al., 2024). We find that Code Llama-34B performs close to GPT-3.5 for FantasyCoref, though a sizable gap persists in the Macro-F1 metric for LitBank , potentially due to its linguistic complexity.

5.2.2 MEI Task Performance with LLMs

In this section, we present the results for the end-to-end MEI task using LLMs. We compare all the approaches from Section 4 and relevant baselines with the results summarized in Table 6. To limit the combinations of LLMs and approaches for our experiments, we first compare all the approaches in tandem with GPT-4 and then present results for the best-performing approach with other LLMs.

The first straightforward approach of using a *Single Prompt* to retrieve all the mentions of major entities in a single pass results in a significant performance drop compared to MEIRa-H (prompt in Table 12 of Appendix). The reason is that while GPT-4 outperforms MEIRa-H at mention linking, its mention detection performance, especially with nested mentions, is much worse compared to MEIRa-H.[7]

To further underscore the importance of mention detection, we compare against *GPT-4 w/ Ext det*, which utilizes an external pre-trained mention detector followed by prompt-based linking (prompt in Table 11 of Appendix). We train the mention detector on the PreCo dataset (Chen et al., 2018), which achieves a 93.8% recall and 53.1% precision on the combined FantasyCoref and LitBank validation sets. *GPT-4 w/ Ext det* performs at par with the fully supervised MEIRa-H, again highlighting the strong mention linking capabilities of GPT-4.

Next, we present the results of our proposed *Two-stage prompt*, motivated by the *Single prompt* method's failure with nested mentions. The first prompt asks GPT-4 to perform word-level MEI, by limiting the task to syntactic heads only. The second prompt then performs the task of mapping the identified syntactic heads to full mention spans. The results strongly validate our proposed approach with a relative improvement of more than 10% over the *Single prompt* method across all metrics and datasets. We also explore replacing the second step, i.e., head-to-span (H2S) retrieval, with an external tool. Specifically, we invert spaCy's span-to-head mapping to obtain a head-to-span retriever.[8]

GPT-4 significantly improves in this setup, outperforming even the supervised model on LitBank. Given the strong performance of *GPT-4 + spaCy H2S*, we evaluate the open-source LLMs in only this setting. We observe a wide gap between GPT-4 and the open-source models. Llama3-8B outperforms other open-source models on both datasets in Micro-F1 and stays competitive with the larger Code Llama-34B in Macro-F1. However, this contrasts with Llama3-8B's significant lag in the idealized golden mention setting, which solely evaluates the model's linking capabilities.

5.3 Error Analysis

We classify MEI errors into five categories: (1) *Missing Major:* Not detecting a mention $m \in \mathcal{M}$. (2) *Major-Major:* Assigning a mention $m \in \mathcal{M}_j$ to any other major entity $\mathcal{E} \setminus e_j$. (3) *Major-Other:* Assigning a mention $m \in \mathcal{M}$ to $\varnothing$.

[7]The failure to detect nested mentions is despite best efforts to provide illustrative examples in the few-shot prompt. Le and Ritter (2023) report similar findings with earlier GPT versions.

[8]For the test set gold mentions of the two datasets, there were only two cases where spans had the same head. We handled these two cases manually.

Golden Mentions	Presently [a small boy] came walking along the path – [an urchin of nine or ten] ......[Winterbourne] had immediately perceived that [he] might have the honor of claiming [him] as a fellow countryman. "Take care [you] don't hurt [your] teeth," [he] said, paternally ......[My] mother counted them last night, and one came out right afterwards. She said she'd slap [me] if any more came out. [I] can't help it. It's this old Europe ......If [you] eat three lumps of sugar, [your] mother will certainly slap [you]," [he] said. "She's got to give [me] some candy, then," rejoined [[his] young interlocutor].
GPT-4 Output	Presently [a small boy] came walking along the path – [an urchin of nine or ten] ......[Winterbourne] had immediately perceived that [he] might have the honor of claiming [him] as a fellow countryman. "Take care you don't hurt your teeth," [he] said, paternally ......[My] mother counted them last night, and one came out right afterwards. [She] said [she]'d slap [me] if any more came out. [I] can't help it. [It]'s this old Europe ......If you eat three lumps of sugar, [your] mother will certainly slap [you]," [he] said. "[She]'s got to give [me] some candy, then," rejoined [his] young interlocutor.
MEIRa-H Output	Presently a small boy came walking along the path – [an urchin of nine or ten] ......[Winterbourne] had immediately perceived that [he] might have the honor of claiming [him] as a fellow countryman. "Take care [you] don't hurt [your] teeth," [he] said, paternally ......[My] mother counted them last night, and one came out right afterwards. She said she'd slap [me] if any more came out. [I] can't help it. It's this old Europe ......If [you] eat three lumps of sugar, [your] mother will certainly slap [you]," [he] said. "She's got to give [me] some candy, then," rejoined [[his] young interlocutor].

Table 8: Qualitative Analysis showcasing different errors made by GPT-4 and MEIRa-H. Errors are color-coded as follows: Missing Major, Others-Major, Extra-Major, Major-Major, and Major-Other.

(4) *Other-Major:* Assigning a mention $m \in \mathcal{M}_{\text{other}}$ to any major entity in $\mathcal{E}$. (5) *Extra-Major:* Detecting extra mentions $m \notin \mathcal{M}_{\text{all}}$ and assigning to any major entity in $\mathcal{E}$.

Results combined over the LitBank and FantasyCoref test sets are presented in Table 7. Missing Major and Extra-Major contribute most of the errors for GPT-4, highlighting the scope for improvement in mention detection and span retrieval. Mention detection also remains a challenge in MEIRa-H, the model making most of the mistakes in the Extra-Major category. GPT-4 distinguishes major entities more clearly than MEIRa-H but tends to over-associate other mentions with major entities, resulting in higher Other-Major and Extra-Major errors. Note that GPT-4 has zero errors in the Major-Other category due to the prompt design, which only allows annotating major entities. Examples of these errors are visualized in Table 8.

6 Related Work

Neural models for CR have become the *de facto* choice in supervised settings (Lee et al., 2017; Kantor and Globerson, 2019; Joshi et al., 2020; Otmazgin et al., 2023). Efforts to enhance model efficiency include reducing candidate mentions to word-level spans (Dobrovolskii, 2021) and using single dense representations for entity clusters (Xia et al., 2021; Toshniwal et al., 2020).

Generalization in CR remains a lingering problem (Moosavi and Strube, 2017; Zhu et al., 2021; Porada et al., 2023). Current solutions include feature addition (Aralikatte et al., 2019; Otmazgin et al., 2023), joint training (Xia and Van Durme, 2021; Toshniwal et al., 2021), and active learning (Zhao and Ng, 2014; Yuan et al., 2022; Gandhi et al., 2023). Rather than relying on additional training data, we argue for an alternative formulation where the burden of domain adaptation is offloaded from training to inference.

LLM evaluation on referential tasks has largely been conducted in limited settings, such as the sentence-level Winograd Schema Challenges (WSC) (Brown et al., 2020), clinical pronoun resolution (Agrawal et al., 2022) and instance-level Q&A (Yang et al., 2022). Le and Ritter (2023) conducted the first document-level evaluation of LLMs for CR but assumed an oracle-mention detector. In contrast, we conduct end-to-end evaluations.

Entity-centric tasks similar to MEI include character identification, where either annotations are restricted to a subset of entities (Baruah and Narayanan, 2023) or custom models are developed to extract mentions of specific characters from TV show transcripts (Chen and Choi, 2016; Zahiri and Choi, 2017). We differ from these works by adopting a generalized task formulation independent of annotation strategies and entity selection. Another task, Entity Linking (Ji et al., 2015) extracts distinct entities from a document and links them to external Knowledge Bases. In contast, MEI focuses on retrieving all mentions (including nominals and pronominals) of a specific set of key entities, extracted solely from the context of the document.

7 Conclusion

CR models are limited in their generalization capabilities owing to annotation differences and general challenges of domain adaptation. We propose MEI as an alternative to CR, where the entities relevant to the input text are provided as input along with the text. Our experiments demonstrate that MEI is more suited for generalization than CR. Additionally, MEI can be viewed as a classification task that enables the use of intuitive metrics. A trivially parallelized variation (MEIRa-S), gives a 25x speedup over a comparable CR model, making it more suitable for longer narratives. Unlike CR, the formulation of MEI allows few-shot prompted LLMs to effectively compete with trained models. Our novel two-stage prompting and robust baseline methods empower top-performing LLMs like GPT-4 to achieve this. Our analysis indicates that this task holds promise for effectively evaluating the long-context referential capabilities of LLMs in an end-to-end manner.

Potential applications of MEI include domains such as film and literature, where metadata about salient entities can be sourced from external databases like IMDb or SparkNotes. Additionally, MEI can be applied to the analysis of documents like of financial and legal reports, when the user is familiar with the relevant entities. Lastly, recent research (Lin and Zeldes, 2024) indicates that LLMs can assist or automate the extraction of salient entities, a direction we intend to explore in future work.

8 Limitations

Major Entity Identification (MEI) is proposed as a generalizable alternative to the coreference resolution (CR) task, and is not a replacement of CR. MEI limits itself to major entities and only caters to applications that are interested in a particular pre-defined set of entities. Our experiments follow certain thresholds that might not be universally applicable, and results and performance might vary slightly along this decision (refer Appendix A.2). Our current few-shot prompting evaluations are limited only to a few models that accommodate a large context window. Optimizing prompts and architecture to allow for a piece-wise aggregation of outputs across chunks of documents is left for future work.

References

Monica Agrawal, Stefan Hegselmann, Hunter Lang, Yoon Kim, and David Sontag. 2022. Large Language Models are Few-Shot Clinical Information Extractors. In *EMNLP*.

Maria Antoniak, Anjalie Field, Jimin Mun, Melanie Walsh, Lauren Klein, and Maarten Sap. 2023. Riveter: Measuring Power and Social Dynamics Between Entities. In *ACL (Volume 3: System Demonstrations)*.

Rahul Aralikatte, Heather Lent, Ana Valeria Gonzalez, Daniel Herschcovich, Chen Qiu, Anders Sandholm, Michael Ringaard, and Anders Søgaard. 2019. Rewarding Coreference Resolvers for Being Consistent with World Knowledge. In *EMNLP-IJCNLP*.

David Bamman, Olivia Lewke, and Anya Mansoor. 2020. An Annotated Dataset of Coreference in English Literature. In *LREC*.

Sabyasachee Baruah and Shrikanth Narayanan. 2023. Character Coreference Resolution in Movie Screenplays. In *Findings of ACL*.

Iz Beltagy, Matthew E Peters, and Arman Cohan. 2020. Longformer: The Long-Document Transformer. *arXiv preprint arXiv:2004.05150*.

Bernd Bohnet, Chris Alberti, and Michael Collins. 2023. Coreference Resolution through a seq2seq Transition-Based System. *TACL*.

Tom B. Brown, Benjamin Mann, Nick Ryder, Melanie Subbiah, Jared Kaplan, Prafulla Dhariwal, Arvind Neelakantan, Pranav Shyam, Girish Sastry, Amanda Askell, Sandhini Agarwal, Ariel Herbert-Voss, Gretchen Krueger, Tom Henighan, Rewon Child, Aditya Ramesh, Daniel M. Ziegler, Jeffrey Wu, Clemens Winter, Christopher Hesse, Mark Chen, Eric Sigler, Mateusz Litwin, Scott Gray, Benjamin Chess, Jack Clark, Christopher Berner, Sam McCandlish, Alec Radford, Ilya Sutskever, and Dario Amodei. 2020. Language Models are Few-Shot Learners. In *NeurIPS*.

Hong Chen, Zhenhua Fan, Hao Lu, Alan Yuille, and Shu Rong. 2018. PreCo: A Large-scale Dataset in Preschool Vocabulary for Coreference Resolution. In *EMNLP*.

Yu-Hsin Chen and Jinho D. Choi. 2016. Character Identification on Multiparty Conversation: Identifying Mentions of Characters in TV Shows. In *Annual Meeting of the Special Interest Group on Discourse and Dialogue*.

Bhuwan Dhingra, Qiao Jin, Zhilin Yang, William Cohen, and Ruslan Salakhutdinov. 2018. Neural Models for Reasoning over Multiple Mentions Using Coreference. In *NAACL-HLT*.

Vladimir Dobrovolskii. 2021. Word-Level Coreference Resolution. In *EMNLP*.

Nupoor Gandhi, Anjalie Field, and Emma Strubell. 2023. Annotating Mentions Alone Enables Efficient Domain Adaptation for Coreference Resolution. In *ACL*.

Sooyoun Han, Sumin Seo, Minji Kang, Jongin Kim, Nayoung Choi, Min Song, and Jinho D. Choi. 2021. FantasyCoref: Coreference Resolution on Fantasy Literature Through Omniscient Writer's Point of View. In *Fourth Workshop on Computational Models of Reference, Anaphora and Coreference*.

Matthew Honnibal, Ines Montani, Sofie Van Landeghem, and Adriane Boyd. 2020. spaCy: Industrial-strength Natural Language Processing in Python.

Naoya Inoue, Charuta Pethe, Allen Kim, and Steven Skiena. 2022. Learning and Evaluating Character Representations in Novels. In *Findings of ACL*.

Heng Ji, Joel Nothman, Ben Hachey, and Radu Florian. 2015. Overview of tac-kbp2015 tri-lingual entity discovery and linking. *Theory and Applications of Categories*.

Albert Q Jiang, Alexandre Sablayrolles, Arthur Mensch, Chris Bamford, Devendra Singh Chaplot, Diego de las Casas, Florian Bressand, Gianna Lengyel, Guillaume Lample, Lucile Saulnier, et al. 2023. Mistral 7B. *arXiv preprint arXiv:2310.06825*.

Mandar Joshi, Danqi Chen, Yinhan Liu, Daniel S. Weld, Luke Zettlemoyer, and Omer Levy. 2020. SpanBERT: Improving Pre-training by Representing and Predicting Spans. *TACL*, 8.

Ben Kantor and Amir Globerson. 2019. Coreference Resolution with Entity Equalization. In *ACL*.

Najoung Kim, Sebastian Schuster, and Shubham Toshniwal. 2024. Code Pretraining Improves Entity Tracking Abilities of Language Models.

Rik Koncel-Kedziorski, Dhanush Bekal, Yi Luan, Mirella Lapata, and Hannaneh Hajishirzi. 2019. Text Generation from Knowledge Graphs with Graph Transformers. In *NAACL-HLT*.

Jonathan K. Kummerfeld and Dan Klein. 2013. Error-Driven Analysis of Challenges in Coreference Resolution. In *EMNLP*.

Nghia T. Le and Alan Ritter. 2023. Are Large Language Models Robust Coreference Resolvers?

Kenton Lee, Luheng He, Mike Lewis, and Luke Zettlemoyer. 2017. End-to-end Neural Coreference Resolution. In *EMNLP*.

Jessica Lin and Amir Zeldes. 2024. GUMsley: Evaluating entity salience in summarization for 12 English genres. In *Proceedings of the 18th Conference of the European Chapter of the Association for Computational Linguistics (Volume 1: Long Papers)*, pages 2575–2588, St. Julian's, Malta. Association for Computational Linguistics.

Jing Lu and Vincent Ng. 2020. Conundrums in Entity Coreference Resolution: Making Sense of the State of the Art. In *EMNLP*.

Nafise Sadat Moosavi and Michael Strube. 2016. Which Coreference Evaluation Metric Do You Trust? A Proposal for a Link-based Entity Aware Metric. In *ACL*.

Nafise Sadat Moosavi and Michael Strube. 2017. Lexical features in coreference resolution: To be used with caution. In *ACL*.

James Munkres. 1957. Algorithms for the assignment and transportation problems. *Journal of the society for industrial and applied mathematics*.

Saul B Needleman and Christian D Wunsch. 1970. A general method applicable to the search for similarities in the amino acid sequence of two proteins. *Journal of molecular biology*.

OpenAI. 2024. GPT-4 Technical Report.

Shon Otmazgin, Arie Cattan, and Yoav Goldberg. 2023. LingMess: Linguistically Informed Multi Expert Scorers for Coreference Resolution. In *EACL*.

Ian Porada, Alexandra Olteanu, Kaheer Suleman, Adam Trischler, and Jackie Chi Kit Cheung. 2023. Investigating Failures to Generalize for Coreference Resolution Models.

Sameer Pradhan, Alessandro Moschitti, Nianwen Xue, Hwee Tou Ng, Anders Björkelund, Olga Uryupina, Yuchen Zhang, and Zhi Zhong. 2013. Towards Robust Linguistic Analysis using OntoNotes. In *CONLL*.

M. Recasens and E. Hovy. 2011. Blanc: Implementing the rand index for coreference evaluation. *Nat. Lang. Eng.*, 17(4):485–510.

Baptiste Rozière, Jonas Gehring, Fabian Gloeckle, Sten Sootla, Itai Gat, Xiaoqing Ellen Tan, Yossi Adi, Jingyu Liu, Romain Sauvestre, Tal Remez, Jérémy Rapin, Artyom Kozhevnikov, Ivan Evtimov, Joanna Bitton, Manish Bhatt, Cristian Canton Ferrer, Aaron Grattafiori, Wenhan Xiong, Alexandre Défossez, Jade Copet, Faisal Azhar, Hugo Touvron, Louis Martin, Nicolas Usunier, Thomas Scialom, and Gabriel Synnaeve. 2024. Code Llama: Open Foundation Models for Code.

Eva Sharma, Luyang Huang, Zhe Hu, and Lu Wang. 2019. An Entity-Driven Framework for Abstractive Summarization. In *EMNLP-IJCNLP*.

Shubham Toshniwal, Sam Wiseman, Allyson Ettinger, Karen Livescu, and Kevin Gimpel. 2020. Learning to Ignore: Long Document Coreference with Bounded Memory Neural Networks. In *EMNLP*.

Shubham Toshniwal, Patrick Xia, Sam Wiseman, Karen Livescu, and Kevin Gimpel. 2021. On Generalization in Coreference Resolution. In *Workshop on Computational Models of Reference, Anaphora and Coreference*.

Brandon T Willard and Rémi Louf. 2023. Efficient Guided Generation for LLMs. *arXiv preprint arXiv:2307.09702*.

Congying Xia, Wenpeng Yin, Yihao Feng, and Philip Yu. 2021. Incremental Few-shot Text Classification with Multi-round New Classes: Formulation, Dataset and System. In *NAACL-HLT*.

Patrick Xia and Benjamin Van Durme. 2021. Moving on from OntoNotes: Coreference Resolution Model Transfer. In *EMNLP*.

Xiaohan Yang, Eduardo Peynetti, Vasco Meerman, and Chris Tanner. 2022. What GPT Knows About Who is Who. In *Workshop on Insights from Negative Results in NLP*.

Michelle Yuan, Patrick Xia, Chandler May, Benjamin Van Durme, and Jordan Boyd-Graber. 2022. Adapting Coreference Resolution Models through Active Learning. In *ACL*.

Sayyed M. Zahiri and Jinho D. Choi. 2017. Emotion Detection on TV Show Transcripts with Sequence-based Convolutional Neural Networks.

Wenzheng Zhang, Sam Wiseman, and Karl Stratos. 2023. Seq2seq is All You Need for Coreference Resolution. In *EMNLP*.

Shanheng Zhao and Hwee Tou Ng. 2014. Domain Adaptation with Active Learning for Coreference Resolution. In *Workshop on Health Text Mining and Information Analysis (Louhi)*.

Yilun Zhu, Sameer Pradhan, and Amir Zeldes. 2021. OntoGUM: Evaluating Contextualized SOTA Coreference Resolution on 12 More Genres. In *ACL-IJCNLP*.

A Appendix

A.1 Linking Speed Comparison

This section compares the computational performance of `longdoc` with the proposed MEIRa-S architecture. The classification formulation and the lack of an update step in MEIRa-S makes it a more efficient alternative to MEIRa-H and CR models. Fig. 3 displays the speed-up obtained in the identification module when assessed across documents with varying numbers of mentions. MEIRa-S consistently clocks a 20x efficiency across all ranges.

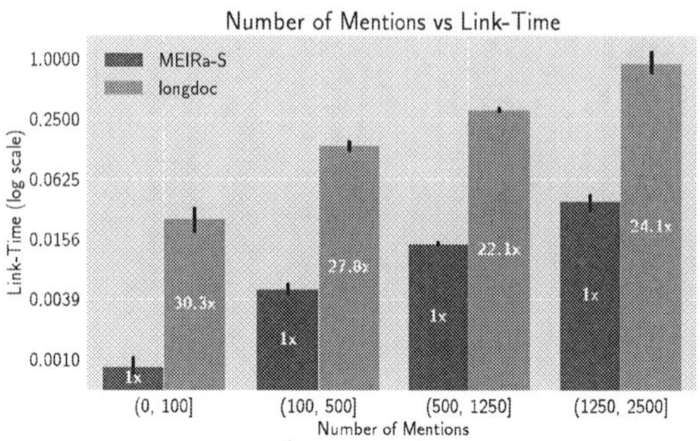

Figure 3: Linking speed comparison between MEIRa-S and `longdoc` for the combined LitBank and Fantasy-Coref test set. There exists 6 documents with (0, 100] mentions, 19 with (100, 500] mentions, 5 with (500, 1250] mentions and 3 with (1250, 2500] mentions.

A.2 Performance across number of entities

For consistency, the experiments of the main paper are evaluated across all the selected major entities (chosen using the thresholds defined in Section 5). A natural extension is to assess the model's performance with varying numbers of entities of choice. For instance, if one is interested in only two key characters, can these models maintain consistency when provided with their designative phrases?

In this section, we address this concern and evaluate the MEI models with varying numbers of input entities. We present the per-entity F1-score of all entities across the AFT dataset. The results for MEIRa-H are showcased in Fig. 4, Fig. 5 and Fig. 6. The first column of the heatmap shows the per-entity F1-score when it is the sole target entity in the document. For e.g., the value in the first column in Fig. 4 corresponding to the entity *Baba Mustapha* (0.93) indicates the performance of the model when *Baba Mustapha* is the only target entity.

As we move across the columns of a particular row (ignoring the first column), the column number indicates the number of target entities used at

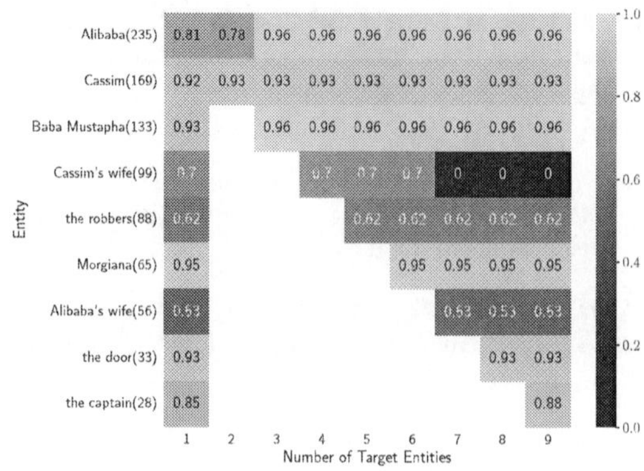

Figure 4: Performance of MEIRa-H across number of target entities for the document Ali Baba and the Forty Thieves.

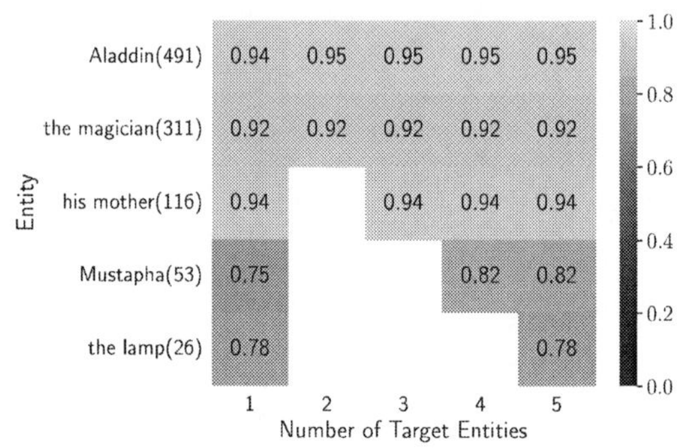

Figure 5: Performance of MEIRa-H across number of target entities for Aladdin.

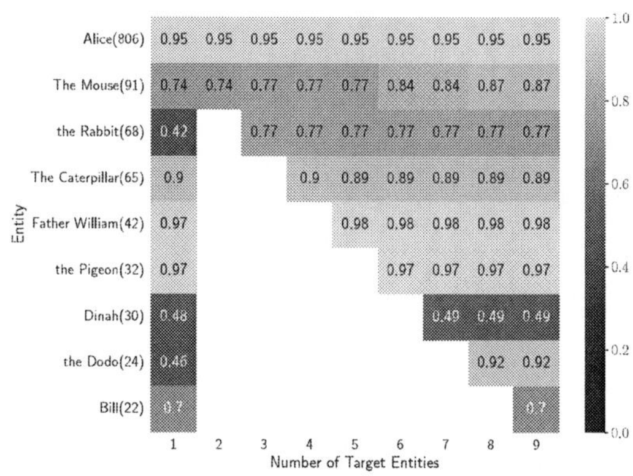

Figure 6: Performance of MEIRa-H across number of target entities for Alice in Wonderland.

inference. For instance, if the column number is k, the target entities are the top-k frequent entities. Again, the 4th column in the row corresponding to *Baba Mustapha* indicates its individual F1-score in the experiment where the four input entities are *Alibaba*, *Cassim*, *Baba Mustapha* and *Cassim's wife*.

There are a few individual cases where the performance significantly varies with modifying the number of input entities. For example, *Cassim's wife* is confused with *Alibaba's wife* after the latter's introduction. However, overall, the per-entity F1-score remains consistent across varying numbers of input entities across all three documents. These results demonstrate the effectiveness of MEIRa-H for applications requiring variable numbers of target entities. This consistency is mainly due to the variable entity training, where a randomly chosen subset of major entities is selected in each iteration. Excluding this procedure leads to significant fluctuation in performance while modifying the number of target entities.

A.3 Prompts

We provide exact prompts for all the few-shot prompting experiments. Please note that not all the major entities listed in the few shot examples are necessary to be present in the text.

A.4 Budget and Hardware details

The supervised models were trained on a 24GB NVIDIA RTX 4090Ti GPU. For experiments with the open source language models, we used two 48GB NVIDIA RTX A6000 GPU's. For GPT-4 and GPT-3.5 experiments, we spent approximately 175$ in total, covering both initial explorations and the computation of final results.

Instruction
You will receive a Text along with a list of Key Entities and their corresponding Cluster IDs as input. Your task is to perform Coreference Resolution on the provided text to categorize "each word belonging to a cluster" with its respective cluster id. Also briefly describe the key entities in 1-2 sentences before starting the coreference task. Follow the format below to label a word with its cluster ID: word#cluster_id Please keep in mind: - Ensure the output adheres to the specified format for easy parsing. - Classify the words in the given text without altering any of the other content.
Example Input:
Key Entities: 1. Katharine Hilbery - #1 2. Mr. Denham - #2 3. Mrs. Hilbery - #3 4. Mr. Hilbery - #4 5. Mr. Fortescue - #5 Text: CHAPTER I It was a Sunday evening in October , and in common with many other young ladies of her class , Katharine Hilbery was pouring out tea . Perhaps a fifth part of her mind was thus occupied , and the remaining parts leapt over the little barrier of day which interposed between Monday morning and this rather subdued moment , and played with the things one does voluntarily and normally in the daylight . But although she was silent , she was evidently mistress of a situation which was familiar enough to her , and inclined to let it take its way for the six hundredth time , perhaps , without bringing into play any of her unoccupied faculties . A single glance was enough to show that Mrs. Hilbery was so rich in the gifts which make tea-parties of elderly distinguished people successful , that she scarcely needed any help from her daughter , provided that the tiresome business of teacups and bread and butter was discharged for her . Considering that the little party had been seated round the tea-table for less than twenty minutes , the animation observable on their faces , and the amount of sound they were producing collectively , were very creditable to the hostess . It suddenly came into Katharine 's mind that if someone opened the door at this moment he would think that they were enjoying themselves ; he would think , " What an extremely nice house to come into ! "
Example Output:
Description of Key Entities present in the text: #1 - Katharine Hilbery: A young and apparently rich lady and the daughter of Mrs. Hilbery. She and Mrs. Hilbery were organising a party for some distinguished elders. #3 - Mrs. Hilbery: She is the mother of Katharine Hilbery and is a well-to-do member of the society and a very efficient and able hostess Coreference: CHAPTER I It was a Sunday evening in October , and in common with many other young ladies of her#1 class , Katharine#1 Hilbery#1 was pouring out tea . Perhaps a fifth part of her#1 mind was thus occupied , and the remaining parts leapt over the little barrier of day which interposed between Monday morning and this rather subdued moment , and played with the things one does voluntarily and normally in the daylight . But although she#1 was silent , she#1 was evidently mistress of a situation which was familiar enough to her#1 , and inclined to let it take its way for the six hundredth time , perhaps , without bringing into play any of her#1 unoccupied faculties . A single glance was enough to show that Mrs.#3 Hilbery#3 was so rich in the gifts which make tea-parties of elderly distinguished people successful , that she#3 scarcely needed any help from her#3 daughter#1 , provided that the tiresome business of teacups and bread and butter was discharged for her#1 . Considering that the little party had been seated round the tea-table for less than twenty minutes , the animation observable on their faces , and the amount of sound they were producing collectively , were very creditable to the hostess#3 . It suddenly came into Katharine#1 's#1 mind that if some one opened the door at this moment he would think that they were enjoying themselves ; he would think , " What an extremely nice house to come into ! "

Table 9: Prompt for WL Coreference

Instruction
Any word marked with # is supposed to be the head of a noun phrase. Expand this head to contain determiner and adjective phrases. Do not remove or add new words while expanding. Stick to the format.
Example Input:
Montraville# was a **Lieutenant#** in the **army#** : **Belcour#** was his brother **officer#** : they had been to take leave of their **friends#** previous to their departure for **America#** , and were now returning to **Portsmouth#** , where the **troops#** waited orders for embarkation
Example Output:
Montraville **(Montraville)** was a Lieutenant **(a Lieutenant in the army)** in the army **(the army)** : Belcour **(Belcour)** was his brother officer **(his brother officer)** : they had been to take leave of their friends **(their friends)** previous to their departure for America **(America)** , and were now returning to Portsmouth **(Portsmouth)** , where the troops **(the troops)** waited orders for embarkation
Example Input:
Arriving at the verge of the **town#** , he dismounted , and sending the **servant#** forward with the horses , proceeded toward the **place#** , where , in the midst of an extensive pleasure **ground#** , stood the **mansion#** which contained the lovely Charlotte **Temple#** .
Example Output:
Arriving at the verge of the town **(the town)** , he dismounted , and sending the servant **(the servant)** forward with the horses , proceeded toward the place **(the place)** , where , in the midst of an extensive pleasure ground **(an extensive pleasure ground)** , stood the mansion **(the mansion which contained the lovely Charlotte Temple)** which contained the lovely Charlotte Temple **(the lovely Charlotte Temple)** .
Example Input:
"You are a benevolent **fellow#** ," said a young **officer#** to him one day and I have a great mind to give you a fine subject to exercise the goodness of your heart upon.
Example Output:
"You are a benevolent fellow **(a benevolent fellow)** ," said a young officer **(a young officer)** to him one day and I have a great mind to give you a fine subject to exercise the goodness of your heart upon.

Table 10: Prompt for H2S Retrieval

Instruction
Annotate all the entity mentions in the following text with coreference clusters. Use Markdown tags to indicate clusters in the output, with the following format [mention] (#cluster_name). Do not modify any text outside (), only add text inside parenthesis. The cluster names of the key entities are already provided, mark the mentions of the entity with the corresponding cluster name. Mark the mentions of the other entities with (#others). Also briefly describe the key entities in 1-2 sentences before starting the coreference task.
Example Input:
Key Entities: 1. Katharine Hilbery (#katharine_hilbery) 2. Mr. Denham (#mr._denham) 3. Mrs. Hilbery (#mrs._hilbery) 4. Mr. Hilbery (#mr._hilbery) 5. Mr. Fortescue (#mr._fortescue) Text: CHAPTER I It was a Sunday evening in October, and in common with [many other young ladies of [her] (#) class] (#) , [Katharine Hilbery] (#) was pouring out tea . Perhaps a fifth part of [her] (#) mind was thus occupied , and the remaining parts leapt over the little barrier of day which interposed between Monday morning and this rather subdued moment , and played with the things one does voluntarily and normally in the daylight . But although [she] (#) was silent , [she] (#) was evidently [mistress] (#) of a situation which was familiar enough to [her] (#) , and inclined to let it take its way for the six hundredth time , perhaps , without bringing into play any of [her] (#) unoccupied faculties . A single glance was enough to show that [Mrs. Hilbery] (#) was so rich in the gifts which make tea-parties of [elderly distinguished people] (#) successful , that [she] (#) scarcely needed any help from [[her] (#) daughter] (#) , provided that the tiresome business of teacups and bread and butter was discharged for [her] (#) . Considering that [the little party] (#) had been seated round the tea-table for less than twenty minutes , the animation observable on [their] (#) faces , and the amount of sound [they] (#) were producing collectively , were very creditable to [the hostess] (#) . It suddenly came into [Katharine 's] (#) mind that if [some one] (#) opened the door at this moment [he] (#) would think that [they] (#) were enjoying [themselves] (#) ; [he] (#) would think , " What [an extremely nice house] (#) to come into ! "
Example Output:
Description of Key Entities present in the text: #katharine_hilbery - Katharine Hilbery: A young and apparently rich lady and the daughter of Mrs. Hilbery. She and Mrs. Hilbery were organising a party for some distinguished elders. #mrs._hilbery - Mrs. Hilbery: She is the mother of Katharine Hilbery and is a well-to-do member of the society and a very efficient and able hostess Coreference: CHAPTER I It was a Sunday evening in October , and in common with [many other young ladies of [her] (#katharine_hilbery) class] (#others) , [Katharine Hilbery] (#katharine_hilbery) was pouring out tea . Perhaps a fifth part of [her] (#katharine_hilbery) mind was thus occupied , and the remaining parts leapt over the little barrier of day which interposed between Monday morning and this rather subdued moment , and played with the things one does voluntarily and normally in the daylight . But although [she] (#katharine_hilbery) was silent , [she] (#katharine_hilbery) was evidently [mistress] (#others) of a situation which was familiar enough to [her] (#katharine_hilbery) , and inclined to let it take its way for the six hundredth time , perhaps , without bringing into play any of [her] (#katharine_hilbery) unoccupied faculties . A single glance was enough to show that [Mrs. Hilbery] (#mrs._hilbery) was so rich in the gifts which make tea-parties of [elderly distinguished people] (#others) successful , that [she] (#mrs._hilbery) scarcely needed any help from [[her] (#mrs._hilbery) daughter] (#katharine_hilbery) , provided that the tiresome business of teacups and bread and butter was discharged for [her] (#katharine_hilbery) . Considering that [the little party] (#others) had been seated round the tea-table for less than twenty minutes , the animation observable on [their] (#others) faces , and the amount of sound [they] (#others) were producing collectively , were very creditable to [the hostess] (#mrs._hilbery) . It suddenly came into [Katharine 's] (#katharine_hilbery) mind that if [some one] (#others) opened the door at this moment [he] (#others) would think that [they] (#others) were enjoying [themselves] (#others) ; [he] (#others) would think , " What [an extremely nice house] (#others) to come into ! "

Table 11: Prompt for evaluating linking performance

Instruction

Annotate all the entity mentions that refer to the key entities provided. The mention needs to include determiners and adjectives, if present. Use Markdown tags to indicate clusters in the output, with the following format [mention] (#cluster_name). The cluster names of the key entitites are already provided. Mark the mentions of the entity with the corresponding cluster name. Also briefly describe the key entities in 1-2 sentences before starting the coreference task.

Example Input:

Key Entities:
1. Katharine Hilbery (#katharine_hilbery)
2. Mr. Denham (#mr._denham)
3. Mrs. Hilbery (#mrs._hilbery)
4. Mr. Hilbery (#mr._hilbery)
5. Mr. Fortescue (#mr._fortescue)

Text:
CHAPTER I It was a Sunday evening in October , and in common with many other young ladies of her class , Katharine Hilbery was pouring out tea . Perhaps a fifth part of her mind was thus occupied , and the remaining parts leapt over the little barrier of day which interposed between Monday morning and this rather subdued moment , and played with the things one does voluntarily and normally in the daylight . But although she was silent , she was evidently mistress of a situation which was familiar enough to her , and inclined to let it take its way for the six hundredth time , perhaps , without bringing into play any of her unoccupied faculties . A single glance was enough to show that Mrs. Hilbery was so rich in the gifts which make tea-parties of elderly distinguished people successful , that she scarcely needed any help from her daughter , provided that the tiresome business of teacups and bread and butter was discharged for her . Considering that the little party had been seated round the tea-table for less than twenty minutes , the animation observable on their faces , and the amount of sound they were producing collectively , were very creditable to the hostess . It suddenly came into Katharine 's mind that if someone opened the door at this moment he would think that they were enjoying themselves ; he would think , " What an extremely nice house to come into ! "

Example Output:

Description of Key Entities present in the text:

#katharine_hilbery - Katharine Hilbery: A young and apparently rich lady and the daughter of Mrs. Hilbery. She and Mrs. Hilbery were organising a party for some distinguished elders.

#mrs._hilbery - Mrs. Hilbery: She is the mother of Katharine Hilbery and is a well-to-do member of the society and a very efficient and able hostess

Coreference:
CHAPTER I It was a Sunday evening in October , and in common with many other young ladies of [her] (#katharine_hilbery) class , [Katharine Hilbery] (#katharine_hilbery) was pouring out tea . Perhaps a fifth part of [her] (#katharine_hilbery) mind was thus occupied , and the remaining parts leapt over the little barrier of day which interposed between Monday morning and this rather subdued moment , and played with the things one does voluntarily and normally in the daylight . But although [she] (#katharine_hilbery) was silent , [she] (#katharine_hilbery) was evidently mistress of a situation which was familiar enough to [her] (#katharine_hilbery) , and inclined to let it take its way for the six hundredth time , perhaps , without bringing into play any of [her] (#katharine_hilbery) unoccupied faculties . A single glance was enough to show that [Mrs. Hilbery] (#mrs._hilbery) was so rich in the gifts which make tea-parties of elderly distinguished people successful , that [she] (#mrs._hilbery) scarcely needed any help from [[her] (#mrs._hilbery) daughter] (#katharine_hilbery) , provided that the tiresome business of teacups and bread and butter was discharged for [her] (#katharine_hilbery) . Considering that the little party had been seated round the tea-table for less than twenty minutes , the animation observable on their faces , and the amount of sound they were producing collectively , were very creditable to [the hostess] (#mrs._hilbery) . It suddenly came into [Katharine 's] (#katharine_hilbery) mind that if some one opened the door at this moment he would think that they were enjoying themselves ; he would think , " What an extremely nice house to come into ! "

Table 12: Prompt for Direct version of E2E MEI

Enriching Conceptual Knowledge in Language Models through Metaphorical Reference Explanation

Zixuan Zhang and **Heng Ji**
University of Illinois Urbana-Champaign
{zixuan11, hengji}@illinois.edu

Abstract

In this paper, we explore a novel approach to concept enrichment in language models (LMs) by leveraging the fundamental similarities between conceptual knowledge enrichment and metaphorical reference resolution. While previous knowledge editing (KE) methods predominantly focus on factual updates, we introduce a method that trains LMs to not only incorporate new conceptual meanings but also generatively explain the connections between original and enriched definitions through metaphorical analogies. To achieve this, we develop a new dataset tailored for concept enrichment tasks and apply it to train an LM capable of updating and reasoning about conceptual knowledge. The proposed method was evaluated on both "is-a" relation classification and metaphorical reference detection. Experimental results show that our approach significantly enhances the model's ability to understand and apply enriched concepts, demonstrating the potential of metaphorical reference identification in improving conceptual knowledge of LMs[1].

1 Introduction

Large language models (LLMs) demonstrate strong capability in serving as a knowledge system efficient in storing, retrieving, and reasoning across different domains of knowledge (Petroni et al., 2019; Zhao et al., 2022; He et al., 2024). Considering that real-world knowledge is constantly evolving, many research efforts focus on post-training knowledge editing and refinement (Meng et al., 2022, 2023; Liu et al., 2024; Wang et al., 2024; Yu and Ji, 2023; Qin et al., 2024), to ensure that the information in language models remains up-to-date. However, most prior KE research primarily focuses on editing factual knowledge. For example, if the LM knows that *Leonardo DiCaprio* is a citizen of the *United States*, previous KE methods would alter the model to respond with a different country (e.g., *Syria*) when queried about his citizenship. While research in cognitive science (Zhao et al., 2024; Rane et al., 2024) suggests that humans typically grasp new information by learning new concepts, some KE methods also focus on editing concept-level knowledge. Basically when a concept's definition is updated, the edited model should reflect a new understanding of both the concept itself and its related instances.

In this paper, we introduce novel insights by identifying the fundamental similarity between enriching the concepts in LMs and a special case of coreference resolution: *metaphors*. Metaphors, or metaphorical references, typically involve using an existing concept to refer to a new one, where the new and old concepts share significant similarities. For example, the concept of ***stream*** originally referred to a "*body of water with a current flowing within its bed and banks*". However, it now also refers to "*a type of real-time digital transmission of video or audio content*", as both meanings involve the "*continuous flow of some contents*". Almost all metaphor cases are essentially enriching older concepts with new meanings, which closely parallels the task of concept enrichment for LMs.

Based on these similarities, we propose a novel and effective method for enriching conceptual knowledge in LMs by training the model to explain metaphorical references. Specifically, when provided with an updated definition of an old concept, our approach trains the model not only to memorize the new meaning, but also to generatively explain the similarity between the old and new meanings, ensuring that the LM gains a deeper understanding of why the enrichment is valid. We develop a new dataset for the task of LM concept enrichment and use it to train a language model for updating conceptual knowledge. Our model is evaluated on both concept definition memorization

[1]Data and code are available at https://github.com/zhangzx-uiuc/ConceptEnrich.

Proceedings of the Seventh Workshop on Computational Models of Reference, Anaphora and Coreference (CRAC 2024), pages 18–22
November 15, 2024.

and sub-instance classification. We also assess its performance on metaphorical reference detection. Experimental results demonstrate the effectiveness of using metaphorical reference generation to enhance LM concept enrichment.

Our contributions can be summarized as follows:

- We propose a new problem setting focused on enriching conceptual knowledge in language models, addressing the realistic need for knowledge to be continuously updated to reflect the dynamic nature of the real world.
- We introduce a novel approach that incorporates metaphorical reference explanation as a training objective, demonstrating its effectiveness both theoretically and empirically.
- We develop and release a new benchmark dataset, *ConceptEnrich*, designed for the task of conceptual knowledge enrichment.

2 Related Work

Conceptual Knowledge Editing Most previous work on knowledge editing in LMs has primarily focused on modifying factual knowledge, with only one prior study, *ConceptEdit* (Wang et al., 2024), addressing the editing of conceptual knowledge in LMs. However, we identify a critical flaw in the basic problem setting of ConceptEdit: the updated concept definitions are often unrealistic, and simply swapped from the definition of other concepts. For example, the model is expected to update the definition of ***stream*** as *a major international multi-sport event* (***Olympics***). We argue that such a setting is not realistic as it never happens in the real world. Additionally, since LMs typically develop understandings of concepts by seeing large amounts of contextual examples during pre-training, an unrealistic edit without providing relevant contexts and examples can break the model's existing knowledge structure, leading to a cascade of related failures in the language model.

Metaphor Detection and Resolution Metaphor detection and resolution have long been central tasks in computational linguistics. With the advent of increasingly powerful language models, researchers have begun to explore how effectively these models can understand metaphors. For instance, (Aghazadeh et al., 2022) investigate the capabilities of current language models in handling metaphors by designing a specific probing task and

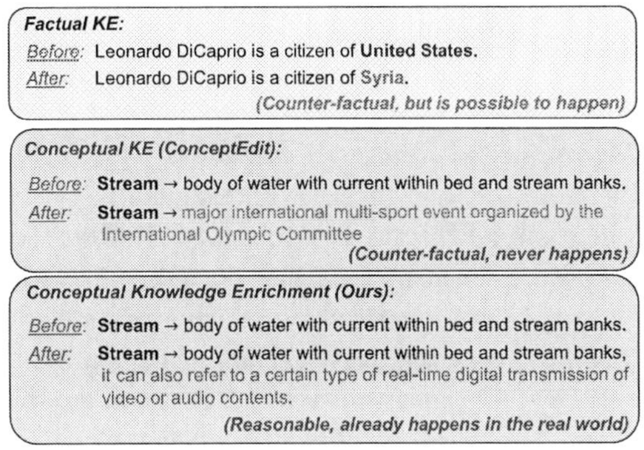

Figure 1: Comparison of the problem settings of traditional factual KE, concept knowledge editing, and concept knowledge enrichment.

dataset. More recently, (Chakrabarty et al., 2023) examined the intersection of visual language models and metaphor detection, evaluating how well diffusion models perform in this complex task.

3 Approach

Problem Formulation We use $p_\theta(\cdot)$ to denote a language model parameterized by θ. Given a set of concepts $\mathcal{C}$, where each concept $c \in \mathcal{C}$ is along with an existing definition $d_{old}(c)$ and a new enriched definition $d_{new}(c)$, our objective is to obtain an updated LM θ_{new} with enriched concept understandings. For example, if c is *tablet*, then $d_{old}(c)$ and $d_{new}(c)$ could be "*a flat piece or slab of stone, clay, wood, or other material, often rectangular in shape, used as a writing surface*" and "*portable touchscreen electronic devices*" respectively.

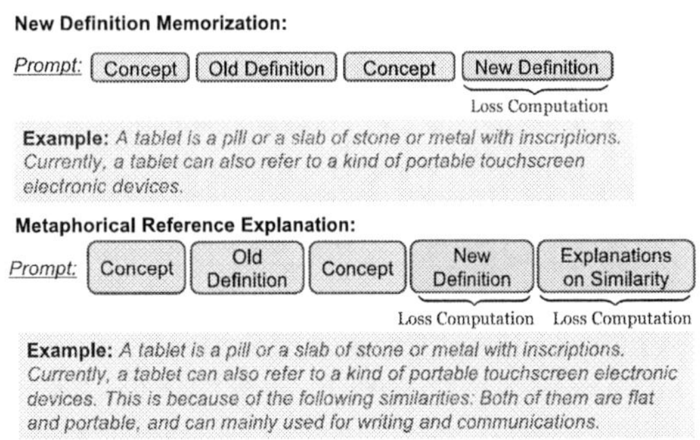

Figure 2: Comparison between the training objectives of *new Definition Memorization* and *Metaphorical Reference Explanation.*

New Definition Memorization We first empower the LM with the fundamental memorization of new definitions of concepts, by directly maximizing the likelihood of new definitions (as illustrated in Figure 2). The loss function can be formulated as a text completion task:

$$\mathcal{L}_{mem}(c) = -\log p_\theta \left(d_{new}(c) \mid c, d_{old}(c) \right). \quad (1)$$

Metaphorical Reference Explanation To further reinforce the model's understanding of the validity of newly enriched concept definitions, we propose a novel method that teaches the model to explain metaphorical references. Specifically, this involves generatively explaining the similarity between the original and new definitions of the concepts. As illustrated in Figure 2, given the concept name and its original definition, we train the model not only to memorize the new definition but also to generate explanations that highlight the similarities between the original and new definitions, clarifying why the enrichment is reasonable. The loss function is formulated as

$$\mathcal{L}_{ref}(c) = -\log p_\theta \left(sim(c) \mid c, d_{new}(c), d_{old}(c) \right),$$

where $sim(c)$ is a textual description on the similarity between the old definition and the new definition. For example, for the original and enriched definitions of ***tablet***, $sim(c)$ could be *"flat and portable, and can mainly used for writing and communications."* Note that such a similarity description can be obtained from the dataset, or generated by the model itself. We evaluate both of these settings in our experiments. The final training objective is a weighted sum of the two loss values.

$$\mathcal{L} = \alpha \cdot \mathcal{L}_{mem} + (1 - \alpha) \cdot \mathcal{L}_{ref}.$$

4 Experiments

4.1 Data

ConceptEnrich Previous work (Wang et al., 2024) develops the *ConceptEdit* dataset that contains a series of concepts with their original and edited definitions. However, as discussed in Section 2, we believe that it is not realistic to directly change the definitions of concepts that are completely unrelated. Therefore, in this paper, we develop a new benchmark dataset, *ConceptEnrich*, which contains 121 concepts that are believed to be substantially enriched recently. The dataset is generated with the assistance of GPT-4, where we prompt the model to brainstorm concepts that have acquired enriched meanings in recent years. The model will also generate their old and new definitions, along with a description of their similarities and some typical instances of the concept. The detailed prompt and one generated example are shown in Figure 3.

Metaphor Detection: VUA Corpus Since we conduct conceptual knowledge enrichment for LMs by training the model to generate explanations for metaphorical reference, it would also be interesting to investigate whether the model with enriched concept understandings can be improved in real linguistic metaphor detection tasks. We adopt the widely-used VUA Corpus (Steen et al., 2010) and test whether our model can perform better.

4.2 Evaluation Metrics

For evaluation metrics, similar to (Wang et al., 2024), we mainly focus on whether the a model taught with enriched concept definitions can perform better in classifying its sub-instances. For example, if the model has already known *"stream"* can be extended to *"digital transmission of audio or video content without the need for downloading"*, can the model correctly identify *"Twitch"* is a certain kind of stream? For each concept and its sub-instances presented in *ConceptEnrich*, we manually construct the same number of negative examples from the sub-instances from other concepts. Then, we use the model to perform a classification task to identify which instances belong to the concept with an enriched meaning. We compute the AUC of the binary classification task and use it to compare the performances of different models. For metaphor reference detection task, we also compute both the accuracy and AUC of metaphor detection.

4.3 Base Model Setup

In this paper, we adopt GPT2-XL (Radford et al., 2019) as our base LM. We choose to use a model released a few years ago because our primary focus in this paper is to evaluate the model's ability to learn updated definitions of concepts. However, many of the most recent open-source language models already include a wide range of concepts in their pre-training data. To ensure a fair comparison and eliminate the influence of existing prior knowledge, we opted for an older model GPT-2. We also adopt the model with the largest available size to ensure that the base model's capability is still robust and strong enough for our evaluations.

4.4 Main Results

To test the effectiveness of our proposed metaphorical reference explanation approach, we mainly compare our final trained model with the baseline

Can you think of some concepts (in English) whose meanings have been enriched or changed in the last 5 years? For example, previously, the concept "tablet" is defined as a flat piece or slab of stone, clay, wood, or other material, often rectangular in shape, used as a writing surface. But now, "tablet" can also refer to a certain kind of touchscreen electronic devices.

Please generate your answers in the following format:
Concept: Tablet
Old Definition: a flat piece or slab of stone, clay, wood, or other material, often rectangular in shape, used as a writing surface
Enriched Definition: a certain kind of touchscreen electronic devices.
Explanation: 1. Both of these are flat and portable. 2. Both of these enables direct interaction with users. 3. Both of these are mainly used for writing and communications.
Examples: Apple iPad, Microsoft Surface Pro, Amazon Kindle

Concept: Stream
1. **Old Definition:** A small, narrow river.
2. **Enriched Definition:** The digital transmission of audio or video content without the need for downloading.
3. **Explanation:**
   1. Both involve the continuous flow of a medium—water in the physical form, data in the digital form.
   2. Both are accessed and utilized as they move along their path.
   3. Both are natural and intuitive ways to receive resources or information.
4. **Examples:**
   Twitch streaming,
   Netflix video streaming,
   Spotify music streaming

Figure 3: The detailed prompt we use to generate data **(left)** and an example generated example from GPT-4 **(right)**.

Models	Accuracy	AUC
GPT2-XL	55.3	50.0
GPT2-XL + Memorization	61.9	64.8
+ *MetaphorExp* (self-generated)	81.0	85.4
+ *MetaphorExp* (GPT4-generated)	**89.5**	**91.3**

Table 1: Performance (%) for sub-instance classification in our proposed *ConceptEnrich* benchmark.

Models	Accuracy	AUC
GPT2-XL	78.3	82.4
GPT2-XL + Memorization	79.0	83.5
+ *MetaphorExp* (self-generated)	79.3	84.4
+ *MetaphorExp* (GPT4-generated)	**81.9**	**86.3**

Table 2: Performance (%) for metaphorical reference detection on the verb-only subset in the VUA corpus.

model only trained with new definition memorization (*GPT2-XL + Memorization*). Additionally, we evaluate the metaphorical reference explanation approach in both of the following settings: using similarity descriptions from the *ConceptEnrich* dataset (*+MetaphorExp* (GPT4-generated)) and those generated by the model itself (*+MetaphorExp* (self-generated)). This allows us to assess whether our approach is robust enough when no predefined similarity descriptions are provided.

From the results in Table 1, we observe that training the model to memorize only the new definitions of concepts enhances its ability to identify

Models	Accuracy	AUC
GPT2-XL	80.3	85.0
GPT2-XL + Memorization	80.5	85.1
+ *MetaphorExp* (self-generated)	81.1	86.0
+ *MetaphorExp* (GPT4-generated)	**85.6**	**89.1**

Table 3: Performance (%) for metaphorical reference detection on the full set of the VUA corpus.

concept sub-instances. Furthermore, our approach, which incorporates metaphorical reference explanations, significantly boosts performance, achieving a 91.3% AUC on the *ConceptEnrich* benchmark. Additionally, even when using self-generated explanations without incorporating any new information, our model still achieves an 85.4% AUC, which is significantly higher than the baseline model that relies solely on memorization. These results demonstrate that using metaphorical reference explanation methods can better help the model to understand and learn enriched meanings of concepts. In Table 2 and Table 3, we can observe similar trends on metaphor detection tasks. These results demonstrate that learning enriched meanings of existing concepts, particularly by exploiting the similarities between old and new definitions, also enhances the language model's ability to detect and understand metaphorical references.

5 Conclusions and Future Work

In this paper, we present a novel and effective approach to concept enrichment in language models by integrating metaphorical reference resolution. The results demonstrate that leveraging metaphorical analogies can significantly enhance a model's ability to comprehend and apply new conceptual knowledge, offering a more nuanced understanding than baseline methods of simply training the model to memorize new concept definitions. The development of a specialized dataset and the successful application of our method to concept sub-instance classification and metaphorical reference detection underscore the potential of our approach.

In future, we plan to explore the scalability of our approach across different domains and languages. Additionally, investigating the integration of our method with other knowledge enrichment techniques, such as continual learning, could further enhance the adaptability and robustness of LMs.

Acknowledgement

We thank the anonymous reviewers for their constructive suggestions. This research is based upon work supported by U.S. DARPA ECOLE Program No. #HR00112390060 and DARPA SemaFor Program No. HR001120C0123. The views and conclusions contained herein are those of the authors and should not be interpreted as necessarily representing the official policies, either expressed or implied, of DARPA, or the U.S. Government. The U.S. Government is authorized to reproduce and distribute reprints for governmental purposes notwithstanding any copyright annotation therein.

References

Ehsan Aghazadeh, Mohsen Fayyaz, and Yadollah Yaghoobzadeh. 2022. Metaphors in pre-trained language models: Probing and generalization across datasets and languages. In *Proceedings of the 60th Annual Meeting of the Association for Computational Linguistics (Volume 1: Long Papers)*, pages 2037–2050, Dublin, Ireland. Association for Computational Linguistics.

Tuhin Chakrabarty, Arkadiy Saakyan, Olivia Winn, Artemis Panagopoulou, Yue Yang, Marianna Apidianaki, and Smaranda Muresan. 2023. I spy a metaphor: Large language models and diffusion models co-create visual metaphors. In *Findings of the Association for Computational Linguistics: ACL 2023*, pages 7370–7388, Toronto, Canada. Association for Computational Linguistics.

Qiyuan He, Yizhong Wang, and Wenya Wang. 2024. Can language models act as knowledge bases at scale? *Preprint*, arXiv:2402.14273.

Jiateng Liu, Pengfei Yu, Yuji Zhang, Sha Li, Zixuan Zhang, and Heng Ji. 2024. Evedit: Event-based knowledge editing with deductive editing boundaries. *Preprint*, arXiv:2402.11324.

Kevin Meng, David Bau, Alex Andonian, and Yonatan Belinkov. 2022. Locating and editing factual associations in GPT. In *Advances in Neural Information Processing Systems 35: Annual Conference on Neural Information Processing Systems 2022, NeurIPS 2022, New Orleans, LA, USA, November 28 - December 9, 2022*.

Kevin Meng, Arnab Sen Sharma, Alex J. Andonian, Yonatan Belinkov, and David Bau. 2023. Mass-editing memory in a transformer. In *The Eleventh International Conference on Learning Representations, ICLR 2023, Kigali, Rwanda, May 1-5, 2023*. OpenReview.net.

Fabio Petroni, Tim Rocktäschel, Sebastian Riedel, Patrick Lewis, Anton Bakhtin, Yuxiang Wu, and Alexander Miller. 2019. Language models as knowledge bases? In *Proceedings of the 2019 Conference on Empirical Methods in Natural Language Processing and the 9th International Joint Conference on Natural Language Processing (EMNLP-IJCNLP)*, pages 2463–2473, Hong Kong, China. Association for Computational Linguistics.

Jiaxin Qin, Zixuan Zhang, Chi Han, Manling Li, Pengfei Yu, and Heng Ji. 2024. Why does new knowledge create messy ripple effects in llms? In *arxiv*.

Alec Radford, Jeff Wu, Rewon Child, David Luan, Dario Amodei, and Ilya Sutskever. 2019. Language models are unsupervised multitask learners.

Sunayana Rane, Polyphony J Bruna, Ilia Sucholutsky, Christopher Kello, and Thomas L Griffiths. 2024. Concept alignment. *arXiv preprint arXiv:2401.08672*.

Gerard J Steen, Aletta G Dorst, J Berenike Herrmann, Anna A Kaal, Tina Krennmayr, Tryntje Pasma, et al. 2010. *A method for linguistic metaphor identification*. John Benjamins Publishing Company Amsterdam.

Xiaohan Wang, Shengyu Mao, Ningyu Zhang, Shumin Deng, Yunzhi Yao, Yue Shen, Lei Liang, Jinjie Gu, and Huajun Chen. 2024. Editing conceptual knowledge for large language models. *Preprint*, arXiv:2403.06259.

Pengfei Yu and Heng Ji. 2023. Self information update for large language models through mitigating exposure bias. In *arxiv*.

Bonan Zhao, Christopher G Lucas, and Neil R Bramley. 2024. A model of conceptual bootstrapping in human cognition. *Nature Human Behaviour*, 8(1):125–136.

Ruilin Zhao, Feng Zhao, Guandong Xu, Sixiao Zhang, and Hai Jin. 2022. Can language models serve as temporal knowledge bases? In *Findings of the Association for Computational Linguistics: EMNLP 2022*, pages 2024–2037, Abu Dhabi, United Arab Emirates. Association for Computational Linguistics.

Polish Coreference Corpus as an LLM Testbed: Evaluating Coreference Resolution within Instruction-Following Language Models by Instruction–Answer Alignment

Karol Saputa and **Angelika Peljak-Łapińska** and **Maciej Ogrodniczuk**

Institute of Computer Science, Polish Academy of Sciences
Warsaw, Poland

karolsaputa@gmail.com,
{angelika.peljak,maciej.ogrodniczuk}@ipipan.waw.pl

Abstract

In this article, we analyse coreference resolution in encoder- and decoder-based approaches in the Polish language. We convert the Polish Coreference Corpus into the instructions suitable for training language models and create supplementary data based on examples that are difficult for encoder-based models, analyse them and create additional questions for more precise mention boundary detection and other ambiguities found.

We propose an evaluation framework for our instructions. The best closed model, Claude 3 Sonnet, achieves 44.52 CoNLL F_1 in instruction following, zero-shot setting, which is surpassed by the fine-tuned Llama 3.1 8B model, which achieves 46.54 F_1.

1 Introduction

Coreference resolution (CR) is traditionally a part of classical natural language processing (NLP) pipeline tasks, treated as a discriminative problem. Until recently, most of the solutions were encoder-based architectures (Liu et al., 2023; Martinelli et al., 2024). Generative approach has been discussed as an alternative, starting with the formulation of coreference resolution as a question answering task (Wu et al., 2020) and the advancements in language models. Thus, a comparison between these two approaches is needed.

A broad focus on large language models with a high number of parameters (Touvron et al., 2023; Dubey et al., 2024), which can be easily trained using human-readable formats of training data, provides an opportunity to reframe the CR problem and improve results. Improvements in encoder-based solutions, which are in exchange much faster (thanks to smaller models), may lead to easier applicability of CR in NLP pipelines.

In this article, we analyse coreference resolution in encoder- and decoder-based approaches and discuss the possible advantages of generative modelling in coreference resolution. Our research case is the Polish language.

For this task, both groups of models are evaluated, an error analysis is conducted, and the potential of providing supplemental Winograd-like finetuning for LLMs is explored.

Smaller LLMs, such as Llama 3.1 8B, finetuned on our instructions achieve results comparable to bigger, commercial, closed models such as Claude 3 Opus. However, these results are far below the levels of custom architectures. These results support the focus of further research on building of new training resources for the Polish language.

2 Related Work

The following Section analyses elements of coreference resolution evaluation related to comparing encoder and decoder approaches.

2.1 Coreference Evaluation

The main resource for CR in the Polish language is the Polish Coreference Corpus (PCC) (Ogrodniczuk et al., 2016) which has been included in the multilingual coreference dataset, CorefUD (Nedoluzhko et al., 2022). The most commonly compared CR metric is the CoNLL F_1 score. This metric, along with others, can be calculated by the coreference scorer (Yu et al., 2023) which evaluates coreference predictions in the CorefUD format and has been used in CR challenges (Žabokrtský et al., 2022, 2023).

Proceedings of the Seventh Workshop on Computational Models of Reference, Anaphora and Coreference (CRAC 2024), pages 23–32

2.2 Language Models in Coreference Resolution

There have been multiple LLM-based coreference resolution systems proposed recently that can be grouped into two categories: (1) LLMs usage is limited to annotating texts in a specific format as in (Hicke and Mimno, 2024; Le and Ritter, 2023; Gan et al., 2024), (2) LLM is incorporated into processing framework as a part of an algorithm e.g. controlling the incremental input to LLM and decoding it (Bohnet et al., 2023), extracting mentions via LM (Skachkova et al., 2023). This system is considered the best known to us solution for the English language.

The first approach (1) requires fewer steps of work. There is no custom data modelling, architecture, or optimisation needed, only supervised fine-tuning of a language model. The annotation schema in this approach can be not expressive enough. For example, the approach of Hicke and Mimno (2024) does not include any texts with minor text alterations in the evaluation, only evaluates exact match scores and requires strict matching of index clusters. Gan et al. (2024) does not analyse the detection of mentions and uses gold mentions instead.

The second approach (2) gives state of the art results thanks to language models' great common sense reasoning about language and world knowledge. Bigger pre-trained models tend to score higher in CR benchmarks (Hicke and Mimno, 2024), as in other tasks. However, in this second approach, there is still a custom architecture needed and coreference reasoning cannot be used directly to improve the general LM performance.

2.3 Encoder-based Solutions

Best-performing solutions for coreference resolutions have moved to an end-to-end, encoder-based approach (Lee et al., 2017), which has been further improved (Kirstain et al., 2021). The Maverick system (Martinelli et al., 2024) presents several improvements to the state-of-the-art encoder-based end-to-end architecture for the English language. Most importantly, it sets the maximum mention span length as a sentence level parameter based on sentence length[1].

These improvements lead Maverick to achieve scores comparable to decoder-based solutions but with a much shorter inference time. However, the benchmark results for coreference resolution plateaued at slightly above 80% CoNLL F_1 score. An encoder-based approach requires modelling of all edge cases in data structures and model architecture. The gains from corrections and inclusion of new edge-cases are small. For example, the CAW system (D'Oosterlinck et al., 2023) improves the score of the earlier model for the 0.9 CoNLL F_1 score.

2.4 Polish Language

Previous attempts to evaluate coreference resolution in the Polish language have been outlined by Saputa (2022) who compares the transformer-based end-to-end approaches with previous systems and discusses dataset-specific modelling for Polish. The performance of models in the Polish language was also discussed as a part of multilingual systems in recent Shared Tasks on Multilingual Coreference Resolution (Žabokrtský et al., 2022, 2023).

3 Challenges for Current Coreference Resolution Systems

3.1 Beyond Annotation in Coreference Resolution

Due to the typical formulation of the task, a prediction of a set of clusters of coreferential mentions, the error analysis of the models is difficult in both qualitative and quantitative way. This was addressed by developing different CR metrics and tools for error analysis, e.g., the taxonomy of errors (Kummerfeld and Klein, 2013). Most importantly, the score of coreference resolution (the correct grouping of mentions into coreferential clusters) cannot be higher than the mention detection score (the correct recognition of all mentions in the text with their proper span limits). This means that mention detection (and the definition of a mention) has a strong impact on the overall coreference resolution score.

[1] It should be noted that the Polish Coreference Corpus contains multi-sentence mentions which are not detected by this architectural approach. The inclusion of longer mentions in the training set, which are more numerous (372 mentions with more than 35 tokens), could yield comparable advantages as in the case of multi-sentence mentions (223 mentions) from a modelling perspective. There is a 91-mention overlap between these two categories: multi-sentence, very long mentions. However, reducing memory overhead is of substantial benefit to the training process.

3.2 Sentence-level Reasoning

One of the frequently occurring errors in mention recognition involves subject clauses, both subordinate (Example 1) and coordinate (Example 2):

(1) *Zresztą fundacje musiałyby rozbudowywać do tych celów jakieś specjalne aparaty urzędniczo-śledcze, co jest absurdem.*
'Besides, NGOs would have to develop some special clerical and investigative apparatus for these purposes, which is absurd.'

(2) *Wydłużyła się droga dzieci do szkół i to także budzi powszechne niezadowolenie.*
'The journey of children to school has lengthened and this, too, is causing widespread dissatisfaction.'

Mentions were often not detected in similar contexts where mention coreferentiality answers the questions of *who?* or *what?*, as in the examples above. The effectiveness of the algorithm is similarly low in the case of mentions in adverbial clauses. Thus, these types of problems were addressed in Section 4.2.

4 Dataset

We convert the Polish Coreference Corpus (Ogrodniczuk et al., 2016) into the instruction format for the evaluation of language models that is suitable for training coreference resolution in the generative approach. The dataset consists of the converted, annotated texts, and two types of supplementary data. The additional data taken from the original collection that is inspired by Winograd-like challenge and post-training approaches to language models: (1) question-answering datasets of examples that are difficult for encoder-based CR model to answer correctly, (2) preferences for answer style and reasoning between models. These supplementary data are motivated by the problems described in Section 3.

4.1 Conversions of PCC into Instructions

The instructions use two formats: bracket-style and list-style. In brackets format, the answer should include the original text of the prompts with mentions annotated in brackets referring to the cluster id (Appendix B.1) e.g.: `[Man]:1`. In list format, the model is asked to construct in its answer a list of clusters with all mentions listed for each cluster (Appendix B.2). The second format is resembling a chain-of-thought, incrementally focusing on next entity in the text. Table 1 presents the number of instructions of each type.

Instructions	Examples		
	Train	Dev	Test
Brackets-style	1463	183	182
List-style	1463	183	182
QA-style	59	7	8
Preferences	59	7	8

Table 1: Details of the instructions provided for LM training. Examples are the entire texts (Brackets/List-style) or sentences (QA-style and Preferences).

4.2 Extracting Difficult Examples from the Corpus

Difficult examples for encoder-based models were selected from the dataset after evaluating the encoder-based model at the sentence level. The sentences with the lowest CoNLL F_1 score were analysed and used to create additional questions for more precise mention boundary detection and more context for other ambiguities found.

QA-style supplemental data (1) is aimed at improving the detection of correct mention boundaries and reasoning about unclear examples in the style of Winograd questions, which require the model to behave as if it was performing commonsense reasoning and possessed knowledge (Cozman and Munhoz, 2020). Preference-style supplementary data (2) is meant to improve the reasoning and explanatory coherence of the model answers, especially when there are multiple possible interpretations, that are resolved by annotators agreement, about which there is no information in a dataset used by encoder-based models. In this context, we refer to the discussion of examples in Section 3.1. In Appendix B.4, an example question is shown with a gold answer and GPT-4o answer that shows both the importance of correct mention boundary detection and coreference reasoning.

4.3 Generating Artificial Examples with LLMs

We used the available language models, GPT 3.5 and LLama 3.1 8B, to generate answers for the prepared questions and assess the preferences between models in terms of correct answer, justification of the answer, precision of citation, and use of appropriate vocabulary.

System	Open	FT	IF rate	MD F$_1$	CoNLL F$_1$ partial match	Precision exact match
GPT-4o	✗	✗	89.80	32.00	24.60	51.06
GPT-4o-mini	✗	✗	64.00	19.32	14.68	23.85
Claude 3 Sonnet	✗	✗	100.00	47.88	44.52	62.22
Claude 3 Opus	✗	✗	100.00	48.30	36.70	69.13
Claude 3 Haiku	✗	✗	84.62	25.94	30.36	38.12
Llama-3.1-70B	✓	✗	26.32	2.99	0.81	3.72
Llama-3.1-8B	✓	✗	1.78	0.56	0.34	0.00
Llama-3.1-8B-FT	✓	✓	100.00	57.80	46.54	62.89
s2e-herbert-large	✓	✓	—	78.40	69.91	73.21
s2e-herbert-base	✓	✓	—	75.53	62.85	70.27

Table 2: Instruction following results of coreference resolution evaluation: Instruction Following (IF) rate, mention detection F_1 (MD), CoNLL F_1 measure on the PCC development set. The following instruction does not apply to `s2e` models as the correct output is asserted by their custom architecture. Evaluation concerns commercial models, open models, and fine-tuned (FT) open models.

5 Evaluation

5.1 Generative Answers Parsing and Alignment

We first tested several prompts on a small development set and then chose one instruction (Appendix B.3) that produced the highest prompt follow-up rate in the tests. This prompt was used in the evaluation of language models in generative coreference resolution.

The text alignment technique (Boyd et al., 2024) was used to match the fragment of each model's generative response to text from the PCC dataset. This is an effective algorithm that allows the modified text (answer) to be matched with the original on the level of individual tokens. Thus, allowing for different tokenization and modifications. Even if the generative answer has a modified version of the texts, the mentions, provided they are intact, should be matched with the original text tokens. This makes it possible to evaluate coreference resolution in general not fine-tuned models whose answers typically include other comments and reasoning in addition to machine-annotated text and have error-prone and alterations-prone evaluation pipelines. This approach also takes into account all possible comments from the model at the beginning and at the end of the text.

The annotation format (Appendix B.1) presents a bracketed format to annotate coreference relations. Such annotated spans are extracted using a regular expression and grouped by cluster id (`[mention_span]:cluster_id`). Text alignment allows for comparison of span indices in each cluster with indices in gold clusters in the dataset, and it also enables writing the prediction back to the conllu file, preserving the original tokenisation. Such conllu files are then evaluated using the coreference scorer.

5.2 Instruction Following

The following instruction is a type of task that does not involve fine-tuning of a model, with only the prompt instructing the model about the task (Zhou et al., 2023). The prompt does not include an example of a complete solution, so it can be described as a zero-shot setting.

The instruction following (IF) rate is a measure of the compliance of a language model with the instructional requirements. We measure IF rate as the correct use of the annotation schema, i.e. non-zero results in the mention detection score. This allows for errors, but reflects at least one correct application of the schema described in the instruction.

In Table 2. we present the results of the evaluation. The IF rate ranges from 26.32% for Llama 3.1 70B to 100% for Claude Opus. Precision scores have been included to demonstrate that the models typically annotate a smaller number of coreference relations than the gold standard annotations, but the predictions are more accurate than the CoNLL F_1 score would suggest. This reflects the issue of task modelling discussed in Section

3.1, which considers the challenge of annotating a large number of relations for each text.

5.3 Instruction Fine-Tuning

We tested the smallest LLama 3.1 model (8B parameters) with supervised fine-tuning for 4 epochs using `SFTTrainer`[2] from the Huggingface ecosystem accustomed to the training infrastructure (see Acknowledgements).

The training used the following default parameters: BF16 precision, batch size of 1, AdamW optimiser, WarmupDecayLR scheduler, maximum sequence length of 8192 tokens, and automatic gradient accumulation. We did not perform any kind of hyper-parameter optimisation apart from tests of prompt instruction formulation (Appendix B.3) that were evaluated on not-tuned models for only a few texts from the training part of the dataset.

In Table 2, we describe results from the development part of the CorefUD Polish dataset, as there is a publicly available gold standard for this part. The fine-tuned model performed better than the best non-tuned model, Claude 3 Sonnet. However, its results are much lower than our reproduction of the results of the start-to-end architecture (Kirstain et al., 2021) that was adapted for the Polish language by Saputa (2022). Table 2 shows scores of non-tuned models, fine-tuned Llama and s2e results[3].

6 Conclusions and Future Work

We proposed a conversion of the Polish Coreference Corpus (PCC) into instructions suitable for generative training, as an adaptation of the coreference resolution for generative models, as well as the evaluation framework for bracket-style answers. There potential for further ablation studies and interaction studies of the proposed resources; for example, we did not provide here an extensive analysis of the difference between training on bracket- and list-style instructions and training on the preferences data. These resources are aimed at reformulation of the coreference resolution dataset format and going beyond standard annotations to handle more fuzziness than is possible using existing available resources.

The first results of the fine-tuning are better than the available commercial and open-source models. The differences in results between open models, commercial models, and the fine-tuned model indicate that commercial models may have been trained on similar types of instructions. Thus, it is important to develop non-commercial datasets and models as alternatives for further advancements of natural language processing in the Polish language.

However, the highest score is much lower than the encoder-based approach discussed for Polish and the decoder-based approaches discussed for English. It means that: (1) custom encoder architectures should be used in specific applications that require coreference resolution, and (2) solving multiple coreference chains during text generation is difficult in the setting proposed in our research.

Acknowledgements

Work completed as part of a project funded by the Polish Minister of Digital Affairs under a special purpose subsidy No. 1/WI/DBiI/202 "Responsible development of the open large language model, PLLuM (Polish Large Language Universal Model) aimed at supporting breakthrough technologies in the public and economic sectors, including an open, Polish-language intelligent assistant for public administration clients."

We would like to thank Piotr Pęzik and Konrad Kaczyński for providing the code for fine-tuning the models that they designed for the LLM training infrastructure used within the PLLuM project.

References

Bernd Bohnet, Chris Alberti, and Michael Collins. 2023. Coreference Resolution through a seq2seq Transition-Based System. *Transactions of the Association for Computational Linguistics*, 11:212–226.

Adriane Boyd, Daniël de Kok, Matthew Honnibal, and Basile Dura. 2024. spacy-alignments. Original-date: 2020-12-08T08:07:25Z.

Fábio Cozman and Hugo Munhoz. 2020. The Winograd Schemas from Hell. In *Encontro Nacional de Inteligência Artificial e Computacional (ENIAC)*, pages 531–542. SBC. ISSN: 2763-9061.

Karel D'Oosterlinck, Semere Kiros Bitew, Brandon Papineau, Christopher Potts, Thomas Demeester, and

[2]`https://huggingface.co/docs/trl/sft_trainer`

[3]It is worth to note that the encoder-based results obtained here are slightly lower than the Shared Tasks state-of-the-art results for Polish. However, since the difference between the performance of the generative modelling is more than 20 points, we did not focus on the improvements.

Chris Develder. 2023. CAW-coref: Conjunction-Aware Word-level Coreference Resolution. In *Proceedings of The Sixth Workshop on Computational Models of Reference, Anaphora and Coreference (CRAC 2023)*, pages 8–14, Singapore. Association for Computational Linguistics.

Abhimanyu Dubey, Abhinav Jauhri, Abhinav Pandey, Abhishek Kadian, Ahmad Al-Dahle, Aiesha Letman, Akhil Mathur, Alan Schelten, Amy Yang, Angela Fan, Anirudh Goyal, Anthony Hartshorn, Aobo Yang, Archi Mitra, Archie Sravankumar, Artem Korenev, Arthur Hinsvark, Arun Rao, Aston Zhang, Aurelien Rodriguez, Austen Gregerson, Ava Spataru, Baptiste Roziere, Bethany Biron, Binh Tang, Bobbie Chern, Charlotte Caucheteux, Chaya Nayak, Chloe Bi, Chris Marra, Chris McConnell, Christian Keller, Christophe Touret, Chunyang Wu, Corinne Wong, Cristian Canton Ferrer, Cyrus Nikolaidis, Damien Allonsius, Daniel Song, Danielle Pintz, Danny Livshits, David Esiobu, Dhruv Choudhary, Dhruv Mahajan, Diego Garcia-Olano, Diego Perino, Dieuwke Hupkes, Egor Lakomkin, Ehab AlBadawy, Elina Lobanova, Emily Dinan, Eric Michael Smith, Filip Radenovic, Frank Zhang, Gabriel Synnaeve, Gabrielle Lee, Georgia Lewis Anderson, Graeme Nail, Gregoire Mialon, Guan Pang, Guillem Cucurell, Hailey Nguyen, Hannah Korevaar, Hu Xu, Hugo Touvron, Iliyan Zarov, Imanol Arrieta Ibarra, Isabel Kloumann, Ishan Misra, Ivan Evtimov, Jade Copet, Jaewon Lee, Jan Geffert, Jana Vranes, Jason Park, Jay Mahadeokar, Jeet Shah, Jelmer van der Linde, Jennifer Billock, Jenny Hong, Jenya Lee, Jeremy Fu, Jianfeng Chi, Jianyu Huang, Jiawen Liu, Jie Wang, Jiecao Yu, Joanna Bitton, Joe Spisak, Jongsoo Park, Joseph Rocca, Joshua Johnstun, Joshua Saxe, Junteng Jia, Kalyan Vasuden Alwala, Kartikeya Upasani, Kate Plawiak, Ke Li, Kenneth Heafield, Kevin Stone, Khalid El-Arini, Krithika Iyer, Kshitiz Malik, Kuenley Chiu, Kunal Bhalla, Lauren Rantala-Yeary, Laurens van der Maaten, Lawrence Chen, Liang Tan, Liz Jenkins, Louis Martin, Lovish Madaan, Lubo Malo, Lukas Blecher, Lukas Landzaat, Luke de Oliveira, Madeline Muzzi, Mahesh Pasupuleti, Mannat Singh, Manohar Paluri, Marcin Kardas, Mathew Oldham, Mathieu Rita, Maya Pavlova, Melanie Kambadur, Mike Lewis, Min Si, Mitesh Kumar Singh, Mona Hassan, Naman Goyal, Narjes Torabi, Nikolay Bashlykov, Nikolay Bogoychev, Niladri Chatterji, Olivier Duchenne, Onur Çelebi, Patrick Alrassy, Pengchuan Zhang, Pengwei Li, Petar Vasic, Peter Weng, Prajjwal Bhargava, Pratik Dubal, Praveen Krishnan, Punit Singh Koura, Puxin Xu, Qing He, Qingxiao Dong, Ragavan Srinivasan, Raj Ganapathy, Ramon Calderer, Ricardo Silveira Cabral, Robert Stojnic, Roberta Raileanu, Rohit Girdhar, Rohit Patel, Romain Sauvestre, Ronnie Polidoro, Roshan Sumbaly, Ross Taylor, Ruan Silva, Rui Hou, Rui Wang, Saghar Hosseini, Sahana Chennabasappa, Sanjay Singh, Sean Bell, Seohyun Sonia Kim, Sergey Edunov, Shaoliang Nie, Sharan Narang, Sharath Raparthy, Sheng Shen, Shengye Wan, Shruti Bhosale, Shun Zhang, Simon Vandenhende, Soumya Batra, Spencer Whitman, Sten Sootla, Stephane Collot, Suchin Gururangan, Sydney Borodinsky, Tamar Herman, Tara Fowler, Tarek Sheasha, Thomas Georgiou, Thomas Scialom, Tobias Speckbacher, Todor Mihaylov, Tong Xiao, Ujjwal Karn, Vedanuj Goswami, Vibhor Gupta, Vignesh Ramanathan, Viktor Kerkez, Vincent Gonguet, Virginie Do, Vish Vogeti, Vladan Petrovic, Weiwei Chu, Wenhan Xiong, Wenyin Fu, Whitney Meers, Xavier Martinet, Xiaodong Wang, Xiaoqing Ellen Tan, Xinfeng Xie, Xuchao Jia, Xuewei Wang, Yaelle Goldschlag, Yashesh Gaur, Yasmine Babaei, Yi Wen, Yiwen Song, Yuchen Zhang, Yue Li, Yuning Mao, Zacharie Delpierre Coudert, Zheng Yan, Zhengxing Chen, Zoe Papakipos, Aaditya Singh, Aaron Grattafiori, Abha Jain, Adam Kelsey, Adam Shajnfeld, Adithya Gangidi, Adolfo Victoria, Ahuva Goldstand, Ajay Menon, Ajay Sharma, Alex Boesenberg, Alex Vaughan, Alexei Baevski, Allie Feinstein, Amanda Kallet, Amit Sangani, Anam Yunus, Andrei Lupu, Andres Alvarado, Andrew Caples, Andrew Gu, Andrew Ho, Andrew Poulton, Andrew Ryan, Ankit Ramchandani, Annie Franco, Aparajita Saraf, Arkabandhu Chowdhury, Ashley Gabriel, Ashwin Bharambe, Assaf Eisenman, Azadeh Yazdan, Beau James, Ben Maurer, Benjamin Leonhardi, Bernie Huang, Beth Loyd, Beto De Paola, Bhargavi Paranjape, Bing Liu, Bo Wu, Boyu Ni, Braden Hancock, Bram Wasti, Brandon Spence, Brani Stojkovic, Brian Gamido, Britt Montalvo, Carl Parker, Carly Burton, Catalina Mejia, Changhan Wang, Changkyu Kim, Chao Zhou, Chester Hu, Ching-Hsiang Chu, Chris Cai, Chris Tindal, Christoph Feichtenhofer, Damon Civin, Dana Beaty, Daniel Kreymer, Daniel Li, Danny Wyatt, David Adkins, David Xu, Davide Testuggine, Delia David, Devi Parikh, Diana Liskovich, Didem Foss, Dingkang Wang, Duc Le, Dustin Holland, Edward Dowling, Eissa Jamil, Elaine Montgomery, Eleonora Presani, Emily Hahn, Emily Wood, Erik Brinkman, Esteban Arcaute, Evan Dunbar, Evan Smothers, Fei Sun, Felix Kreuk, Feng Tian, Firat Ozgenel, Francesco Caggioni, Francisco Guzmán, Frank Kanayet, Frank Seide, Gabriela Medina Florez, Gabriella Schwarz, Gada Badeer, Georgia Swee, Gil Halpern, Govind Thattai, Grant Herman, Grigory Sizov, Guangyi, Zhang, Guna Lakshminarayanan, Hamid Shojanazeri, Han Zou, Hannah Wang, Hanwen Zha, Haroun Habeeb, Harrison Rudolph, Helen Suk, Henry Aspegren, Hunter Goldman, Igor Molybog, Igor Tufanov, Irina-Elena Veliche, Itai Gat, Jake Weissman, James Geboski, James Kohli, Japhet Asher, Jean-Baptiste Gaya, Jeff Marcus, Jeff Tang, Jennifer Chan, Jenny Zhen, Jeremy Reizenstein, Jeremy Teboul, Jessica Zhong, Jian Jin, Jingyi Yang, Joe Cummings, Jon Carvill, Jon Shepard, Jonathan McPhie, Jonathan Torres, Josh Ginsburg, Junjie Wang, Kai Wu, Kam Hou U, Karan Saxena, Karthik Prasad, Kartikay Khandelwal, Katayoun Zand, Kathy Matosich, Kaushik Veeraraghavan, Kelly Michelena, Keqian Li, Kun Huang, Kunal Chawla, Kushal Lakhotia, Kyle Huang, Lailin Chen, Lakshya Garg, Lavender A, Leandro Silva, Lee Bell, Lei Zhang, Liangpeng Guo, Licheng Yu, Liron Moshkovich, Luca Wehrstedt, Madian Khabsa, Manav Avalani, Manish Bhatt, Maria Tsimpoukelli, Martynas Mankus, Matan Hasson, Matthew Lennie, Matthias Reso, Maxim Groshev, Maxim Naumov, Maya Lathi, Meghan Keneally, Michael L. Seltzer, Michal Valko, Michelle Restrepo, Mihir Patel, Mik Vyatskov, Mikayel Samvelyan, Mike Clark, Mike Macey, Mike Wang, Miquel Jubert Hermoso, Mo Metanat, Mohammad Rastegari, Munish Bansal, Nandhini Santhanam, Natascha Parks, Natasha White, Navyata Bawa, Nayan Singhal, Nick Egebo, Nicolas Usunier, Nikolay Pavlovich Laptev, Ning Dong, Ning Zhang, Norman Cheng, Oleg Chernoguz, Olivia Hart, Omkar Salpekar, Ozlem Kalinli, Parkin Kent, Parth Parekh, Paul Saab, Pavan Balaji, Pedro Rittner, Philip Bontrager, Pierre Roux, Piotr Dollar, Polina Zvyagina, Prashant Ratanchandani, Pritish Yuvraj, Qian Liang, Rachad Alao, Rachel Rodriguez, Rafi Ayub, Raghotham Murthy, Raghu Nayani, Rahul Mitra, Raymond Li, Rebekkah Hogan, Robin Battey, Rocky Wang, Rohan Maheswari, Russ Howes, Ruty Rinott, Sai Jayesh Bondu, Samyak Datta, Sara Chugh, Sara Hunt, Sargun Dhillon, Sasha Sidorov, Satadru Pan, Saurabh Verma, Seiji Yamamoto, Sharadh Ramaswamy, Shaun Lindsay, Shaun Lindsay, Sheng Feng, Shenghao Lin, Shengxin Cindy Zha, Shiva Shankar, Shuqiang Zhang, Shuqiang Zhang, Sinong Wang, Sneha Agarwal, Soji Sajuyigbe, Soumith Chintala, Stephanie Max, Stephen Chen, Steve Kehoe, Steve Satterfield, Sudarshan Govindaprasad, Sumit Gupta, Sungmin Cho, Sunny Virk, Suraj Subramanian, Sy Choudhury, Sydney Goldman, Tal Remez, Tamar Glaser, Tamara Best, Thilo Kohler, Thomas Robinson, Tianhe Li, Tianjun Zhang, Tim Matthews, Timothy Chou, Tzook Shaked, Varun Vontimitta, Victoria Ajayi, Victoria Montanez, Vijai Mohan, Vinay Satish Kumar, Vishal Mangla, Vlad Ionescu, Vlad Poenaru, Vlad Tiberiu Mihailescu, Vladimir Ivanov, Wei Li, Wenchen Wang, Wenwen Jiang, Wes Bouaziz, Will Constable, Xiaocheng Tang, Xiaofang Wang, Xiaojian Wu, Xiaolan Wang, Xide Xia, Xilun Wu, Xinbo Gao, Yanjun Chen, Ye Hu, Ye Jia, Ye Qi, Yenda Li, Yilin Zhang, Ying Zhang, Yossi Adi, Youngjin Nam, Yu, Wang, Yuchen Hao, Yundi Qian, Yuzi He, Zach Rait, Zachary DeVito, Zef Rosnbrick, Zhaoduo Wen, Zhenyu Yang, and Zhiwei Zhao. 2024. The Llama 3 Herd of Models. arXiv:2407.21783 [cs].

Denis Emelin and Rico Sennrich. 2021. Wino-X: Multilingual Winograd Schemas for Commonsense Reasoning and Coreference Resolution. In *Proceedings of the 2021 Conference on Empirical Methods in Natural Language Processing*, pages 8517–8532, Online and Punta Cana, Dominican Republic. Association for Computational Linguistics.

Yujian Gan, Massimo Poesio, and Juntao Yu. 2024. Assessing the Capabilities of Large Language Models in Coreference: An Evaluation. In *Proceedings of the 2024 Joint International Conference on Computational Linguistics, Language Resources and Evaluation (LREC-COLING 2024)*, pages 1645–1665, Torino, Italia. ELRA and ICCL.

Rebecca Hicke and David Mimno. 2024. [Lions: 1] and [Tigers: 2] and [Bears: 3], Oh My! Literary Coreference Annotation with LLMs. In *Proceedings of the 8th Joint SIGHUM Workshop on Computational Linguistics for Cultural Heritage, Social Sciences, Humanities and Literature (LaTeCH-CLfL 2024)*, pages 270–277, St. Julians, Malta. Association for Computational Linguistics.

Yuval Kirstain, Ori Ram, and Omer Levy. 2021. Coreference Resolution without Span Representations. In *Proceedings of the 59th Annual Meeting of the Association for Computational Linguistics and the 11th International Joint Conference on Natural Language Processing (Volume 2: Short Papers)*, pages 14–19, Online. Association for Computational Linguistics.

Jonathan K. Kummerfeld and Dan Klein. 2013. Error-Driven Analysis of Challenges in Coreference Resolution. In *Proceedings of the 2013 Conference on Empirical Methods in Natural Language Processing*, pages 265–277, Seattle, Washington, USA. Association for Computational Linguistics.

Nghia T. Le and Alan Ritter. 2023. Are Large Language Models Robust Coreference Resolvers? arXiv:2305.14489 [cs].

Kenton Lee, Luheng He, Mike Lewis, and Luke Zettlemoyer. 2017. End-to-end Neural Coreference Resolution. In *Proceedings of the 2017 Conference on Empirical Methods in Natural Language Processing*, pages 188–197, Copenhagen, Denmark. Association for Computational Linguistics.

Ruicheng Liu, Rui Mao, Anh Tuan Luu, and Erik Cambria. 2023. A brief survey on recent advances in coreference resolution. *Artificial Intelligence Review*, 56(12):14439–14481.

Giuliano Martinelli, Edoardo Barba, and Roberto Navigli. 2024. Maverick: Efficient and Accurate Coreference Resolution Defying Recent Trends. In *Proceedings of the 62nd Annual Meeting of the Association for Computational Linguistics (Volume 1: Long Papers)*, pages 13380–13394, Bangkok, Thailand. Association for Computational Linguistics.

Anna Nedoluzhko, Michal Novák, Martin Popel, Zdeněk Žabokrtský, Amir Zeldes, and Daniel Zeman. 2022. CorefUD 1.0: Coreference Meets Universal Dependencies. In *Proceedings of the Thirteenth Language Resources and Evaluation Conference*, pages 4859–4872, Marseille, France. European Language Resources Association.

Maciej Ogrodniczuk, Katarzyna Głowińska, Mateusz Kopeć, Agata Savary, and Magdalena Zawisławska. 2016. Polish Coreference Corpus. In *Human Language Technology. Challenges for Computer*

Science and Linguistics, pages 215–226, Cham. Springer International Publishing.

Karol Saputa. 2022. Coreference Resolution for Polish: Improvements within the CRAC 2022 Shared Task. In *Proceedings of the CRAC 2022 Shared Task on Multilingual Coreference Resolution*, pages 18–22, Gyeongju, Republic of Korea. Association for Computational Linguistics.

Natalia Skachkova, Tatiana Anikina, and Anna Mokhova. 2023. Multilingual coreference resolution: Adapt and Generate. In *Proceedings of the CRAC 2023 Shared Task on Multilingual Coreference Resolution*, pages 19–33, Singapore. Association for Computational Linguistics.

Hugo Touvron, Louis Martin, Kevin Stone, Peter Albert, Amjad Almahairi, Yasmine Babaei, Nikolay Bashlykov, Soumya Batra, Prajjwal Bhargava, Shruti Bhosale, Dan Bikel, Lukas Blecher, Cristian Canton Ferrer, Moya Chen, Guillem Cucurull, David Esiobu, Jude Fernandes, Jeremy Fu, Wenyin Fu, Brian Fuller, Cynthia Gao, Vedanuj Goswami, Naman Goyal, Anthony Hartshorn, Saghar Hosseini, Rui Hou, Hakan Inan, Marcin Kardas, Viktor Kerkez, Madian Khabsa, Isabel Kloumann, Artem Korenev, Punit Singh Koura, Marie-Anne Lachaux, Thibaut Lavril, Jenya Lee, Diana Liskovich, Yinghai Lu, Yuning Mao, Xavier Martinet, Todor Mihaylov, Pushkar Mishra, Igor Molybog, Yixin Nie, Andrew Poulton, Jeremy Reizenstein, Rashi Rungta, Kalyan Saladi, Alan Schelten, Ruan Silva, Eric Michael Smith, Ranjan Subramanian, Xiaoqing Ellen Tan, Binh Tang, Ross Taylor, Adina Williams, Jian Xiang Kuan, Puxin Xu, Zheng Yan, Iliyan Zarov, Yuchen Zhang, Angela Fan, Melanie Kambadur, Sharan Narang, Aurelien Rodriguez, Robert Stojnic, Sergey Edunov, and Thomas Scialom. 2023. Llama 2: Open Foundation and Fine-Tuned Chat Models. arXiv:2307.09288 [cs].

Wei Wu, Fei Wang, Arianna Yuan, Fei Wu, and Jiwei Li. 2020. CorefQA: Coreference Resolution as Query-based Span Prediction. In *Proceedings of the 58th Annual Meeting of the Association for Computational Linguistics*, pages 6953–6963, Online. Association for Computational Linguistics.

Juntao Yu, Michal Novák, Abdulrahman Aloraini, Nafise Sadat Moosavi, Silviu Paun, Sameer Pradhan, and Massimo Poesio. 2023. The Universal Anaphora Scorer 2.0. In *Proceedings of the 15th International Conference on Computational Semantics*, pages 183–194, Nancy, France. Association for Computational Linguistics.

Jeffrey Zhou, Tianjian Lu, Swaroop Mishra, Siddhartha Brahma, Sujoy Basu, Yi Luan, Denny Zhou, and Le Hou. 2023. Instruction-Following Evaluation for Large Language Models.

Zdeněk Žabokrtský, Miloslav Konopik, Anna Nedoluzhko, Michal Novák, Maciej Ogrodniczuk, Martin Popel, Ondrej Prazak, Jakub Sido, and Daniel Zeman. 2023. Findings of the Second Shared Task on Multilingual Coreference Resolution. In *Proceedings of the CRAC 2023 Shared Task on Multilingual Coreference Resolution*, pages 1–18, Singapore. Association for Computational Linguistics.

Zdeněk Žabokrtský, Miloslav Konopík, Anna Nedoluzhko, Michal Novák, Maciej Ogrodniczuk, Martin Popel, Ondřej Pražák, Jakub Sido, Daniel Zeman, and Yilun Zhu. 2022. Findings of the Shared Task on Multilingual Coreference Resolution. In *Proceedings of the CRAC 2022 Shared Task on Multilingual Coreference Resolution*, pages 1–17, Gyeongju, Republic of Korea. Association for Computational Linguistics.

A Other methods

A.1 Adaptation of English Winograd Schema

Translating the English Winograd Schema into Polish proved unsuccessful in most respects due to structural differences between the languages. Those differences do not concern the English-Polish pair exclusively. Emelin and Sennrich (2021), working with German, French, and Russian, found "that not all WinoGrande samples are suitable for the inclusion in Wino-X, as replacing the "gap" [token in place of an ambiguous pronoun in each schema, which can be filled by one of two preceding nouns] with "it" can yield ungrammatical or disfluent sequences" (p. 8518)

Emelin and Sennrich also used certain heuristics to filter out cases that would be difficult to translate, but most of those heuristics, however, do not apply to the Polish language. Moreover, the WinoMT dataset was quality checked with the use of Python grammar checker, also known as OpenOffice spellchecker, and it proved to be insensitive to syntax and stylistic errors, which usually disqualify most Polish translations of Winograd Schema Challenge examples.

Translation attempts revealed that only a handful of ambiguous structures present in the original schema are in fact ambiguous and both grammatically and stylistically correct in Polish.

In our search for difficult examples of coreference, we also carried out a literature review, aimed specifically at finding sentences and texts containing mentions that should be ambiguous for the language model but should not pose a challenge for a human. This method also gave unsatisfactory results.

A.2 Creating New Examples based on Samples Found in Previous Efforts

We got a handful of examples that proved difficult for an existing model, but there was no apparent pattern connecting those instances.

B Instruction Details

B.1 Generative Answer Schema

This is a fragment of text with id 307 (with original punctuation). Mentions with cluster index appearing only once appear later in the text. Singletons (mentions appearing only once, not coreferential) are omitted.

> kompletnie nie [zgadzam]:0 się z tą interpretacją że ruch. To wskazanie [Marka Belki]:1 jest obliczone na pozyskanie przez [Bronisława Komorowskiego]:2 [elektoratu centrolewicowego]:3 wszystkie badania pokazują że [ten elektorat centrolewicowy]:3 jest zdecydowany głosować na. [Komorowskiego]:2. SLD z całym szacunkiem ma te między pięć a siedem procent twardego elektor elektoratu lewicowego a nie [centrolewicowego]:3 to po pierwsze po drugie wydaje [mi]:0 się że. akurat [mam]:0. prawo bronić [decyzji. [marszałka Komorowskiego]:2 żeby już teraz zgłaszać [kandydata na [prezesa [banku]:7]:6]:5]:4 bo po pierwsze od początku [mówiłem]:0 że akurat [ta instytucja]:7 w przeciwieństwie do niektórych innych.

Following English translation of the above fragment:

> [I]:0 completely disagree with this interpretation that the movement. This indication of [Marek Belka]:1 is calculated to win over [Bronisław Komorowski]:2 [the centre-left electorate]:3 all polls show that [this centre-left electorate]:3 is determined to vote for. [Komorowski]:2. The SLD with all due respect has those between five and seven percent of the hard left electorate and not [centre-left electorate]:3 this is first of all, secondly it seems to [me]:0 that. just [I]:0 have. the right to defend [the decision of. [Speaker Komorowski]:2 to announce [a candidate for [the president of the [bank]:7]:6]:5]:4 already now because firstly from the beginning [I]:0 said that exactly [this institution]:7 unlike some others.

B.2 List-style Instruction

This is fragment of the list-style answer generated for text 307. Singletons (mentions appearing only once, not coreferential) are omitted.

> grupa (1): *zgadzam, mi, mam, mówiłem, ja, moja, ja, przyjmowałem, mi*
>
> grupa (2): *Marka Belki, Marek Belka*
>
> grupa (3): *Bronisława Komorowskiego,*

Komorowskiego, marszałka Komorowskiego, marszałka Komorowskiego, marszałek

grupa (4): *elektoratu centrolewicowego, ten elektorat centrolewicowy, centrolewicowego*

grupa (5): *decyzji marszałka Komorowskiego żeby już teraz zgłaszać kandydata na prezesa banku, ta decyzja*

grupa (6): *kandydata na prezesa banku, jakiejś kandydatury*

grupa (7): *prezesa banku, tym prezesem*

grupa (8): *banku, ta instytucja, ta instytucja, bank, on*

Following English translation of the above fragment:

group (1): *I, me, I have, I said, I, my, I, I accepted, me*

group (2): *Mark Belka, Marek Belka*

group (3): *Bronislaw Komorowski, Komorowski, marshal Komorowski, marshal Komorowski, marshal*

group (4): *centre-left electorate, this centre-left electorate, centre-left*

group (5): *the decision of Marshal Komorowski to already put forward a candidate for bank president, this decision*

group (6): *a candidate for bank president, some candidacy*

group (7): *the bank president, this president*

group (8): *the bank, this institution, this institution, the bank, it*

B.3 Instruction Following Prompt

Zaznacz relacje koreferencji w poniższym tekście za pomocą nawiasów kwadratowych i indeksów wspólnej referencji - `[zakres wzmianki]:indeks_grupy` np. `[syn [jednej z [Polek]:3]:2]:1`. Zwróć uwagę na dokładne granice wzmianek i ich kolejność. Tekst:

Following English translation of the above fragment:

Mark the coreference relations in the following text using square brackets and subscripts of the common reference - `[mention range]:index_group` e.g. `[son of [one of [Poles]:3]:2]:1`. Note the exact boundaries of the mentions and their order. Text:

B.4 Winograd-like Questions

Below we include one exemplary sentence-level question in the Winograd style from the development part of the QA-style dataset that has a wrong answer from the GPT-4o model.

Question: Odpowiedz na poniższe pytanie. Napisz wyłącznie samą odpowiedź lub przynajmniej powtórz dokładną odpowiedź osobno w ostatniej linii. Zacytuj dokładny fragment, do którego odnosi się 'to' w zdaniu: "Wprawdzie już zapoznał się z naszymi broszurami, ale to mu nie wystarcza, chciałby przeprowadzić wywiady z dostojnikami, przyjrzeć się naszemu życiu z bliska". Odpowiedz wyłącznie cytatem z tekstu.

GPT-4o answer: ...ale to mu nie wystarcza...

Gold answer: zapoznał się z naszymi broszurami

Following English translation of the above fragment:

Question:. Answer the following question. Write only the answer itself or at least repeat the exact answer separately on the last line. Quote the exact passage to which 'it' refers in the sentence: 'Although he has already familiarised himself with our brochures, but this is not enough for him, he would like to interview the dignitaries, take a close look at our life'. Respond with a quote from the text only.

GPT-4o answer: ...but that is not enough for him...

Gold answer: has familiarised himself with our brochures

MSCAW-coref: Multilingual, Singleton and Conjunction-Aware Word-Level Coreference Resolution

Houjun Liu*, **John Bauer, Karel D'Oosterlinck**
Christopher Potts, Christopher D. Manning
Stanford University
*houjun@stanford.edu

Abstract

Modern multi-lingual coreference resolution approaches largely focus on the clustering of mention spans, leading to quartic complexity in the choice of both spans and span links. The recently published CAW-coref reduces coreference complexity to quadratic while still attaining 97.9% of SOTA performance through a word-level approach on the English OntoNotes slice. Naively extending the CAW-coref algorithm towards multiple languages on the CorefUD dataset results in a lackluster 77.4% of SOTA performance. We find this is due to annotation differences across OntoNotes and CorefUD—the latter features singletons which CAW-coref is not able to classify. In response, we introduce MSCAW-coref, which extends CAW-coref to work in a multilingual setting and accounts for singleton mentions. We demonstrate that MSCAW-coref attains 95.7% of SOTA performance on CorefUD while being substantially more efficient. Our algorithmic contribution towards accounting for singletons is a major driver of performance. Finally, we discuss the cross-linguistic generalization capability of our approach. We release the models, code, and a package for performing coreference analysis for the community as a part of Stanza (https://github.com/stanfordnlp/stanza).

1 Introduction

Coreference resolution ("coref") is the task of finding textual spans within a document that refer to the same entity in the real world. It is an important parsing step with many applications in NLP (Jurafsky and Martin, 2021). Coref is especially difficult when processing long documents with corresponding long chains of dependencies. Classical end-to-end neural approaches (Lee et al., 2017) often use a procedure that resolves coref by first identifying spans and then linking them together, leading to an $O(n^4)$ computation for n tokens. Worse yet, state-of-the-art (SOTA) coref approaches are often transition parsers (Bohnet et al., 2023), which require multiple forward passes of a language model (LM) to resolve all chains. Such inefficient computation is often untenable, especially in long documents.

Dobrovolskii (2021) and D'Oosterlinck et al. (2023) introduce WL-coref and CAW-coref, which are two iterations of an approach which (1) creates word-level bilinear links for head-word identification, (2) filters the links for likely coreference, and (3) extracts the spans surrounding each headword. This only-once-bilinear approach reduces the complexity of the coref computation to $O(n^2)$ while causing little loss in coref performance.

While these approaches are promising for high-efficiency coref computations, two limitations remain: first, these current approaches only focus on English, usually using the OntoNotes corpus (Weischedel et al., 2011); second, the identification of singleton mentions are beneficial across application domains of coreference (Recasens et al., 2013) but cannot be represented with existing word-level approaches due to the current heuristic of non-mentions being words with no antecedents.

In response, we introduce MSCAW-coref, an extension of the word-level coreference approach that addresses both of these challenges. To support singleton links, we revise the head-word linking step in CAW-coref to include a "sequence start" antecedent link for all first references in a chain, thereby supporting singletons through having at least one antecedent link; to support multilinguality, we apply a low-rank adaptation parameter-efficient fine-tuning scheme to XLM-RoBERTa (Hu et al., 2021; Conneau et al., 2020) to create contextual embeddings with multilingual support.

We train our approach on CorefUD, a multilingual coreference dataset with annotated singletons (Nedoluzhko et al., 2022), and demonstrate 95.7% performance compared to the best-reported quartic multilingual results while maintaining the

Proceedings of the Seventh Workshop on Computational Models of Reference, Anaphora and Coreference (CRAC 2024), pages 33–40
November 15, 2024.

dramatically more efficient modeling approach of word-level coref. We further demonstrate that our approach can zero-shot generalize to unseen languages at training time at a slight cost to performance.

2 Related Work

2.1 Modeling Approaches

Transition and Sequence-to-Sequence Parses The current state-of-the-art in coref (Bohnet et al., 2023) is formulated as an autoregressive, transition-based parser which creates each link with a forward pass of a 13B parameter LM until the reference chains are built. These methods have been demonstrated to generalize well over structured language parsing tasks (Paolini et al., 2021) and can be reformulated as autoregressive language modeling tasks either by identifying coreferences directly (Zhang et al., 2023) or through many surrogate tasks such as question-answering (Wu et al., 2020) or even language model prompting (Le and Ritter, 2023). While the performance of these approaches is strong, processing n tokens corresponds to worst-case n forward passes with a time complexity of $O(n)$ of a full (possibly very large, as in the case of Bohnet et al., 2023) LM required building all transitions, which introduces significant inefficiencies for long documents.

Span-Level Parses Despite the significant performance gains of recent Seq2Seq approaches, the vast majority of modern approaches are span-level parses which first formulate likely mentions before linking them together. The first end-to-end coreference model (Lee et al., 2017) follows this approach, which was later improved with an LM for contextual embeddings (Joshi et al., 2019) and multilingualism (Pražák et al., 2021). In addition to span-level linking, later work such as SpanBERT (Joshi et al., 2020) improved the performance even further by incorporating span-level representations. While being significantly more scalable than transition-based parses, these approaches still require the LM to disambiguate coref decisions, scaling by a factor of $O(n^4)$ for n input tokens (with pruning to optimize runtime performance at the cost of accuracy and to keep the problem from being intractable) due to the need to first create spans $O(n^2)$ then link them together $O(n^2)$.

Word-Level Parses In response to these inefficiencies, approaches emerged that link words together first prior to detecting spans. Kirstain et al. (2021) achieved promising span-level results without using spans at all, by formulating a word-level link to the end of each span instead. In this work, we build most directly upon `WL-coref` and `CAW-coref` (Dobrovolskii, 2021; D'Oosterlinck et al., 2023)—approaches that link head-words together before expanding each into spans.

2.2 Multilinguality

Recent approaches that demonstrated performance gains in handling multilinguality vary from language-specific fine-tuning (Skachkova et al., 2023), monolingual training from scratch (Pražák et al., 2021), or joint training with a multilingual LM (Straka, 2023). Despite the gains from specific fine-tuning demonstrated by prior approaches, the joint training method currently holds the best result for the multilingual coreference shared task (Žabokrtský et al., 2023) and is extended upon in this work.

3 `MSCAW-coref`

3.1 Data Preprocessing

To create head-word coreference data via annotated span-level entities, we follow `CAW-coref`. We use the dependency parse information given in the source dataset to pick the headword that is (1) dependent on a word outside the span or, if available, (2) coordinating conjunction within each span, if less than two dependency steps away from the head-word from (1). We discuss concerns of soundness for maintaining conjunction-awareness across languages in appendix C.

3.2 Modeling

Our `MSCAW-coref` extends `CAW-coref` (D'Oosterlinck et al., 2023). We now describe our approach here while additionally summarizing the aspects of `CAW-coref` left unchanged.

Word-Level Representations `CAW-coref` leveraged a monolingual LM backbone, specifically `RoBERTa-large` (Liu et al., 2019), for contextual word-level representations by performing a single forward pass of the input document. To support multilingualism, we elected to use the larger 561M parameter `XLM-RoBERTa-large` (Conneau et al., 2020) as our LM backbone. To improve training time performance, we tune our approach using Low-Rank adaptations (Hu et al., 2021).

Coarse Scoring Without change from `CAW-coref`, a *coarse antecedent score* is created by a bilinear mapping between each of the input word embeddings obtained in the previous step. For each word, then, the top k coarse antecedents' embeddings are then passed to the next step.

Final Scoring and Singleton Prediction We first apply a small feed-forward network to compute a *fine antecedent score* for each word against its top k coarse antecedents, with higher values representing headwords that are more likely to be coreferential.

Second, we formulate an additional binary classification task whereby the fine antecedent scores of all words, including those in the future, are used as input features to predict whether or not each word is the first occurrence of a coreference chain.

After this is complete, for each word in the document, we obtain (1) k real-valued *antecedent scores*—computed as the sum of the rough and fine antecedent scores—for being a possible antecedent corresponding to k candidate antecedents in the document as well as (2) a single real-valued score for that word being the first member of a mention.

Coref Chain Construction We perform a greedy breadth-first search procedure using the scores computed in the fine-scoring step to chain corefs. We first examine the highest score for each word and delineate three cases—(1) if all of its scores are negative, we consider the word not coreferent and ignore it; (2) if any of its top-k antecedent scores are the highest of all scores, we add the corresponding antecedent word to our search stack; (3) if the first-mention score is the highest, we mark that word as the first mention in our search tree and add it to the search stack. After emptying the search stack, we obtain chains of coreferent words by retracing antecedent links, with the first token of each chain marked as "first-mention".

Notably, we can detect singletons by distinguishing cases (1) and (3)—words could have no valid antecedents (i.e., fitting case (2)), yet still, be added to our search/coref stack—even if size 1—due to its first-mention score.

Span Extraction Finally, exactly following `CAW-coref`, for each coreferent word, a span is extracted using a feed-forward neural network followed by a 1-dimensional convolutional layer which marks the start and end of each span. Coreference cluster information is not given to this step.

4 Experiments

4.1 Data

Most current approaches to coref are trained on OntoNotes (Weischedel et al., 2011) (including previously `CAW-coref` and `WL-coref`), which is a corpus which both does not include support for singletons and have fairly shallow coverage of both languages and linguistic phenomena (Nedoluzhko et al., 2022; Zeldes); the dataset includes only English, Arabic, and Chinese sections.

However, recent advances in universal syntactical tagging (de Marneffe et al., 2021) resulted in much more standardized annotations of morphological features as well as dependencies (necessary for our approach) across languages, leading to the development of CorefUD (Nedoluzhko et al., 2022): a multilingual corpus for coreference resolution. This corpus is suitable for training our current task as CorefUD has support for a variety of languages (10) spanning across the Germanic, Slavic, and Romance families, and has annotations for singleton mentions. Further, as described in section 4.2, the corpus has been widely used in shared tasks for multilingual coref.

To train and evaluate our model, we select the entire publically available subset of CorefUD published for the CRAC shared task, and prepare the dataset in the manner described further in section 4.2. We use train/dev splits provided by the shared task, and make no modification in terms of the data subset selection; if multiple datasets were available for a particular language, we mixed together all of them and trained jointly.

4.2 Baseline Study

Baselines The CRAC shared task on multilingual coreference resolution (Žabokrtský et al., 2023) directly uses the CorefUD (Nedoluzhko et al., 2022) dataset; approaches presented in the task, therefore, provide suitable and timely baselines for multilingual coreference resolution. We therefore elect to score our approach against the top-performing approaches presented in that shared task. We also benchmark applying `CAW-coref` directly with a multilingual backbone without the proposed changes for coref chain construction and singletons.

Scoring `MSCAW-coref` follows a *different* definition of head-words (due to conjunction resolution described in section 3.1). This makes exact

	efficiency		MUC			B^3			$ceaf_e$			mean
	complexity	LM params	R	P	F1	R	P	F1	R	P	F1	F1
ours	$O(n^2)$	561M	0.782	0.760	0.771	0.74	0.748	0.744	0.717	**0.764**	0.740	0.752
ours (naive CAW-coref)†	$O(n^2)$	561M	0.777	0.773	0.775	0.530	0.729	0.613	0.306	0.746	0.434	0.608
Straka, 2023	$O(n^4)$	1.2B	**0.810**	**0.814**	**0.812**	**0.779**	**0.780**	**0.78**	**0.788**	0.741	**0.763**	**0.785**
Anonymous‡	-	-	0.751	0.803	0.776	0.715	0.773	0.743	0.750	0.725	0.737	0.750
Pražák and Konopik, 2022*	$O(n^4)$	561M	0.728	0.762	0.745	0.658	0.639	0.649	0.637	0.523	0.574	0.656
Pražák et al., 2021	$O(n^4)$	179M	0.642	0.776	0.703	0.422	0.714	0.531	0.255	0.702	0.374	0.536

Table 1: Performance of our approach on the CorefUD 1.1 dataset against baseline and top performers from the 2023 CRAC multilingual shared task, dev slice (Nedoluzhko et al., 2022). **mean F1** is the main metric being evaluated. Scores are calculated with the official scorer of the CRAC shared task but using **exact span matches** and **including singletons**. Where possible, the published dev predictions from the shared task are used. †: implementation of `CAW-coref` with our proposed multi-lingual backbone without novel singleton scorer. ‡: anonymous submission to 2023 challenge without corresponding publication. *: results presented are an iteration included in the 2023 shared task. Model optimization details are given in appendix B.

Span LEA / Held Out		Germanic			Romance			Slavic			Uralic
	all	no	de	en	es	fr	ca	pl	ru	cs	hu
none	0.689	0.734	0.638	0.656	0.712	0.503	0.693	0.68	0.677	0.715	0.569
no	-0.075	-0.054	-0.144	-0.038	+0.043	+0.061	+0.033	+0.037	+0.001	+0.008	+0.084
de	-0.085	-0.106	-0.317	-0.072	+0.059	+0.060	-0.010	+0.033	+0.020	+0.020	+0.067
en	-0.074	-0.086	-0.146	-0.148	+0.088	+0.084	-0.003	+0.026	+0.008	+0.041	+0.058
es	-0.092	-0.080	-0.100	-0.062	-0.008	+0.043	+0.022	+0.032	+0.024	-0.007	+0.005
fr	-0.163	-0.052	-0.106	-0.054	+0.050	-0.098	+0.001	+0.012	+0.031	+0.017	+0.042
ca	-0.076	-0.081	-0.119	-0.025	-0.007	+0.067	-0.066	-0.001	+0.022	+0.039	+0.035
pl	-0.091	-0.084	-0.073	-0.049	+0.034	+0.056	+0.046	-0.307	-0.009	+0.012	+0.042
ru	-0.097	-0.073	-0.106	-0.046	+0.043	+0.063	-0.011	-0.008	-0.312	+0.025	+0.089
cs	-0.100	-0.095	-0.037	-0.029	+0.046	+0.058	+0.049	+0.022	+0.039	-0.467	+0.061
hu	-0.086	-0.095	-0.092	-0.027	+0.075	+0.049	-0.015	-0.012	+0.024	+0.017	-0.136

Table 2: Ablation of performance of `MSCAW-coref` across languages and when generalizing to unseen languages. The top row of the table shows percentage performance in span-match LEA (Moosavi and Strube, 2016); the colored rows show the percentage change in performance when the language outlined in the row is withheld from training. Results reported balanced per language. Model optimization details are given in appendix B.

head-word match (used originally in the shared task) an unsuitable metric for scoring the results obtained here; furthermore, the comparison score in the shared task does not account for singletons, which have important and distinct uses in discourse (De Marneffe et al., 2015) from regular mentions. As such, our baseline scores against CorefUD use the *exact span level matches* which also *includes singletons* instead of the head-word-only and non-singleton scores used as the primary metric of the CRAC shared task.

Notably, there is an exact algorithmic solution provided by the shared task[1] to derive the head-word from the dependency tree, so the exact span resolution task (unlike previously the partial span resolution task) is a superset of the metric usually given in the shared task.

Scores are computed with the official scoring system given in the shared task, and recomputed from published dev set outputs of shared task participants when needed.

4.3 Ablation Study

We also evaluate the performance of our model across languages and its ability to generalize to unseen languages. To do this, we sample a 10% test split from the train split of CorefUD, controlling for an equivalent representation of each language across all datasets. Then, we withhold one language at a time during training and report evaluation results across all languages (including the withheld language).

5 Results

Table 1 gives the results of our baseline study. While our approach achieves 96% of the performance of the leading solution of the shared task (Straka, 2023) on the CoNLL-2012 metric evaluated with singletons and exact span matches, we did so with significantly reduced computational complexity from $O(n^4)$ to $O(n^2)$ as well as lowered constant-time performance due to the reduc-

[1] https://github.com/udapi/udapi-python/blob/master/udapi/block/corefud/movehead.py

tion of parameters in the LM backbone. Notably, the highest-performing approach in the shared task using our same LM backbone (Pražák and Konopik, 2022) achieved a dramatically lower performance of 65.6% compared to our 75.2%. Furthermore, naively applying the original `CAW-coref` using a multi-lingual backbone, on the other hand, only results in 60.8% mean F1 compared to our 75.2% mean F1 (row 2).

We further investigate the language-specific and out-of-domain generalization results of our scheme in table 2. Results appear to be roughly clustered by language family. Romance languages generalize well amongst each other: holding out French entirely during training but including Spanish and Catalan only results in a 9.8% reduction in French performance, and holding out Spanish or Catalan at training only results in less than 1% reduction in the test performance of the other; Germanic languages appears to benefit from inclusion of all data; and Slavic and Uralic languages benefited from the *removal* of other families' languages during training. We find the performance degradation between language family lines qualitatively supported by previous work (Pražák et al., 2021)—in part due to differing annotation standards (Porada et al., 2024)—and also underscore our approach's ability to generalize zero-shot to unseen languages.

6 Conclusion

In this work, we extend `CAW-coref` (D'Oosterlinck et al., 2023), an instance of `WL-coref` (Dobrovolskii, 2021), to add support for singleton mentions and non-English languages. We did so by introducing `MS-CAW` coref, a modeling approach that retains word-level time-complexity while achieving performance that is within 5% of the best-performing multilingual model on the CorefUD multilingual dataset in span-match metrics. We further release our trained multilingual models and corresponding source code for use by the wider community.

Limitations

Our approach predicts singletons through disambiguation of the starts of mention chains, yet prior work (De Marneffe et al., 2015) discussed the reduction of modeling complexity through predicting coreferent sequences and singletons as separate objects. Early empirical results (appendix A) indicate that our approach performs slightly better compared to using the cluster start classifier to predict singletons only; yet, further investigations into these results would add to the understanding of coreference modeling.

Furthermore, we inherit the choice from `CAW-coref` that each span can be isomorphically mapped to a headword—this is not true: there will always be more spans than headwords in a sequence. Further investigations into the deduplication of overlapping spans will likely bring further gains in performance to our approach.

Recent work highlights that differing annotation standards between datasets may contribute to variations in performance in coreference tasks (Porada et al., 2024). Correspondingly, we did observe generalization differences across datasets. A systemic error analysis that takes into account these different standards can help improve the generalization performance of the approach.

Lastly, as discussed in appendix C, we note that the conjunction-awareness properties of `CAW-coref` did not result in performance gains of similar magnitude in the multilingual setting. Further work can investigate language-specific properties of CAW and adapt the approach for further performance improvements.

Acknowledgments

We thank our anonymous reviewers for their valuable and gracious feedback on our work. Our model is implemented for and with the tooling provided by Stanza (Qi et al., 2020).

References

Bernd Bohnet, Chris Alberti, and Michael Collins. 2023. Coreference resolution through a seq2seq transition-based system. *Transactions of the Association for Computational Linguistics*, 11:212–226.

Alexis Conneau, Kartikay Khandelwal, Naman Goyal, Vishrav Chaudhary, Guillaume Wenzek, Francisco Guzmán, Edouard Grave, Myle Ott, Luke Zettlemoyer, and Veselin Stoyanov. 2020. Unsupervised cross-lingual representation learning at scale. In *Proceedings of the 58th Annual Meeting of the Association for Computational Linguistics*, pages 8440–8451, Online. Association for Computational Linguistics.

Marie-Catherine de Marneffe, Christopher D. Manning, Joakim Nivre, and Daniel Zeman. 2021. Universal Dependencies. *Computational Linguistics*, 47(2):255–308.

Marie-Catherine De Marneffe, Marta Recasens, and Christopher Potts. 2015. Modeling the lifespan of discourse entities with application to coreference resolution. *Journal of Artificial Intelligence Research*, 52:445–475.

Vladimir Dobrovolskii. 2021. Word-level coreference resolution. In *Proceedings of the 2021 Conference on Empirical Methods in Natural Language Processing*, pages 7670–7675, Online and Punta Cana, Dominican Republic. Association for Computational Linguistics.

Karel D'Oosterlinck, Semere Kiros Bitew, Brandon Papineau, Christopher Potts, Thomas Demeester, and Chris Develder. 2023. CAW-coref: Conjunction-aware word-level coreference resolution. In *Proceedings of The Sixth Workshop on Computational Models of Reference, Anaphora and Coreference (CRAC 2023)*, pages 8–14, Singapore. Association for Computational Linguistics.

Edward J Hu, Phillip Wallis, Zeyuan Allen-Zhu, Yuanzhi Li, Shean Wang, Lu Wang, Weizhu Chen, et al. 2021. Lora: Low-rank adaptation of large language models. In *International Conference on Learning Representations*.

Mandar Joshi, Danqi Chen, Yinhan Liu, Daniel S. Weld, Luke Zettlemoyer, and Omer Levy. 2020. SpanBERT: Improving pre-training by representing and predicting spans. *Transactions of the Association for Computational Linguistics*, 8:64–77.

Mandar Joshi, Omer Levy, Luke Zettlemoyer, and Daniel Weld. 2019. BERT for coreference resolution: Baselines and analysis. In *Proceedings of the 2019 Conference on Empirical Methods in Natural Language Processing and the 9th International Joint Conference on Natural Language Processing (EMNLP-IJCNLP)*, pages 5803–5808, Hong Kong, China. Association for Computational Linguistics.

Daniel Jurafsky and James H Martin. 2021. Speech and language processing: An introduction to natural language processing, computational linguistics, and speech recognition.

Yuval Kirstain, Ori Ram, and Omer Levy. 2021. Coreference resolution without span representations. In *Proceedings of the 59th Annual Meeting of the Association for Computational Linguistics and the 11th International Joint Conference on Natural Language Processing (Volume 2: Short Papers)*, pages 14–19, Online. Association for Computational Linguistics.

Nghia T. Le and Alan Ritter. 2023. Are large language models robust coreference resolvers? *Preprint*, arxiv:2305.14489 [cs].

Kenton Lee, Luheng He, Mike Lewis, and Luke Zettlemoyer. 2017. End-to-end neural coreference resolution. In *Proceedings of the 2017 Conference on Empirical Methods in Natural Language Processing*, pages 188–197, Copenhagen, Denmark. Association for Computational Linguistics.

Yinhan Liu, Myle Ott, Naman Goyal, Jingfei Du, Mandar Joshi, Danqi Chen, Omer Levy, Mike Lewis, Luke Zettlemoyer, and Veselin Stoyanov. 2019. Roberta: A robustly optimized bert pretraining approach. *arXiv preprint arXiv:1907.11692*.

Nafise Sadat Moosavi and Michael Strube. 2016. Which coreference evaluation metric do you trust? a proposal for a link-based entity aware metric. In *Proceedings of the 54th Annual Meeting of the Association for Computational Linguistics (Volume 1: Long Papers)*, pages 632–642, Berlin, Germany. Association for Computational Linguistics.

Anna Nedoluzhko, Michal Novák, Martin Popel, Zdeněk Žabokrtský, Amir Zeldes, and Daniel Zeman. 2022. CorefUD 1.0: Coreference meets Universal Dependencies. In *Proceedings of the Thirteenth Language Resources and Evaluation Conference*, pages 4859–4872, Marseille, France. European Language Resources Association.

Giovanni Paolini, Ben Athiwaratkun, Jason Krone, Ma Jie, Alessandro Achille, Rishita Anubhai, Cicero Nogueira dos Santos, Bing Xiang, Stefano Soatto, et al. 2021. Structured prediction as translation between augmented natural languages. In *ICLR 2021-9th International Conference on Learning Representations*, pages 1–26. International Conference on Learning Representations, ICLR.

Ian Porada, Alexandra Olteanu, Kaheer Suleman, Adam Trischler, and Jackie Cheung. 2024. Challenges to evaluating the generalization of coreference resolution models: A measurement modeling perspective. In *Findings of the Association for Computational Linguistics ACL 2024*, pages 15380–15395, Bangkok, Thailand and virtual meeting. Association for Computational Linguistics.

Ondřej Pražák and Miloslav Konopik. 2022. End-to-end multilingual coreference resolution with mention head prediction. In *Proceedings of the CRAC 2022 Shared Task on Multilingual Coreference Resolution*, pages 23–27, Gyeongju, Republic of Korea. Association for Computational Linguistics.

Ondřej Pražák, Miloslav Konopík, and Jakub Sido. 2021. Multilingual coreference resolution with harmonized annotations. In *Proceedings of the International Conference on Recent Advances in Natural Language Processing (RANLP 2021)*, pages 1119–1123, Held Online. INCOMA Ltd.

Peng Qi, Yuhao Zhang, Yuhui Zhang, Jason Bolton, and Christopher D. Manning. 2020. Stanza: A python natural language processing toolkit for many human languages. In *Proceedings of the 58th Annual Meeting of the Association for Computational Linguistics: System Demonstrations*, pages 101–108, Online. Association for Computational Linguistics.

Marta Recasens, Marie-Catherine de Marneffe, and Christopher Potts. 2013. The life and death of discourse entities: Identifying singleton mentions. In

Proceedings of the 2013 Conference of the North American Chapter of the Association for Computational Linguistics: Human Language Technologies, pages 627–633, Atlanta, Georgia. Association for Computational Linguistics.

Natalia Skachkova, Tatiana Anikina, and Anna Mokhova. 2023. Multilingual coreference resolution: Adapt and generate. In *Proceedings of the CRAC 2023 Shared Task on Multilingual Coreference Resolution*, pages 19–33, Singapore. Association for Computational Linguistics.

Milan Straka. 2023. ÚFAL CorPipe at CRAC 2023: Larger context improves multilingual coreference resolution. In *Proceedings of the CRAC 2023 Shared Task on Multilingual Coreference Resolution*, pages 41–51, Singapore. Association for Computational Linguistics.

Ralph Weischedel, Eduard Hovy, Mitchell Marcus, Martha Palmer, Robert Belvin, Sameer Pradhan, Lance Ramshaw, and Nianwen Xue. 2011. OntoNotes: A large training corpus for enhanced processing.

Thomas Wolf, Lysandre Debut, Victor Sanh, Julien Chaumond, Clement Delangue, Anthony Moi, Pierric Cistac, Tim Rault, Remi Louf, Morgan Funtowicz, Joe Davison, Sam Shleifer, Patrick von Platen, Clara Ma, Yacine Jernite, Julien Plu, Canwen Xu, Teven Le Scao, Sylvain Gugger, Mariama Drame, Quentin Lhoest, and Alexander Rush. 2020. Transformers: State-of-the-art natural language processing. In *Proceedings of the 2020 Conference on Empirical Methods in Natural Language Processing: System Demonstrations*, pages 38–45, Online. Association for Computational Linguistics.

Wei Wu, Fei Wang, Arianna Yuan, Fei Wu, and Jiwei Li. 2020. CorefQA: Coreference resolution as query-based span prediction. In *Proceedings of the 58th Annual Meeting of the Association for Computational Linguistics*, pages 6953–6963, Online. Association for Computational Linguistics.

Zdeněk Žabokrtský, Miloslav Konopik, Anna Nedoluzhko, Michal Novák, Maciej Ogrodniczuk, Martin Popel, Ondrej Prazak, Jakub Sido, and Daniel Zeman. 2023. Findings of the second shared task on multilingual coreference resolution. In *Proceedings of the CRAC 2023 Shared Task on Multilingual Coreference Resolution*, pages 1–18, Singapore. Association for Computational Linguistics.

Amir Zeldes. Opinion piece: Can we fix the scope for coreference?: Problems and solutions for benchmarks beyond OntoNotes. 13(1):41–62.

Wenzheng Zhang, Sam Wiseman, and Karl Stratos. 2023. Seq2seq is all you need for coreference resolution. In *Proceedings of the 2023 Conference on Empirical Methods in Natural Language Processing*, pages 11493–11504, Singapore. Association for Computational Linguistics.

A Singletons vs. Starts of Sequences

Table 3 highlights that our approach performs slightly worse when using the cluster-start classification scheme discussed in section 3.2 to learn starts of sequences and singletons separately. Note that, while our strong performance is maintained in both approaches, predicting singletons resulted in a slight decrease in dev set accuracy.

B Implementation

We train all reported instances of our model using Huggingface's implementation of `xlm-roberta-large` (Wolf et al., 2020), leaving $k = 50$ rough antecedents before fine scoring. To improve training time efficiency, we restrict trainable parameters in the LM backbone using LoRA ($r = 32, \alpha = 16$) (Hu et al., 2021). The rest of the model is tuned fully. We chose a reduced learning rate for our LM backbone at $LR = 2.5 \times 10^{-5}$ with our parsing head being tuned at $LR = 3 \times 10^{-4}$.

C Scaling Conjuction Awareness to a Multilingual Setting

The conjuction-aware data preparation scheme, described in section 3.1, was originally designed with the OntoNotes English dataset (Weischedel et al., 2011). Therefore, it is apt to investigate whether the dependency-based head-word revision scheme is appropriate as the model is scaled across new languages.

Table 4 highlights that the CAW scheme empirically creates minimal (but non-zero) improvements in span-level LEA. We elected to preserve this method across all languages as a word-level approach without CAW would be unable to simultaneously resolve conjoined mentions and their constituent parts such as "Tom and Mary" simultaneously with "Tom" and "Mary" (D'Oosterlinck et al., 2023)—a condition made more frequent by the awareness of singleton mentions in the dataset.

	MUC			B^3			$ceaf_e$			mean
	R	P	F1	R	P	F1	R	P	F1	F1
ours	**0.782**	0.76	**0.771**	**0.74**	0.748	**0.744**	0.717	**0.764**	0.74	**0.752**
ours (singletons seperate)	0.78	0.76	0.77	0.739	0.748	0.743	**0.722**	0.758	0.74	0.751

Table 3: Performance of our approach on the CorefUD 1.1 dataset against our approach but while predicting singletons separately from mention chain starts, dev slice (Nedoluzhko et al., 2022). **mean F1** is the main metric being evaluated. Scores are calculated with the shared task scorer using **exact span matches** and **including singletons**.

	Span-Level LEA
ours	**0.689**
ours (non-CAW)	0.681

Table 4: Performance of our conjunction-aware approach on the CorefUD 1.1 dataset against our approach but while using CorefUD gold head-words.

Unifying the Scope of Bridging Anaphora Types in English: Bridging Annotations in ARRAU and GUM

Lauren Levine and **Amir Zeldes**
Georgetown University
Department of Linguistics
{lel76, amir.zeldes}@georgetown.edu

Abstract

Comparing bridging annotations across coreference resources is difficult, largely due to a lack of standardization across definitions and annotation schemas and narrow coverage of disparate text domains across resources. To alleviate domain coverage issues and consolidate schemas, we compare guidelines and use interpretable predictive models to examine the bridging instances annotated in the GUM, GENTLE and ARRAU corpora. Examining these cases, we find that there is a large difference in types of phenomena annotated as bridging. Beyond theoretical results, we release a harmonized, subcategorized version of the test sets of GUM, GENTLE and the ARRAU Wall Street Journal data to promote meaningful and reliable evaluation of bridging resolution across domains.

1 Introduction

The term "bridging" has been used to describe a broad set of associative coreference phenomena, where the interpretation of an anaphor is in some way dependent on the comprehension of a non-identical antecedent. While considerably less studied than identity coreference, bridging anaphora have been increasingly included in the creation of recent coreference resources, including in recent shared task settings (Khosla et al., 2021; Yu et al., 2022). However, bridging annotations are difficult to compare between resources, as corpora frequently differ not only in their text-types and domains, but also in their definitions of bridging as a phenomenon and their annotation schemas for categorizing bridging subtypes (Kobayashi and Ng, 2020).[1]

Due to this difference in both content and schema, it becomes difficult to establish a reliable standard bench-mark for the evaluation of bridging resolution tasks. In this paper we analyze two of the largest available bridging resources for English: GUM (Zeldes, 2017) and its accompanying test corpus GENTLE (Aoyama et al., 2023), and the sub-corpora of ARRAU (Poesio and Artstein, 2008; Uryupina et al., 2019), with a focus on its largest sub-corpus, ARRAU WSJ, which is composed of Wall Street Journal data. We compare the contents and bridging schemas of these corpora with an eye towards creating more cross resource compatible, high quality bridging data in the future.

In order to determine significant differences between the corpora, we first find categorical differences in their annotation guidelines and technical formats, and then train predictive models on each corpus, performing error analysis on the cross-corpus prediction results. We also conduct a feature analysis of the predictive models to examine the environmental differences between the occurrences of bridging in the corpora under investigation. Finally, we provide harmonized test sets for GUM/GENLTE and ARRAU WSJ, providing revised bridging annotations which integrate ARRAU style bridging subtype annotations into GUM and unify the categories for entity type annotations. It is our hope that this effort at harmonization will promote interest in the cross compatibility of bridging resources.

2 Background

Clark (1975) offers the first theoretical account of bridging as a phenomenon, covering a broad range of discourse inference, including overlap with identity coreference. There have subsequently been various theoretical accounts of bridging which have provided different perspectives (Hawkins, 1978; Asher and Lascarides, 1998; Baumann and Riester, 2012). There have similarly been a number efforts to create annotated resources for bridging, each with its own theoretical understanding of what

[1]The same can also be said of definitions of identity coreference, see Zeldes (2022); Poesio et al. (2024); the case of markable span definitions in particular concerns both types of anaphora alike.

Proceedings of the Seventh Workshop on Computational Models of Reference, Anaphora and Coreference (CRAC 2024), pages 41–51

bridging encompasses as a linguistic phenomenon.

Kobayashi and Ng (2020) give a survey of currently available bridging datasets, with a focus on English, and list 7 corpora (including 4 sub-corpora of ARRAU), additionally mentioning GUM in passing (the paper predates the release of GENTLE). Table 1 gives an overview of these datasets, and adds and compares some essential properties of their coverage for bridging phenomena.

In terms of token count and bridging instances, the news section of ARRAU (ARRAU WSJ; 229k tokens, 3.7k bridging instances) and GUM (228k tokens, 1.9k bridging instances as of version 10) are the largest.[2] While the ARRAU WSJ is only a single genre, GUM includes 16 different genres (academic writing, biographies, courtroom transcripts, essays, fiction, how-to guides, interviews, letters, news, online forum discussions, podcasts, political speeches, spontaneous face to face conversations, textbooks, travel guides, and vlogs), with its extended test corpus GENTLE spanning an additional 8 genres (dictionary entries, live esports commentary, legal documents, medical notes, poetry, mathematical proofs, course syllabuses, and threat letters). Additionally, ARRAU is one of the few corpora which includes subtype annotations for bridging, a feature that GUM and GENTLE lack. The complimentary attributes of these two datasets and their relatively large size of bridging instances makes them prime candidates for comparison and harmonization. As such, in this paper we focus on comparing and unifying between these two bridging schemas, leaving a broader harmonization with other resources for future work. The following section breaks down the categorical differences in these two annotation formalisms.

3 Categorical Differences

Some of the most substantial differences between the datasets come from their theoretical underpinnings and technical infrastructure. In ARRAU, bridging is considered to be a type of "anaphoric reference which links the object being referred to by the markable to an already established discourse entity ... via a semantic relation other than coreference" (Poesio et al., 2021). This focus on semantic relations takes a more lexically grounded approach, laying out specific types of semantic relations to be marked as bridging, including *part-of* and *set* relations. GUM/GENTLE, by contrast, approach bridging from the perspective of information status, broadly laying out bridging as any newly introduced entity which is in some way underspecified, but whose identity is interpretable/inferable thanks to a non-identical antecedent entity (Zeldes, 2024). The main structural differences that emerge from a comparison of the datasets' guidelines and annotations are laid out below:

Previously mentioned anaphors While in GUM/GENTLE the entity of a bridging anaphor must be mentioned for the first time after its antecedent has already been introduced, ARRAU considers bridging to apply even if the entity in question has already been introduced, as in (1).

(1) *Could I move .. [engine E two]$_i$ .. there should be [one engine]$_j$ at Corning .. [engine E two]$_i$ is there*

In this example, the second mention of *engine E two* is annotated in ARRAU as a bridging anaphor to *one engine*; however the entity *engine E two* was already introduced into the discourse earlier, and is also annotated as a coref antecedent to the bridging anaphor. Such examples are prohibited in GUM/GENTLE where bridging anaphora can only occur with non-given (i.e. non-aforementioned) mentions.

Split bridging antecedents ARRAU allows bridging from one anaphor to multiple antecedents as in (2).

(2) *FOREIGN PRIME RATES: [Canada 13.50%]$_i$; [Germany 8.50%]$_j$; [Japan 4.875%]$_k$; [Switzerland 8.50%]$_l$; [Britain 15%]$_m$ .. lending practices vary widely by [location]$_n$*

Here the mention *location* is taken as an anaphor bridging to all pairs of country and prime rate. While it is true that it refers to the location of a loan, we question whether the antecedent is truly split: if the location is the countries, then this is split antecedent coreference (and not bridging); if it is inferrable from the existence of a rate, which has a jurisdiction location which is conceptually distinct from the country, then the antecedent should simply be *FOREIGN PRIME RATES*. Regardless, such split bridging antecedents are categorically

[2]We include the Reddit subset of GUM for which we obtain the underlying texts using the API (Behzad and Zeldes, 2020), and use the original markable definitions from GUM, as opposed to the OntoGUM version which is harmonized with OntoNotes definitions (Zhu et al., 2021).

		Domain	Docs	Tokens	Mentions	Bridging	Definite Anaphora	Indefinite Anaphora	Entity Antecedent	Event Antecedent	Referential Bridging	Lexical Bridging	Information Status	Subtypes	Comparative Anaphora	Gold Treebank
Corpora	ISNotes	WSJ news	50	40k	11k	663	✓	✓	✓	✓	✓	✗	✓	✓	✗	✓
	BASHI	WSJ news	50	58k	19k	459	✓	✓	✓	✓	✓	✗	✗	✗	✓	✓
	ARRAU RST	news	413	229k	72k	3.7k	✓	✓	✓	✗	✓	✓	✓	✓	✓	✓
	ARRAU GNOME	medical, art history	5	21k	6.5k	692	✓	✓	✓	✗	✓	✓	✓	✓	✓	✗
	ARRAU PEAR	spoken narratives	20	14k	4k	333	✓	✓	✓	✗	✓	✓	✓	✓	✓	✗
	ARRAU TRAINS	dialogues	114	84k	17k	710	✓	✓	✓	✗	✓	✓	✓	✓	✓	✗
	SciCorp	scientific text	14	61k	9.4k	1.3k	✓	✗	✓	✗	✓	✗	✓	✗	✓	✗
	GUM (V10.1.0)	16 genres	235	228k	64k	1.9k	✓	✓	✓	✓	✓	✓	✓	✗	✓	✓
	GENTLE (V2.0.0)	8 genres	26	18k	5.6k	58	✓	✓	✓	✓	✓	✓	✓	✗	✓	✓

(Column group heading: Corpus Characteristics)

Table 1: Survey of English Bridging Resources

excluded in GUM.

Discontinuous mention spans In ARRAU entity spans are allowed to be discontinuous spans of tokens, while GUM's representation format does not support discontinuous mentions. This allows for a more appropriate handling of spans such as "$[Mr.]_{i1}$ *and* $[Mrs.\ [Smith]_{i2}]_j$", where the indices *i1* and *i2* indicate the two parts of the discontinuous mention "Mr. Smith". In GUM/GENTLE, continuous spans represent both mentions, spuriously including 'Mrs.' in the first mention: "$[Mr.\ and\ [Mrs.\ Smith]_j]_i$".

Entity types ARRAU allows for a coreference cluster to contain multiple entity types amongst its members (e.g. ORGANIZATION and LOCATION for a country), while GUM requires that all members of a coreference cluster have the same entity type. Additionally and unlike GUM, ARRAU does not assign an entity type for coordinate entity mentions, for instance in (3):

(3) [[*wildlife*]$_{\text{ANIMATE}}$ *and* [*the fishing industry*]$_{\text{ABSTRACT}}$]$_{\text{NONE}}$

Even though the entities within the coordination have types (ANIMATE and ABSTRACT), the entity type of the coordinate phrase is NONE. In GUM, coordinate entities only receive a shared markable if they are also referred to in aggregate elsewhere in the text. In the case of a mixed type coordinate markable, the coordinate phrase and related aggregate mention will both be labeled with the entity type ABSTRACT.

Unified Types	Original Entity Types: GUM	Original Entity Types: ARRAU
PERSON	PERSON	PERSON
PLACE	PLACE	SPACE
ORGANIZATION	ORGANIZATION	ORGANIZATION
CONCRETE	OBJECT, PLANT	CONCRETE
EVENT	EVENT	PLAN
TIME	TIME	TIME
SUBSTANCE	SUBSTANCE	SUBSTANCE, MEDICINE
ANIMATE	ANIMAL	ANIMATE
ABSTRACT	ABSTRACT	ABSTRACT, UNDERSP-ONTO, DISEASE, NUMERICAL, NONE

Table 2: Unified entity types between the GUM and ARRAU schemas

The inventory of possible entity types in ARRAU and GUM also have some minor differences. For our purposes, we create a unified set of entity categories and collapse the inventories of the individual resources as shown in Table 2.

Bridging subtypes While GUM does not attempt to subcategorize different varieties of bridging, ARRAU WSJ has an inventory of 9 subtype labels which can be applied to bridging annotations. Table 3 lists the different bridging subtype labels used in ARRAU, along with a brief explanation for each. Further explanation can be found in ARRAU's annotation guidelines (Poesio et al., 2021).

Reflecting on these categorical differences, we favor GUM's more structurally restrictive approach, which is based on the information status of mentions, since it links the phenomenon to the cognitive act of bridging as a form of information fetching:

Subtype	Description
POSS	anaphor is a part/attribute of the antecedent
POSS-INV	antecedent is a part/attribute of the anaphor
ELEMENT	anaphor is an element of the antecedent set
ELEMENT-INV	antecedent is an element of the anaphor set
SUBSET	anaphor is a subset of the antecedent set
SUBSET-INV	antecedent is subset of the anaphor set
OTHER	anaphor marked with "other"
OTHER-INV	antecedent marked with "other"
UNDERSP-REL	sense anaphora, situational reference
(unmarked)	no subtype annotation was provided

Table 3: Bridging subtype labels used in ARRAU

if an anaphor requires back reference to resolve but has not been mentioned before, then bridging has occurred. Semantic criteria, by contrast, are less easy to apply, since we find many NPs whose extensions can be considered to form set-member relations but are not annotated as bridging in ARRAU, from 'people' to any person mentioned in a text to ontological categories (e.g. 'time' in general vs. specific times), and we would like to exclude such cases on principled grounds.

Additionally, we like that GUM's approach casts a wider scope in terms of possible bridging varieties because it does not depend on a finite set of pre-defined semantic relations to identify instances of bridging, whereas ARRAU appears to depend on such pre-defined relations. However, we do find the additional granularity of the bridging subtypes in ARRAU to be desirable. As such, we advocate for a less restrictive approach to identifying bridging relations, as in GUM, which can then be categorized with more granular subtype relations, such as those used in ARRAU. This view is reflected in our test set harmonization effort detailed in Section 7.

4 Predictive Models

Although the differences outlined in Section 3 are the most striking, and responsible for the largest discrepancies in bridging frequency and included subtypes, a long tail of less obvious differences distinguishes much of the data in the different corpora. In order to identify such subtle differences, we train and test bridging mention classifiers across corpora, starting with gold standard mention spans and trying to answer the question: which bridging instances in one corpus would not be considered ones in the other, and which instances does one corpus miss, which another might include? Given the sparseness of the data, exacerbated by the need to fine-tune a separate model on each dataset, we use statistical machine learning models and attempt to extract consistent features for mention spans from each corpus.

4.1 Data

Based on the categorical differences outlined in Section 3, we remove cases annotated as bridging in ARRAU WSJ which we believe are structurally ineligible to be instances of bridging in GUM, and which would otherwise compromise compatibility between datasets. From the ARRAU WSJ data, we remove 297 cases of bridging with multiple antecedents, and 957 instances where the bridging anaphor already had an identity coreference antecedent. Although this reduction of over 1,200 cases necessarily loses information, we observe that the much tighter information structural definition of bridging leads to more consistency in example types, and note that this already accounts for most of the difference in bridging prevalence between the datasets, leaving ARRAU WSJ with about 12 bridging instances per 1K tokens (and not the unfiltered 18.2), compared to GUM's 8.3 instances per 1K tokens.

We also found that there are 864 instances of discontinuous entity span instances which we include, but for consistency treat as continuous, emulating the behavior in GUM/GENTLE.[3] A count of the remaining bridging instances in each dataset is shown in Table 4. The harmonized test sets presented in Section 7 are composed of this reduced set of bridging annotations.

We compose separate train and test datasets for GUM/GENTLE and ARRAU, so we may analyze their bridging environments separately. The training data for the GUM classifier contains documents from GUM's given train and dev partitions, while the test data contains documents from GUM's test partition and GENTLE, to test texts that are out-of-domain in both datasets. The training data for the ARRAU classifier contains documents from ARRAU WSJ's given train and dev partitions, and test contains documents from ARRAU WSJ's given test partition.

In order to train and evaluate our predictive models for bridging, we formulate the task as a binary judgement: given a pair of mentions and their accompanying linguistic features, predict whether the

[3]Though out of scope for this paper, we believe that discontinuous mentions are the more accurate analysis and could be introduced into the GUM data, possibly using the gold syntax trees.

	GUM/GENTLE	ARRAU WSJ
Train	1611	779
Test	280	176

Table 4: Counts of bridging instances in classifier training and evaluation data

pair is an instance of bridging. We first extract all mention instances from the GUM/GENTLE and ARRAU data, and then enumerate all possible pairs, tracking whether they are instances of bridging, identity coreference, or non-coreference pairs. For each extracted mention, we track the entity type (which has been collapsed to be compatible between the two corpora, as in Table 2), information status, definiteness, phrase length, distance, and the following attributes of the syntactic head of each entity: dependency relation (deprel), part of speech (xpos), lemma, and number (plural vs. singular). To obtain dependency relations for ARRAU WSJ, we convert the gold constituent trees to dependencies using CoreNLP (Manning et al., 2014).

Due to the relative scarcity of bridging instances, we construct each train and test set with balanced classes of bridging, identity coreference, and non-coreference pairs. We first take all of the bridging pairs in the documents from each section of the data partitions (counts shown in Table 4), and then we take a random selection of an equal quantity for identity coreference and non-coreference pairs. In order to have reasonable candidate pairs in this selection, pronoun anaphora are excluded, as they are almost always instances of identity coreference, and non-bridging cases are limited to anaphor-antecedent pairs that are within the maximum distance of an attested bridging pair.

4.2 Models

Using the data partitions for each corpus outlined in Section 4.1, we train two XGBoost classifiers[4]: one trained on the train data from GUM, and the other trained on the train data from ARRAU WSJ. Each of these classifiers was trained and optimized with a grid search with 5 fold cross validation on the training data, using a subset of the linguistic features extracted during the creation of the mention pair data partitions. For both the antecedent and the anaphor of the mention pair, features included entity type, definiteness, phrase length, and syntactic dependency relation, part of speech, number, and lemma of the mention's syntactic head. Additionally, the information status of the antecedent and antecedent-anaphor distance were included as features.

Table 5 shows the performance of each classifier on its own test data and the test data of the other corpus, along with the performance of a random baseline on both test sets (averaged from 5 runs). The random baseline has a 33% chance of predicting an antecedent-anaphor pair as bridging, reflecting the balanced classes of bridging, identity coreference, non-coreference pairs in the test sets. Even with the classes balanced in the train and test data, we see that each classifier's performance on predicting the positive class of bridging on their own test data is relatively low, with the GUM classifier giving an F-score of 0.71, and the ARRAU classifier giving an F-score of 0.67. Still, we see that these both substantially outperform the random baseline, which gives an F-score of 0.32 on GUM/GENTLE test and an F-score of 0.33 on ARRAU WSJ test.

The performance of each classifier on the test data of the other corpus is lower than on its own, with the ARRAU classifier giving an F-score of 0.56 on the GUM/GENTLE eval data and the GUM classifier giving an F-score of just 0.22 (worse than the random baseline), on the ARRAU WSJ eval data. Given the substantial differences in the approach to bridging annotations between the two corpora, performance degradation on cross-corpus prediction is expected. However, it is worth noting that the performance degradation is steeper for the GUM classifier than the ARRAU classifier, to the point where the GUM classifier performs worse than random chance. This suggests that ARRAU may have more varieties of bridging not seen in the GUM data than vice versa. In order to investigate the differences in bridging varieties in the two corpora more closely, we conduct an analysis of the feature importance of the predictive models in Section 5, and an error analysis of the cross-corpus prediction results in Section 6.

5 Feature Analysis

Feature importance is an indication of the relative contribution of a particular feature for the decision of a model. By examining the feature importances of our predictive models from Section 4.2,

[4]https://xgboost.readthedocs.io/en/latest/index.html

Classifiers	Eval Data	P	R	F
GUM	GUM/GENTLE	0.74	0.68	0.71
	ARRAU WSJ	0.41	0.15	0.22
ARRAU WSJ	GUM/GENTLE	0.57	0.55	0.56
	ARRAU WSJ	0.66	0.69	0.67
Random Baseline	GUM/GENTLE	0.32	0.32	0.32
	ARRAU WSJ	0.33	0.34	0.33

Table 5: XGBoost classifier performance and random baseline on predicting the positive class of bridging cases

	Bridge	Non-bridge
Def	13.3	-9.4
Ind	-7.4	5.3
	GUM/GENLTE	

	Bridge	Non-bridge
Def	0.7	-0.5
Ind	-0.3	0.2
	ARRAU WSJ	

Table 6: Chi-square residuals for definiteness of the anaphor (definite vs. indefinite) being an indicator of bridging in GUM/GENTLE and ARRAU WSJ

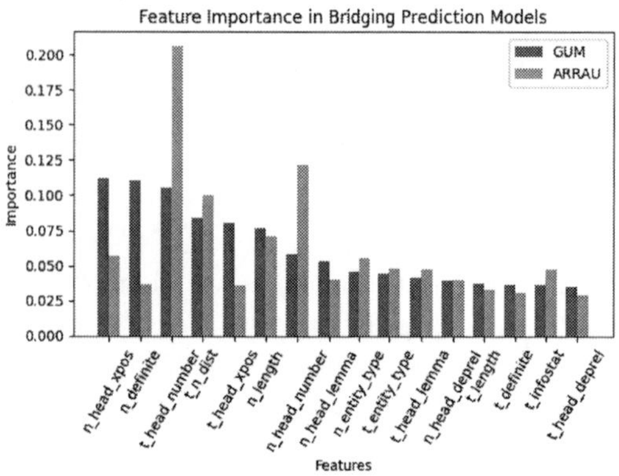

Figure 1: Feature importance of XGBoost classifiers trained on GUM and ARRAU WSJ

we can gain insight into which linguistic features are characteristic of the varieties of bridging captured in each of the corpora used for model training. The feature importance results of the GUM classifier and the ARRAU classifier are shown in Figure 1. Importance is measured using XGBoost's importance type "gain", which indicates the average contribution of the corresponding feature over the trees in the model based on the purity metric Gini. For comparison, we include the feature importance of the models using Mean Decrease in Accuracy (MDA) as a metric in Appendix A. Looking at Figure 1, we see that the part of speech of the anaphor and the definiteness of the anaphor are the features of most import for the GUM classifier, while the number (plural vs. singular) of the antecedent and the anaphor are the most important features for the ARRAU classifier. Number is perhaps such an important feature in the ARRAU classifier due to the focus on capturing the pre-defined set-element and set-subset relations as instances of bridging.

As definiteness of a newly introduced entity is a strong signal of some form of referential bridging, it is logical to see definitenss of the anaphor as an important feature for the GUM classifier. It has a much lower relative importance for the ARRAU classifier, possibly because ARRAU is not limited to newly introduced entities as candidates for bridging, focusing more on semantic part-whole or subset relations. In Table 6, we show the chi-square residuals for definiteness of the anaphor as an indication of an entity pair being an instance of bridging. We see that in both GUM/GENTLE and ARRAU WSJ, a definite anaphor is a positive indicator for bridging and an indefinite anaphor is negative indicator for bridging. However, the magnitude of the residuals for the GUM/GENTLE data is notably larger than those of the ARRAU WSJ. This confirms that definiteness of the anaphor is a stronger indication of whether something is bridging in the GUM/GENTLE data than in the ARRAU WSJ data.

The entity types of the antecedent and the anaphor of a bridging instance are a set of categorical features with similar feature importance in the two classifiers. To investigate these features jointly, in Figures 2 and 3 we provide heatmaps of the distributions of antecedent-anaphor entity type combinations in bridging instances in each dataset. We can see that in both datasets it is common for bridging to occur to and from entities of the same type. We also see that bridging to and from ABSTRACT entities is common in both datasets. However, we also see that in GUM bridging instances of entity type PLACE-PLACE are one of the more common combinations (10% compared to 3% in ARRAU), while in ARRAU WSJ bridging instances of entity type ORGANIZATION-ORGANIZATION are of higher frequency (16% compared to 2% in GUM). Such differences in distribution indicate that there is variation between the resources, either due to differences in corpus content or differences in bridging varieties annotated. In the following section, we investigate some concrete examples within the test sets of each corpus.

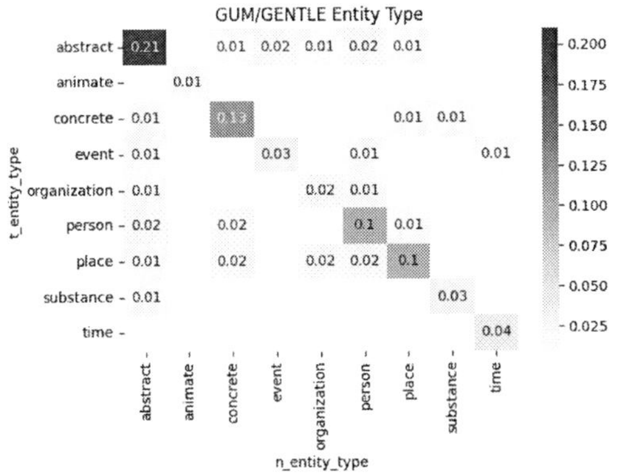

Figure 2: Distribution for antecedent-anaphor entity type combinations for GUM/GENTLE (only combinations with a proportion of 1% or higher are visualized)

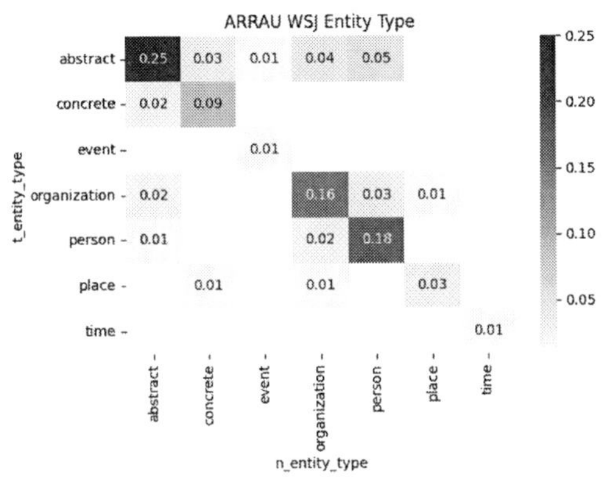

Figure 3: Distribution for antecedent-anaphor entity type combinations for ARRAU WSJ (only combinations with a proportion of 1% or higher are visualized)

6 Cross-Corpus Error Analysis

As we can see from observing the prediction scores of the models in Table 5, the GUM and ARRAU classifiers have moderate success in predicting instances of bridging in their own test sets, but see performance degrade when applied to the test set of the other corpus. This tells us that the classifiers have learned some characteristic features of their respective training datasets. Using the decision probabilities outputted from the classifiers as a confidence measure, we can look at examples which the classifiers are most confident about but predicted incorrectly in order to look for characteristic differences between the bridging instances included in each dataset. Below we look at some of the most confident mistakes of the classifiers on the test data of the opposite corpus.

Memorization of specific noun pairs, such as "house"–"door" or "country"–"capital" is an important tool in predicting bridging relations in unseen data, which is unsurprisingly more effective for common nouns. It therefore comes as no surprise that many of the GUM classifier's errors on the ARRAU test set seem to stem from out of vocabulary (OOV) items, due to the large number of named entities unique to the WSJ domain. In fact, 10.1% of RST-DT tokens are proper nouns, compared to just 5.8% in GUM. This creates a large amount of noise in the error pool, which made it difficult to find example cases that exposed characteristic differences between the datasets. Additionally, it is worth noting that the low performance of the GUM classifier on the ARRAU data (worse than chance) brings into question the utility of analyzing individual examples of incorrect predictions. However, mistakes of the ARRAU classifier on the GUM test set highlighted several common bridging situations which are present in GUM due to its genre diversity, but are missing from ARRAU WSJ, which only has news data. Out of the 280 samples in the GUM/GENTLE test set, there are 18 instances which the ARRAU classifier gives a <10% probability of being instances of bridging even though they actually are instances of bridging.

For example, the ARRAU classifier gives a <1% probability that the boxed entities in (4) are an example of bridging, though it is annotated as such in GUM.

(4) *Escape The Room Employees, what is the weirdest thing [you]'ve seen someone do in one of the rooms?*

OH WAIT [I] THOUGHT OF ANOTHER ONE

GUM allows bridging in cases where multiple addressees are later referenced individually, as in the case above where a question to multiple addresses on an online discussion forum is answered by an individual's post.

Another genre specific example comes from person-to-heading bridging instances in GUM, which are common in the biography genre of the corpus. For instance, the ARRAU classifier gives example (5) from a biography text in GUM only a 5% probability of being bridging.

(5) *Jens Otto Harry Jespersen...was [a Danish linguist who specialized in the grammar of*

the English language]

[*Early life*]

The above example is an instance of bridging from a person (a Danish linguist), to a heading which one infers is a reference to that individual due to the expected structure of a biographical text (early life = the early life of the Danish linguist under discussion).

Similarly, in GUM's academic genre, bridging instances to and from various captions and citations are a direct result of the graphical organization of the text type. For example, the ARRAU classifier gives the following example of bridging a probability of only 7%:

(6) [*Figure 2.2*]

A pre-1982 copper penny ([left]) contains approximately 3 ×× 10 22 copper atoms...

In the example above, a figure citation is bridging to an entity within the caption of the figure, which references an internal part of the figure itself (the left part of the figure). While these sort of part-whole relations are a very common form of bridging, the application to graphical references is a genre specific phenomenon that one would not necessarily observe in any given corpus of bridging.

From the examples above, we can see that the genre of a text can play a big role in the types of bridging that will be present. As the ARRAU corpus does not include online forum discussions, biographies, and academic texts, it is not able to represent the varieties of bridging which are characteristic to these genres. This gap in coverage contributes to the motivation to have a larger number of comparable bridging resources from a diverse set of domains.

7 Harmonized Test Sets

In order to promote the comparability of cross-corpus evaluation results for bridging resolution systems (see Hou 2020; Kobayashi and Ng 2021), we present harmonized test sets for GUM/GENTLE and ARRAU WSJ[5]. For these revised test sets, we harmonize on the following three points: categorical differences regarding the scope of bridging, categories for entity types, and bridging subtype annotations.

As discussed in Section 3, there are several categorical differences in the definitions of what counts as bridging in GUM and ARRAU. For the purpose of unifying the scope of bridging between these two corpora, we favor GUM's more structurally restrictive approach. As such, we remove cases of bridging with multiple antecedents and cases where the bridging anaphor has an identity coreference antecedent from the ARRAU WSJ test set. This leaves us with 176 instances of bridging in the revised ARRAU WSJ test set.

As ARRAU and GUM have relatively similar entity type categories in their original schemas for entity annotations, we are able to combine them into a single condensed set as shown in Table 2. While entity types are not integral to the comparability of bridging annotations, they are a relevant feature for analysis, so we choose to include them in this harmonization effort. The distribution of bridging anaphor entity types in each of the test sets is shown in Table 7.

As noted in Section 3, ARRAU has a schema for categorizing subtypes of bridging (shown in Table 3), while GUM does not make any attempt to differentiate sub-varieties of bridging. As such, we harmonize the bridging annotations by manually annotating the GUM/GENTLE test set with ARRAU style bridging subtypes. This annotation was completed by the authors of this paper. While manually annotating the bridging instances in the GUM/GENTLE test set with ARRAU style bridging subtypes, 8 instances of bridging were thrown out as annotation errors, leaving 272 instances of bridging in the GUM/GENTLE test set.

The distribution of bridging subtypes in each of the test sets is shown in Table 8. In both test sets, ELEMENT and SUBSET are common bridging subtypes, but we see that GUM/GENTLE have larger proportions of the POSS and UNDERSP-REL categories. This suggests some difference in the bridging varieties between the two corpora, but is likely also partially explained by the large portion of bridging instances in the ARRAU test set which did not receive a bridging subtype annotation (36%). We leave experimental evaluation of systems on these harmonized test sets for future work and hope that their availability will promote more meaningfully comparable research on bridging resolution across a range of text types.

[5] https://github.com/lauren-lizzy-levine/bridging_test_sets

Entity Types	GUM/GENTLE	ARRAU WSJ
PERSON	40 (15%)	41 (23%)
PLACE	45 (17%)	11 (6%)
ORGANIZATION	18 (7%)	55 (31%)
CONCRETE	57 (21%)	22 (13%)
EVENT	20 (7%)	2 (1%)
TIME	15 (6%)	2 (1%)
SUBSTANCE	6 (2%)	0
ANIMATE	6 (2%)	0
ABSTRACT	63 (23%)	43 (24%)

Table 7: Distribution of bridging anaphor entity types in harmonized GUM/GENTLE test and ARRAU WSJ test.

Bridging Subtype	GUM/GENTLE	ARRAU WSJ
POSS	78 (29%)	9 (5%)
POSS-INV	4 (1%)	2 (1%)
ELEMENT	81 (30%)	49 (28%)
ELEMENT-INV	17 (6%)	5 (3%)
SUBSET	21 (8%)	33 (19%)
SUBSET-INV	5 (2%)	9 (5%)
OTHER	11 (4%)	3 (2%)
OTHER-INV	6 (2%)	1 (<1%)
UNDERSP-REL	49 (18%)	1 (<1%)
(unmarked)	0	64 (36%)

Table 8: Distribution of bridging subtypes in harmonized GUM/GENTLE test and ARRAU WSJ test.

8 Conclusion

In this paper, we compared the bridging annotations from two of the largest English language corpora with such annotations: ARRAU and GUM. We examined the categorical differences between the scope of their definitions for bridging, and the subtypes annotated within each corpus. We also used predictive models to analyze the linguistic environments and finding examples of interesting differences between the bridging varieties included in each corpus. These differences stem from not only the different genre composition of the corpora, but also the approach towards bridging taken by each corpus. This finding encourages the creation of more genre diverse resources for bridging that are readily comparable with existing resources for bridging. To this end, we have also provided harmonized versions of the GUM/GENTLE test set and the ARRAU WSJ test set, which include unified entity types and ARRAU style bridging subtype annotations added to GUM/GENTLE test. We intend for these harmonized test sets to be the beginning of a larger effort to create a more unified, cross compatible ecosystem of bridging resources for linguistic research and work on automatic bridging resolution.

Limitations

This project is the beginning of an effort to create a more uniform and cross-compatible ecosystem of bridging resources, so it naturally leaves much for future work. In this work, we only examine two of the existing English resources for bridging, and we do not consider the annotation schemas of resources for other languages (such as for German (Grishina, 2016; Eckart et al., 2012)). Subsequent work will require a broader consideration of the various phenomena captured under the label of bridging in various resources and their accompanying categorization schemas.

References

Tatsuya Aoyama, Shabnam Behzad, Luke Gessler, Lauren Levine, Jessica Lin, Yang Janet Liu, Siyao Peng, Yilun Zhu, and Amir Zeldes. 2023. GENTLE: A genre-diverse multilayer challenge set for English NLP and linguistic evaluation. In *Proceedings of the 17th Linguistic Annotation Workshop (LAW-XVII)*, pages 166–178, Toronto, Canada. Association for Computational Linguistics.

Nicholas Asher and Alex Lascarides. 1998. Bridging. *Journal of Semantics*, 15(1):83–113.

Stefan Baumann and Arndt Riester. 2012. Referential and lexical givenness: Semantic, prosodic and cognitive aspects. *Prosody and meaning*, 25:119–162.

Shabnam Behzad and Amir Zeldes. 2020. A cross-genre ensemble approach to robust Reddit part of speech tagging. In *Proceedings of the 12th Web as Corpus Workshop*, pages 50–56, Marseille, France. European Language Resources Association.

Herbert H. Clark. 1975. Bridging. In *Theoretical Issues in Natural Language Processing*.

Kerstin Eckart, Arndt Riester, and Katrin Schweitzer. 2012. *A Discourse Information Radio News Database for Linguistic Analysis*, pages 65–76. Springer Berlin Heidelberg, Berlin, Heidelberg.

Yulia Grishina. 2016. Experiments on bridging across languages and genres. In *Proceedings of the Workshop on Coreference Resolution Beyond OntoNotes (CORBON 2016)*, pages 7–15, San Diego, California. Association for Computational Linguistics.

John A. Hawkins. 1978. Definiteness and indefiniteness: A study in reference and grammaticality prediction. *Journal of Linguistics*, 27:405–442.

Yufang Hou. 2020. Bridging anaphora resolution as question answering. In *Proceedings of the 58th Annual Meeting of the Association for Computational Linguistics*, pages 1428–1438, Online. Association for Computational Linguistics.

Sopan Khosla, Juntao Yu, Ramesh Manuvinakurike, Vincent Ng, Massimo Poesio, Michael Strube, and Carolyn Rosé. 2021. The CODI-CRAC 2021 shared task on anaphora, bridging, and discourse deixis in dialogue. In *Proceedings of the CODI-CRAC 2021 Shared Task on Anaphora, Bridging, and Discourse Deixis in Dialogue*, pages 1–15, Punta Cana, Dominican Republic. Association for Computational Linguistics.

Hideo Kobayashi and Vincent Ng. 2020. Bridging resolution: A survey of the state of the art. In *Proceedings of the 28th International Conference on Computational Linguistics*, pages 3708–3721, Barcelona, Spain (Online). International Committee on Computational Linguistics.

Hideo Kobayashi and Vincent Ng. 2021. Bridging resolution: Making sense of the state of the art. In *Proceedings of the 2021 Conference of the North American Chapter of the Association for Computational Linguistics: Human Language Technologies*, pages 1652–1659, Online. Association for Computational Linguistics.

Christopher D. Manning, Mihai Surdeanu, John Bauer, Jenny Finkel, Steven J. Bethard, and Davide McClosky. 2014. The Stanford CoreNLP natural language processing toolkit. In *Proceedings of ACL 2014: System Demonstrations*, pages 55–60, Baltimore, MD.

Massimo Poesio and Ron Artstein. 2008. Anaphoric annotation in the ARRAU corpus. In *Proceedings of the Sixth International Conference on Language Resources and Evaluation (LREC'08)*, Marrakech, Morocco. European Language Resources Association (ELRA).

Massimo Poesio, Maris Camilleri, Paloma Carretero-Garcia, and Ron Artstein. 2021. *ARRAU 3 Annotation Manual.*

Massimo Poesio, Maciej Ogrodniczuk, Vincent Ng, Sameer Pradhan, Juntao Yu, Nafise Sadat Moosavi, Silviu Paun, Amir Zeldes, Anna Nedoluzhko, Michal Novák, Martin Popel, Zdeněk Žabokrtský, and Daniel Zeman. 2024. Universal anaphora: The first three years. In *Proceedings of the 2024 Joint International Conference on Computational Linguistics, Language Resources and Evaluation (LREC-COLING 2024)*, pages 17087–17100, Torino, Italia. ELRA and ICCL.

Olga Uryupina, Ron Artstein, Antonella Bristot, Federica Cavicchio, Francesca Delogu, Kepa Joseba Rodríguez, and Massimo Poesio. 2019. Annotating a broad range of anaphoric phenomena, in a variety of genres: the ARRAU corpus. *Natural Language Engineering*, 26:95 – 128.

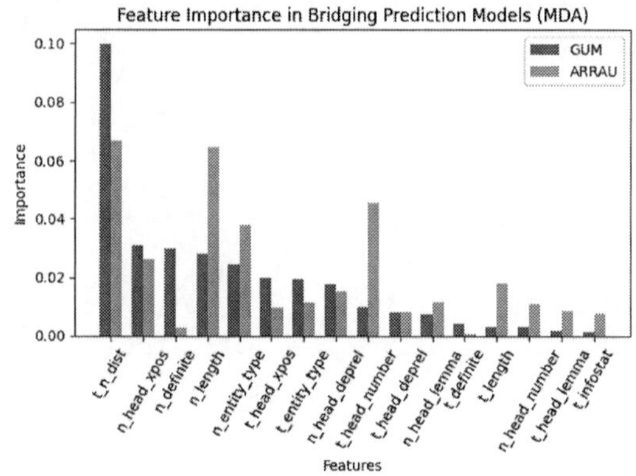

Figure 4: Feature importance of XGBoost classifiers trained on GUM and ARRAU WSJ for Mean Decrease Accuracy (MDA)

Juntao Yu, Sopan Khosla, Ramesh Manuvinakurike, Lori Levin, Vincent Ng, Massimo Poesio, Michael Strube, and Carolyn Rosé. 2022. The CODI-CRAC 2022 shared task on anaphora, bridging, and discourse deixis in dialogue. In *Proceedings of the CODI-CRAC 2022 Shared Task on Anaphora, Bridging, and Discourse Deixis in Dialogue*, pages 1–14, Gyeongju, Republic of Korea. Association for Computational Linguistics.

Amir Zeldes. 2017. The GUM Corpus: Creating Multilayer Resources in the Classroom. *Language Resources and Evaluation*, 51(3):581–612.

Amir Zeldes. 2022. Can we fix the scope for coreference? problems and solutions for benchmarks beyond OntoNotes. *Dialogue & Discourse*, 13(1):41–62.

Amir Zeldes. 2024. Entity and Information Status Annotation. GUM Annotation Wiki.

Yilun Zhu, Sameer Pradhan, and Amir Zeldes. 2021. OntoGUM: Evaluating contextualized SOTA coreference resolution on 12 more genres. In *Proceedings of the 59th Annual Meeting of the Association for Computational Linguistics and the 11th International Joint Conference on Natural Language Processing (Volume 2: Short Papers)*, pages 461–467, Online. Association for Computational Linguistics.

A Mean Decrease Accuracy Feature Importance

For the sake of comparison with our original feature importance analysis shown in Figure 1, we include the feature importance of the models using Mean Decrease in Accuracy (MDA) as a metric in Figure 4. Comparing the two figures, we see that the feature importance results are somewhat different between the two metrics. Using MDA as a metric, in both the GUM classifier and the ARRAU classifier, the feature with the most importance is the distance between the antecedent and the anaphor (t_a_dist), which was not the case using the Gini based metric. However, by analyzing the feature importance for our models using two different metrics and examining their overlap, we can also see which features are consistently important for each model. The part of speech of the anaphor head (n_head_xpos) and the definiteness of the anaphor (n_definite) remain in the top three most important features for the GUM classifier when using MDA as a metric. Additionally, the number (plural vs. singular) of the antecedent (t_head_number) remains in the three most important features for the ARRAU classifier when using MDA as a metric.

WINOPRON: Revisiting English Winogender Schemas for Consistency, Coverage, and Grammatical Case

Vagrant Gautam[1] **Julius Steuer**[1] **Eileen Bingert**[1]
Ray Johns[2] **Anne Lauscher**[3] **Dietrich Klakow**[1]
[1]Saarland University, Germany [2]Independent Researcher, USA
[2]Data Science Group, University of Hamburg, Germany
vgautam@lsv.uni-saarland.de

Abstract

While measuring bias and robustness in coreference resolution are important goals, such measurements are only as good as the tools we use to measure them. Winogender Schemas (Rudinger et al., 2018) are an influential dataset proposed to evaluate gender bias in coreference resolution, but a closer look reveals issues with the data that compromise its use for reliable evaluation, including treating different pronominal forms as equivalent, violations of template constraints, and typographical errors. We identify these issues and fix them, contributing a new dataset: WINOPRON. Using WINOPRON, we evaluate two state-of-the-art supervised coreference resolution systems, SpanBERT, and five sizes of FLAN-T5, and demonstrate that accusative pronouns are harder to resolve for all models. We also propose a new method to evaluate pronominal bias in coreference resolution that goes beyond the binary. With this method, we also show that bias characteristics vary not just across pronoun sets (e.g., *he* vs. *she*), but also across surface forms of those sets (e.g., *him* vs. *his*).

Winogender Schemas (Rudinger et al., 2018)

(a) **The counselor** disclosed to the patient that *he/she/they* was professionally mandated to report certain issues.

(b) **The patient** disclosed to the counselor that *he/she/they* had a history of substance abuse.

WinoPron (ours)

(1a) **The counselor** told the patient that *he/she/they/xe* had a professional duty to report certain issues.

(1b) The counselor told **the patient** that *he/she/they/xe* did not have to pay out of pocket for the sessions.

(2a) **The counselor** and the patient agreed on having biweekly sessions for *him/her/them/xem* to be able to closely monitor progress.

(2b) The counselor and **the patient** agreed on having biweekly sessions for *him/her/them/xem* to be able to afford it.

(3a) **The counselor** informed the patient that *his/her/their/xyr* qualifications were in psychology.

(3b) The counselor informed **the patient** that *his/her/their/xyr* insurance fully covered the cost of the sessions.

Fix #1: Add 2 missing grammatical cases

Fix #2: Fix structural violations, e.g, non-parallel templates

Fix #3: Ensure templates support all pronouns

Fix #4: Add neopronoun xe/xem/xyr to the evaluation

Figure 1: Problems with Winogender Schemas that we fix in our new coreference resolution dataset, WINOPRON. Correct antecedents appear in **bold**.

1 Introduction

Third-person pronouns (*he*, *she*, *they*, etc.) help us refer to people in conversation. Since they mark referential gender in English, gender bias affects how coreference resolution systems map these pronouns to people. Rudinger et al. (2018) demonstrated this by introducing Winogender Schemas, a challenge dataset to evaluate occupational gender bias in coreference resolution systems. The dataset has become popular due to its careful construction; it has been translated to other languages (Hansson et al., 2021; Stanovsky et al., 2019) and used in framings beyond coreference resolution, e.g., to evaluate natural language inferences (Poliak et al., 2018) and intrinsic bias in language models (Kurita et al., 2019).

However, a closer look at the dataset reveals weaknesses that compromise its use for reliable evaluation (see Figure 1), which we hypothesize would affect both performance and bias evaluation.

In this paper, we identify issues with the original dataset and fix them to create a new dataset we call WINOPRON (§3).[1] We then empirically show how our fixes affect coreference resolution system performance (§4) as well as bias (§5), with a novel method we propose to evaluate pronominal bias in coreference resolution that goes beyond the binary and focuses on linguistic rather than social gender (Cao and Daumé III, 2021).

[1]Data and code available at github.com/uds-lsv/winopron.

Proceedings of the Seventh Workshop on Computational Models of Reference, Anaphora and Coreference (CRAC 2024), pages 52–66
November 15, 2024.

(a) The cashier told **the customer** that *his / her / their* card was declined.
(b) **The cashier** told the customer that *his / her / their* shift ended soon.

Figure 2: Winogender Schemas for *cashier*, *customer* and possessive pronouns, with the antecedent bolded.

Our fixes reveal that grammatical case, which we balance for in WINOPRON, does indeed matter for both performance and bias results; accusative pronouns are harder to resolve than nominative or possessive pronouns, and system pronominal bias is not always consistent across different grammatical cases of the same pronoun set. We find that singular *they* and the neopronoun *xe* are extremely hard for supervised coreference resolution systems to resolve, but surprisingly easy for FLAN-T5 models of a certain size. We put forth hypotheses for these patterns and look forward to future work testing them.

2 Background: Winogender Schemas

Winogender Schemas (Rudinger et al., 2018) are a widely-used dataset consisting of paired sentence templates in English, with slots for two human entities (an occupation and a participant), and a third person singular pronoun. As Figure 2 shows, the second part of each template disambiguates which of the two entities the pronoun uniquely refers to, similar to Winograd schemas (Levesque et al., 2012). Changing the pronoun (e.g., from *his* to *her*) maintains the coreference, allowing us to measure whether coreference resolution systems are worse at resolving certain pronouns to certain entities. Rudinger et al. (2018) use the gendered associations of these pronouns to show that gender bias affects coreference resolution performance.

The entities consist of 60 occupation-participant pairs (e.g., *accountant* is paired with *taxpayer*). A pair of templates is created for each occupation-participant pair, resulting in a total of 120 unique templates. The template pairs are designed to be parallel until the pronoun, such that only the ending can be used to disambiguate how to resolve the pronoun: it should resolve to the occupation in one template, and to the participant in the other. Each template can be instantiated with three pronoun sets (*he*, *she*, and singular *they*), for a total of 120 x 3 = 360 sentences for evaluation.

Grammatical case	WS	WP
Nominative (*he, she, they, xe*)	89	120
Accusative (*him, her, them, xem*)	4	120
Possessive (*his, her, their, xyr*)	27	120

Table 1: Number of templates per grammatical case in Winogender Schemas (WS) and WINOPRON (WP).

3 WinoPron Dataset

Although Winogender Schemas are established in the coreference resolution literature, we find issues with the dataset that compromise its use for reliable evaluation (see Figure 1 for examples). We first motivate these issues and our fixes, and then describe how we create and systematically validate our new dataset, WINOPRON.

We mostly reuse the occupation-participant pairs from Winogender Schemas (see Appendix A for the full list of pairings), but add 240 templates to cover missing grammatical cases, for a total of 360 templates. We also include a neopronoun set (*xe/xem/xyr*), giving us 360 templates x 4 pronoun sets = 1,440 sentences for evaluation.

3.1 Issues and Solutions

Support for 3 Grammatical Cases We hypothesize that systems have different performance and bias characteristics with pronouns in different grammatical cases.[2] However, as Table 1 shows, Winogender Schemas have a variable number of pronouns per grammatical case, and treat them all as equivalent. To enable more granular evaluation, we balance this distribution in WINOPRON.

Consistency Fixes Winograd-like schemas have strict structural constraints so that models cannot inflate performance through heuristics. However, when analyzing Winogender Schemas, we found constraint violations, e.g., non-parallel paired templates. We fixed these along with typographical errors to ensure robust and reliable evaluation.

Support for All English Pronouns For a controlled evaluation comparing pronouns, it is common to use templates that only vary the pronoun. However, 17% of Winogender Schemas must be modified to work with singular *they* due to its different verbal agreement ("he was" but "they were"). To ensure a fair comparison between pronouns, we modify these templates to work with any pronouns.

[2]Here, we mean the surface form of the pronoun.

Single-Entity Versions When evaluating large language models on coreference resolution when they have not explicitly been trained for it, poor performance could mean that the model simply cannot perform the task (with a given prompt). In its current form, Winogender Schemas do not allow us to disentangle *why* bad model performance is bad. In WINOPRON, we create single-entity sentences that are parallel to the traditional, more complex double-entity sentences, for a simple setting to test this, and a useful baseline for all systems.

3.2 Data Creation

Two authors with linguistic training iteratively created sentence templates until we reached consensus on their grammaticality and correct, unique coreferences. We found template construction to be particularly challenging and time-consuming, due to ambiguity and verbal constraints.

Ambiguity Our biggest source of ambiguity during template creation was singular *they*, as *they* is also a third person plural pronoun. For example, if an *advisor* and *student* were meeting to discuss *their* future, this could potentially refer to their future *together*. This problem applied across grammatical cases. In addition, possessive sentences were potentially ambiguous across all pronoun series; when discussing a *doctor* and a *patient* and someone's diagnosis, this could be the *doctor*'s diagnosis (i.e., the diagnosis made by the doctor), or the *patient*'s diagnosis (i.e., the diagnosis the patient received). All ambiguous templates were discarded and subsequently reworked.

Verbal Constraints The structural constraint of template pairs being identical until the pronoun led to some difficulties in finding appropriate (logically and semantically plausible) endings for the two sentences, particularly with accusative pronouns. With nominative pronouns, we had to ensure we used verbs in the past tense and avoid was/were, so that our templates could be used with both *he/she/xe* and singular *they*. It was also sometimes difficult to create single-entity sentences that were semantically close to the double-entity versions because the latter only made sense with two entities (e.g., "X gave Y something").

3.3 Data Validation

As WINOPRON templates have structural constraints that can be programmatically validated, we wrote automatic checks for these. In addition, we performed human annotation of the sentences for grammaticality, and unique, correct coreferences.

Automatic Checks We automatically checked our data for completeness first, i.e., that every occupation-participant pair had sentence templates for nominative, accusative, and possessive pronouns. We then automatically checked structural constraints, e.g., that a pair of templates must always be identical until the pronoun slot, and that no additional pronouns appeared in the sentence.

Human Annotation Both authors who created the schemas systematically annotated them, rating 100% of the final instances as grammatical and 100% of them as having unique, correct coreferences. We confirmed the uniqueness of coreferences by marking each data instance as coreferring with the appropriate antecedent and *not* coreferring with the other antecedent. An additional annotator independently verified the final templates, rating 100% of them as grammatical, and 98.2% as having unique, correct coreferences.

4 Performance and Consistency

To demonstrate the effects of our changes, we evaluate performance and consistency on WINOPRON with a range of models with different levels of training for coreference resolution.

4.1 Models

LingMess (Otmazgin et al., 2023) is a state-of-the-art, linguistically motivated, mixture-of-experts system for coreference resolution.

CAW-coref (D'Oosterlinck et al., 2023) is a state-of-the-art word-level coreference resolution system based on an encoder-only model.

SpanBERT (Joshi et al., 2020) is an encoder-only language model pre-trained with a span prediction objective and further enhanced for coreference resolution with fine-tuning data. We use both available model sizes (base and large) for evaluation.

FLAN-T5 (Chung et al., 2024) is an instruction-tuned language model which is not trained for coreference resolution. We evaluate on five model sizes (small, base, large, xl, and xxl), with prompts from the FLAN collection (Longpre et al., 2023). See Appendix D for details on prompting.

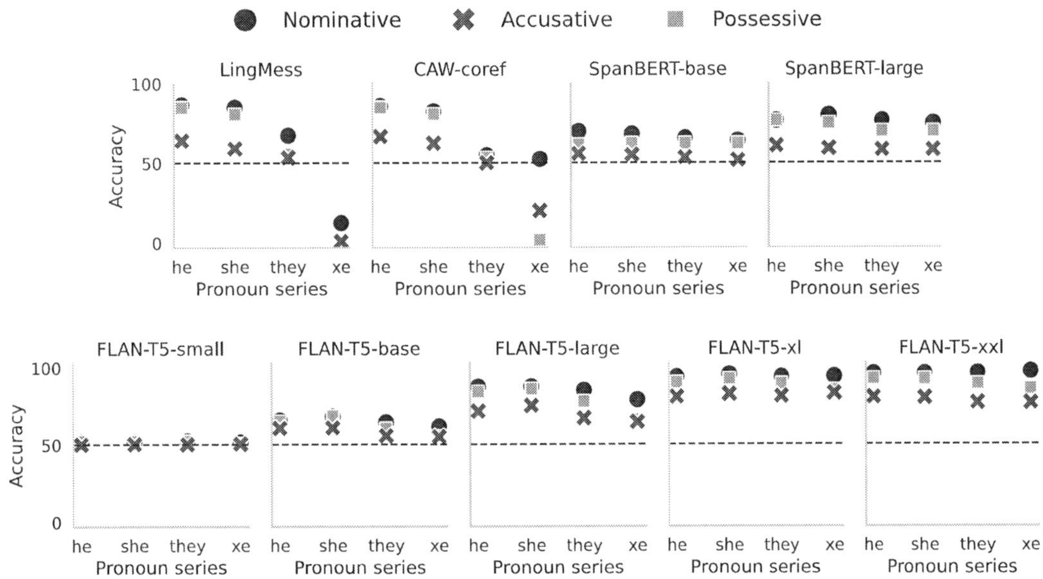

Figure 3: Accuracy on WINOPRON by case and pronoun series with supervised coreference resolution systems (CAW-coref and LingMess), and language models fine-tuned for coreference resolution (SpanBERT) and prompted zero-shot (FLAN-T5), compared to random performance (50%). Accusative pronoun performance is worse than other grammatical cases, and singular *they* and the neopronoun *xe* are challenging for several models.

System	WS	WP	ΔF_1
LingMess	85.5	64.4	-21.1
CAW-coref	81.3	67.3	-14.0
SpanBERT-base	71.8	61.6	-10.2
SpanBERT-large	82.0	70.1	-11.9
FLAN-T5-small	52.2	51.6	-0.6
FLAN-T5-base	66.6	62.4	-4.2
FLAN-T5-large	89.2	78.0	-11.2
FLAN-T5-xl	97.4	89.0	-8.4
FLAN-T5-xxl	97.5	88.8	-8.7

Table 2: Overall performance (F_1) of coreference resolution systems on Winogender Schemas (WS) and WINOPRON (WP). WINOPRON is harder for all systems.

4.2 Performance Results

We first show how our changes affect overall performance between Winogender Schemas and WINOPRON. Then we use WINOPRON to investigate differences across case (which we have balanced for) and pronoun sets (which can now be evenly compared). Additional results are in Appendix E.

WINOPRON is harder than Winogender Schemas. As Table 2 shows, all the systems we evaluate perform worse on WINOPRON, with F1 dropping on average by 10 percentage points compared to Winogender Schemas. Patterns of performance across models are similar between Winogender Schemas and WINOPRON, with similar scaling behaviour for both SpanBERT and FLAN-T5. Notably, scale seems to supercede supervision, as the largest FLAN-T5 models perform the best overall. Smaller FLAN-T5 models perform at chance level, which is likely a reflection of the "demand gap" induced through prompting (Hu and Frank, 2024).

Accusative pronouns are harder. When model accuracy is split by grammatical case and pronoun series, we see that *all* models struggle with accusative pronouns. In general, systems perform best at resolving nominative pronouns, with a slight decrease for possessive pronouns and a large drop for accusative pronouns, as seen in Figure 3. This finding holds even for the best performing models on WINOPRON, FLAN-T5-xl and FLAN-T5-xxl, where accuracy with accusative pronouns (81.9% and 78.6%) is much lower than with nominative (94.3% and 96.3%) or possessive (89.3% and 90.0%) pronouns. We hypothesize that the performance gap for accusative pronouns is partially an effect of frequency; *him* tokens appear roughly half as often in large pre-training corpora as *he* and *his* tokens (Elazar et al., 2024).

Performance with singular *they* and neopronouns is bimodal. For the supervised coreference resolution systems (LingMess and CAW-coref), performance with singular *they* is close to chance, and performance with the neopronoun *xe* is far below chance, despite good performance with *he/him/his* and *she/her/her*. SpanBERT performance also shows a gap between singular *they* and neopronoun performance compared to data-rich pronouns, although the gap is much smaller. These findings mirror those of Cao and Daumé III (2020); Lauscher et al. (2022) and Gautam et al. (2024a). However, in contrast to Gautam et al.'s (2024a) findings with encoder-only and decoder-only models, there is no large difference in accuracy across pronoun sets with FLAN-T5 models. As FLAN-T5 has been instruction fine-tuned for the task of coreference resolution but not pronoun fidelity (Chung et al., 2024), this could explain the model's ability to generalize to new pronouns in our setting.

4.3 Consistency Results

Next, we evaluate system consistency on groups of closely related instances in WINOPRON, in order to dissect performance results and examine if systems are really right for the right reasons. We follow Ravichander et al. (2022) in operationalizing consistency by taking the score of the lowest-performing instance in the group as the group's score. We consider two groups, illustrated in Figure 4: (a) *pronoun consistency*, and (b) *disambiguation consistency*, inspired by Abdou et al.'s (2020) pair accuracy on Winograd Schemas. In both cases, we report the percentage of groups for which a model performs consistently.

Pronoun consistency measures model robustness across pronoun sets, i.e., if a model fails with even one pronoun set on a given template, then its score for that template is zero. As we consider four pronoun sets, chance is $50\%^4$, or 6.25%. Disambiguation consistency measures a system's ability to resolve a fixed pronoun to competing antecedents in paired templates. Chance is thus 0.5^2, or 0.25.

SpanBERT-large is more robust to pronoun variation. As Table 3 shows, LingMess and the small and base sizes of FLAN-T5 score below chance, the former due to near-zero performance on *xe/xem/xyr*, and the latter due to poor performance overall. Interestingly, SpanBERT-large is more consistent (60.0%) than FLAN-T5-xl (55.3%) and FLAN-T5-xxl (43.9%). This indicates that despite its lower overall performance in Section 4.2, SpanBERT-large is more robust to pronominal variation.

Pronoun consistency

(a) **The counselor** informed the patient that *his* qualifications were in psychology.
(b) **The counselor** informed the patient that *her* qualifications were in psychology.
(c) **The counselor** informed the patient that *their* qualifications were in psychology.
(d) **The counselor** informed the patient that *xyr* qualifications were in psychology.

Disambiguation consistency

(a) **The counselor** informed the patient that xyr *qualifications were in psychology*.
(b) The counselor informed **the patient** that xyr *insurance covered the cost of the sessions*.

Figure 4: Example groups for scoring consistency metrics using WINOPRON templates for *counselor*, *patient* and possessive pronouns, with the antecedent bolded.

Model	PronounC	DisambigC
LingMess	*4.2*	33.3
CAW-coref	18.3	34.7
SpanBERT-base	50.0	*24.3*
SpanBERT-large	**60.0**	41.2
FLAN-T5-small	*3.9*	*0.0*
FLAN-T5-base	*0.8*	*0.0*
FLAN-T5-large	14.4	*5.4*
FLAN-T5-xl	55.3	**51.4**
FLAN-T5-xxl	43.9	43.3

Table 3: Consistency results on WINOPRON. Chance is 6.25% for pronoun consistency (PronounC) and 25% for disambiguation consistency (DisambigC). *Red, italicized numbers* are worse than chance.

The best model can only disambiguate half of the sentence pairs. Following from its high overall performance, FLAN-T5-xl has the highest disambiguation consistency score at 51.4%, just over half the template pairs we evaluate. In contrast, SpanBERT-base has disambiguation consistency below chance (24.3%). Given its reasonable overall performance, this result could stem from model bias, i.e., over-resolving a pronoun to a particular antecedent, disregarding the disambiguating context. We thus investigate bias in more detail next.

5 Pronominal Bias

So far, we have focused on coreference resolution performance and consistency and found that accusative forms and less frequent pronoun sets are harder, and models are mostly non-robust to pronominal variation and antecedent disambiguation. However, we have not established the extent to which models fail because they simply cannot perform the task, or if they are over-resolving a pronoun to a particular antecedent due to biased associations between them. Thus, we aim to disentangle performance and bias in this section.

Winogender Schemas were originally proposed to measure gender bias in coreference resolution by using pronouns (a form of lexical gender) as a proxy for social gender. Rudinger et al. (2018) then correlate incorrect resolution of English masculine and feminine pronouns with occupational statistics from the USA. By conflating lexical and social gender (see Cao and Daumé III (2021) for a critical discussion), their analysis is subject to the same limitations as their data: treating different grammatical cases of the same pronoun as equivalent, and focusing only on *he* and *she*. We thus propose a new method for evaluating pronominal bias in coreference resolution, correcting for these issues, and we then apply our method to investigate bias in SpanBERT models on WINOPRON.

5.1 Evaluating Pronominal Bias

When proposing a new method to evaluate pronominal bias in coreference resolution systems, our primary goal is to disentangle performance and bias. In other words, we should have reason to believe that the model can perform the task, and that the reason it gets an instance wrong is specifically due to bias. Additionally, we would like our method to work with an arbitrary set of pronouns of interest, and multiple surface forms of those pronouns.

Measuring Performance We first **(1)** isolate template pairs where the system attempts the task of coreference resolution as intended, i.e., the system resolves each pronoun to the occupation or participant (regardless of correctness). Next, we **(2)** focus on the template pairs that the model can *correctly* disambiguate with at least one pronoun set, p_a. We deem the model capable of performing coreference resolution on this set of template pairs if it can resolve them with at least one pronoun set.

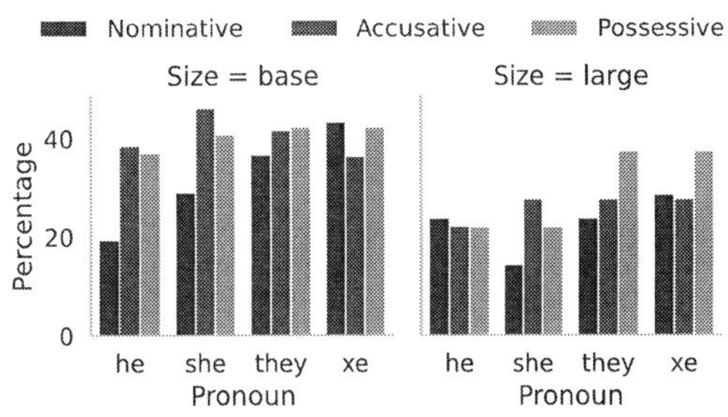

Figure 5: Percentage of model-attempted templates that show bias, for SpanBERT-base and SpanBERT-large.

Measuring Bias Of the template pairs that a model can successfully disambiguate with at least one pronoun p_a, we then **(3)** focus on cases where the model fails to disambiguate the exact same template pair with a different pronoun $p_b \neq p_a$, as this is likely due to bias. If the model over-resolves p_b to the occupation, we posit that the model has a *positive bias* between p_b and that occupation. On the other hand, if it over-resolves p_b to the participant, the model is biased against associating p_b with the occupation, i.e., it has a *negative bias*.

Comparing Results With sets of positively and negatively biased occupations for each pronoun form, we want to quantify how many of a model's reasonable attempts to resolve a pronoun gave biased outputs. We thus compute the percentage of templates that result in bias (see Measuring Bias) of the total templates that a model attempts to resolve with that pronoun, given that it can correctly solve it with at least one pronoun (see Measuring Performance). This gives us a quantitative measure of "how biased" a model is which also controls for whether a model is attempting the task and can perform the task with another pronoun. In addition, we can quantify whether two models or two surface forms of a pronoun set have similar occupational biases by computing the Jaccard index (Jaccard, 1912), i.e., the size of the intersection of the biased occupation sets divided by the size of their union.

5.2 Results

We apply our method to SpanBERT-base and SpanBERT-large and collect all instances of positive and negative bias between a pronoun form and an occupation. Aggregated bias results for both models are shown in Figure 5, and Table 4 shows a sample of biased occupations for SpanBERT-large.

Pronouns	Nominative case		Accusative case		Possessive case	
	Positive	Negative	Positive	Negative	Positive	Negative
he/him/his	*engineer painter*	*receptionist secretary*	–	*dietitian secretary*	*practitioner chef*	*hairdresser secretary*
she/her/her	*hairdresser painter*	*accountant plumber*	*cashier*	*firefighter mechanic*	*practitioner painter*	*accountant surgeon*
they/them/their	–	*accountant plumber*	–	*cashier dietitian*	*advisor baker*	*accountant surgeon*
xe/xem/xyr	–	*hairdresser engineer*	–	*mechanic cashier*	*advisor baker*	*engineer supervisor*

Table 4: A sample of SpanBERT-large's biases when resolving pronouns to occupations. Positive bias: the model over-resolves the pronoun to that occupation. Negative bias: the model under-resolves the pronoun to the occupation.

Grammatical case	he	she	they	xe
Nominative	0.14	0.15	0.17	0.32
Accusative	0.12	0.10	0.25	0.29
Possessive	0.12	0.18	0.24	0.24

Table 5: Similarity of biased occupations between SpanBERT-base and SpanBERT-large, quantified with the Jaccard index (0.0 -1.0; higher is more similar).

SpanBERT-base is more biased than SpanBERT-large. As Figure 5 shows, a larger percentage of SpanBERT-base's attempted and resolvable templates show biased behaviour when compared to SpanBERT-large. This pattern holds even when examining positive and negative biases separately. However, there are more negatively biased occupations than positively biased ones for both models.

Bias is qualitatively different across model sizes. In addition to being quantitatively different, we find that despite being trained and fine-tuned on the same data, there is low overlap between the occupational biases acquired by SpanBERT-base and SpanBERT-large (see Table 5). For instance, the former positively associates *she* with *machinist*, while the latter positively associates *she* with *hairdresser* and *painter*. Only *they/them/their* and *xe/xem/xyr* have slightly higher overlap, mostly due to negative bias, as these models under-resolve these particular pronouns to all occupations.

Bias does not match qualitatively across grammatical case. In other words, positive bias with *she* for an occupation does not entail positive bias with *her*. We quantify this systematically by computing Jaccard indices in Table 6, where we find

Case pairings	he	she	they	xe
SpanBERT-base				
Nom-Acc	0.10	0.00	0.00	0.00
Acc-Poss	0.07	0.13	0.14	0.07
Nom-Poss	0.07	0.11	0.10	0.09
SpanBERT-large				
Nom-Acc	0.10	0.00	0.07	0.06
Acc-Poss	0.22	0.00	0.06	0.06
Nom-Poss	0.17	0.29	0.15	0.19

Table 6: Similarity of biased occupations across pairings of grammatical case (nom: nominative, acc: accusative, poss: possessive) of a pronoun set, quantified with the Jaccard index (0.0 -1.0; higher is more similar).

that most pairings of grammatical case have very low overlap in their biases. In fact, even contradictory associations are possible; SpanBERT-base has a positive bias between *manager* and *them*, but a negative bias betweeen *manager* and *their*. Only nominative and possessive occupational biases in SpanBERT-large appear to somewhat consistently overlap with each other. Although some of these instances (e.g., negative bias for *secretary* with *he*, *him*, and *his*) align with social stereotypes (Haines et al., 2016), the overall pattern provides evidence that grammatical case in pronouns has its own set of biases that should be examined in their own right.

Bias is not additive. Even though SpanBERT-large has positive bias for *baker* and *her*, *their* as well as *xyr*, this does not imply that the model must have a negative bias between *baker* and *his*; it does not. This further highlights the need for evaluation that goes beyond binary, oppositional operationalizations of gender via pronouns.

6 Discussion

By systematically identifying and fixing issues with Winogender Schemas (Rudinger et al., 2018), we create a new dataset, WINOPRON, and find that: **(1)** different grammatical cases of pronouns show vastly different performance and bias characteristics, **(2)** pronominal biases are rich and varied, of which *he* and *she* are only the tip of the iceberg, and **(3)** model biases are complex and do not necessarily match our intuitions about them. Based on our findings, we make some recommendations for researchers who study coreference resolution and those who study bias and fairness via pronouns.

First, grammatical case is a dimension of pronominal performance and bias that warrants more study (Munro and Morrison, 2020). In particular, we hope that future work further investigates *why* accusative pronouns are harder. The patterns we demonstrate (both for performance and bias) could arise from a number of sources beyond mere frequency, including quirks of our dataset, or the distribution of semantic roles in training data for coreference resolution systems.

Second, we echo prior calls for fairness researchers to attend to the differences between social gender and terms that index it (Cao and Daumé III, 2021; Gautam et al., 2024b), to include more diversity in pronouns (Baumler and Rudinger, 2022; Lauscher et al., 2022; Hossain et al., 2023), and to move towards richer operationalizations of gender (Devinney et al., 2022; Ovalle et al., 2023) and bias (Blodgett et al., 2020). Specifically, future work on bias in coreference resolution should treat pronominal bias as distinct from (social) gender bias, defend how and why pronouns are mapped to social gender, and move beyond binary, oppositional methods of evaluation.

Lastly, as our work is a case study in how careful data curation and operationalization affects claims about system performance and bias, we emphasize the need for thoughtful data work (Sambasivan et al., 2021), and encourage the use of automatic checks when feasible, as in our work.

7 Related work

Besides Rudinger et al. (2018), there are a number of papers that tackle gender bias in coreference resolution, all of which differ from ours. Similar to Winogender Schemas, WinoBias (Zhao et al., 2018) proposes Winograd-like schemas that focus on occupations to evaluate gender bias in coreference resolution. However, WinoBias only covers *he* and *she*, rather than our coverage of all English pronoun sets by design. In addition, like Winogender, WinoBias also treats pronouns in all grammatical cases the same way. WinoNB schemas (Baumler and Rudinger, 2022) evaluate how coreference resolution systems handle singular they and plural they with similar schemas. Beyond these constructed schemas, there also exist datasets of challenging sentences found "in the wild," such as BUG (Levy et al., 2021), GAP (Webster et al., 2018), and GICOREF (Cao and Daumé III, 2021). However, as these natural datasets are not carefully constructed like Winograd-like schemas, pronouns cannot be swapped in dataset instances and still be assumed to be grammatical or coherent.

Our work is also one among several papers that investigate datasets for problems including low quality or noisy data (Elazar et al., 2024; Abela et al., 2024), artifacts (Shwartz et al., 2020; Herlihy and Rudinger, 2021; Elazar et al., 2021; Dutta Chowdhury et al., 2022), contamination (Balloccu et al., 2024; Deng et al., 2024), and issues with conceptualization and operationalization of bias (Blodgett et al., 2021; Selvam et al., 2023; Nighojkar et al., 2023; Subramonian et al., 2023; Gautam et al., 2024b). We cover many of these areas, but do not control for dataset artifacts, which we explain further in our Limitations section.

8 Conclusion

We demonstrate a number of issues with the well-known Winogender Schemas dataset, which we fix in our new, expanded WINOPRON dataset. In addition, we propose a novel way to evaluate pronominal bias in coreference resolution that goes beyond the binary and focuses on lexical gender. With our new dataset, we evaluate both supervised coreference resolution systems and language models, and find that the grammatical case of pronouns affects model performance and bias, and that bias varies widely across models, pronoun sets and grammatical cases. Our work demonstrates that measurements of bias and robustness are only as good as the datasets and metrics we use to measure them, and we call for careful attention when developing future resources for evaluating bias and coreference resolution, with attention to grammatical case, more careful operationalizations of bias, and greater diversity in the pronouns we consider.

Limitations

As in Winogender Schemas, our schemas are not "Google-proof" and could conceivably be solved with heuristics, including word co-occurrences, which is a primary concern when creating and evaluating *Winograd* schemas (Levesque et al., 2012; Amsili and Seminck, 2017; Elazar et al., 2021). The fact that we do not control for this means that our dataset gives *generous* estimates of system performance, particularly for strong language models like FLAN-T5, but it also means that this dataset is inappropriate to test "reasoning." Our dataset construction instead controls for simple system heuristics that are relevant for coreference resolution, such as always picking the first entity in the sentence, or always picking the second.

We take steps to prevent data contamination (Jacovi et al., 2023), including not releasing our data in plain text, and not evaluating with language models behind closed APIs that do not guarantee that our data will not be used to train future models (Balloccu et al., 2024). However, as we cannot guarantee a complete absence of data leakage unless we never release the dataset, we encourage caution in interpreting results on WINOPRON with models trained on data after August 2024.

Finally, we note that as our evaluation set only contains one set of templates per occupation-participant pair, our results represent a point in the distribution of bias related to that occupation. We thus echo Rudinger et al.'s (2018) view of Winogender Schemas as having "high positive predictive value and low negative predictive value" for bias. In other words, they may demonstrate evidence of pronominal bias in systems, but not prove its absence. In the case of large language models in particular, using a small number of templates for templatic evaluation is known to be brittle even to small, meaning-preserving changes to the template (Seshadri et al., 2022; Selvam et al., 2023). Our dataset's small size is a result of us requiring a tightly controlled and structured dataset to evaluate how coreference resolution varies. Thus, it may differ from realistic examples (which would have other differences that confound bias results). We wish to emphasize that in addition to controlled datasets like ours, realistic evaluation is also necessary for holistically evaluating performance, robustness and bias in coreference resolution.

Acknowledgements

The authors thank Timm Dill for several rounds of patient annotation, and are grateful to Rachel Rudinger, Benjamin Van Durme, and our CRAC reviewers for their comments. Vagrant Gautam received funding from the BMBF's (German Federal Ministry of Education and Research) SLIK project under the grant 01IS22015C. Anne Lauscher's work is funded under the Excellence Strategy of the German Federal Government and States.

References

Mostafa Abdou, Vinit Ravishankar, Maria Barrett, Yonatan Belinkov, Desmond Elliott, and Anders Søgaard. 2020. The sensitivity of language models and humans to Winograd schema perturbations. In *Proceedings of the 58th Annual Meeting of the Association for Computational Linguistics*, pages 7590–7604, Online. Association for Computational Linguistics.

Kurt Abela, Kurt Micallef, Marc Tanti, and Claudia Borg. 2024. Tokenisation in machine translation does matter: The impact of different tokenisation approaches for Maltese. In *Proceedings of the Seventh Workshop on Technologies for Machine Translation of Low-Resource Languages (LoResMT 2024)*, pages 109–120, Bangkok, Thailand. Association for Computational Linguistics.

Pascal Amsili and Olga Seminck. 2017. A Google-proof collection of French Winograd schemas. In *Proceedings of the 2nd Workshop on Coreference Resolution Beyond OntoNotes (CORBON 2017)*, pages 24–29, Valencia, Spain. Association for Computational Linguistics.

Simone Balloccu, Patrícia Schmidtová, Mateusz Lango, and Ondrej Dusek. 2024. Leak, cheat, repeat: Data contamination and evaluation malpractices in closed-source LLMs. In *Proceedings of the 18th Conference of the European Chapter of the Association for Computational Linguistics (Volume 1: Long Papers)*, pages 67–93, St. Julian's, Malta. Association for Computational Linguistics.

Connor Baumler and Rachel Rudinger. 2022. Recognition of they/them as singular personal pronouns in coreference resolution. In *Proceedings of the 2022 Conference of the North American Chapter of the Association for Computational Linguistics: Human Language Technologies*, pages 3426–3432, Seattle, United States. Association for Computational Linguistics.

Su Lin Blodgett, Solon Barocas, Hal Daumé III, and Hanna Wallach. 2020. Language (technology) is power: A critical survey of "bias" in NLP. In *Proceedings of the 58th Annual Meeting of the Association for Computational Linguistics*, pages 5454–

5476, Online. Association for Computational Linguistics.

Su Lin Blodgett, Gilsinia Lopez, Alexandra Olteanu, Robert Sim, and Hanna Wallach. 2021. Stereotyping Norwegian salmon: An inventory of pitfalls in fairness benchmark datasets. In *Proceedings of the 59th Annual Meeting of the Association for Computational Linguistics and the 11th International Joint Conference on Natural Language Processing (Volume 1: Long Papers)*, pages 1004–1015, Online. Association for Computational Linguistics.

Yang Trista Cao and Hal Daumé III. 2020. Toward gender-inclusive coreference resolution. In *Proceedings of the 58th Annual Meeting of the Association for Computational Linguistics*, pages 4568–4595, Online. Association for Computational Linguistics.

Yang Trista Cao and Hal Daumé III. 2021. Toward gender-inclusive coreference resolution: An analysis of gender and bias throughout the machine learning lifecycle*. *Computational Linguistics*, 47(3):615–661.

Hyung Won Chung, Le Hou, Shayne Longpre, Barret Zoph, Yi Tay, William Fedus, Yunxuan Li, Xuezhi Wang, Mostafa Dehghani, Siddhartha Brahma, Albert Webson, Shixiang Shane Gu, Zhuyun Dai, Mirac Suzgun, Xinyun Chen, Aakanksha Chowdhery, Alex Castro-Ros, Marie Pellat, Kevin Robinson, Dasha Valter, Sharan Narang, Gaurav Mishra, Adams Yu, Vincent Zhao, Yanping Huang, Andrew Dai, Hongkun Yu, Slav Petrov, Ed H. Chi, Jeff Dean, Jacob Devlin, Adam Roberts, Denny Zhou, Quoc V. Le, and Jason Wei. 2024. Scaling instruction-finetuned language models. *Journal of Machine Learning Research*, 25(70):1–53.

Chunyuan Deng, Yilun Zhao, Xiangru Tang, Mark Gerstein, and Arman Cohan. 2024. Investigating data contamination in modern benchmarks for large language models. In *Proceedings of the 2024 Conference of the North American Chapter of the Association for Computational Linguistics: Human Language Technologies (Volume 1: Long Papers)*, pages 8706–8719, Mexico City, Mexico. Association for Computational Linguistics.

Hannah Devinney, Jenny Björklund, and Henrik Björklund. 2022. Theories of "gender" in nlp bias research. In *Proceedings of the 2022 ACM Conference on Fairness, Accountability, and Transparency*, FAccT '22, page 2083–2102, New York, NY, USA. Association for Computing Machinery.

Karel D'Oosterlinck, Semere Kiros Bitew, Brandon Papineau, Christopher Potts, Thomas Demeester, and Chris Develder. 2023. CAW-coref: Conjunction-aware word-level coreference resolution. In *Proceedings of The Sixth Workshop on Computational Models of Reference, Anaphora and Coreference (CRAC 2023)*, pages 8–14, Singapore. Association for Computational Linguistics.

Koel Dutta Chowdhury, Rricha Jalota, Cristina España-Bonet, and Josef Genabith. 2022. Towards debiasing translation artifacts. In *Proceedings of the 2022 Conference of the North American Chapter of the Association for Computational Linguistics: Human Language Technologies*, pages 3983–3991, Seattle, United States. Association for Computational Linguistics.

Yanai Elazar, Akshita Bhagia, Ian Helgi Magnusson, Abhilasha Ravichander, Dustin Schwenk, Alane Suhr, Evan Pete Walsh, Dirk Groeneveld, Luca Soldaini, Sameer Singh, Hannaneh Hajishirzi, Noah A. Smith, and Jesse Dodge. 2024. What's in my big data? In *The Twelfth International Conference on Learning Representations*.

Yanai Elazar, Hongming Zhang, Yoav Goldberg, and Dan Roth. 2021. Back to square one: Artifact detection, training and commonsense disentanglement in the Winograd schema. In *Proceedings of the 2021 Conference on Empirical Methods in Natural Language Processing*, pages 10486–10500, Online and Punta Cana, Dominican Republic. Association for Computational Linguistics.

Vagrant Gautam, Eileen Bingert, Dawei Zhu, Anne Lauscher, and Dietrich Klakow. 2024a. Robust pronoun fidelity with english llms: Are they reasoning, repeating, or just biased?

Vagrant Gautam, Arjun Subramonian, Anne Lauscher, and Os Keyes. 2024b. Stop! in the name of flaws: Disentangling personal names and sociodemographic attributes in NLP. In *Proceedings of the 5th Workshop on Gender Bias in Natural Language Processing (GeBNLP)*, pages 323–337, Bangkok, Thailand. Association for Computational Linguistics.

Elizabeth L. Haines, Kay Deaux, and Nicole Lofaro. 2016. The times they are a-changing ... or are they not? a comparison of gender stereotypes, 1983–2014. *Psychology of Women Quarterly*, 40(3):353–363.

Saga Hansson, Konstantinos Mavromatakis, Yvonne Adesam, Gerlof Bouma, and Dana Dannélls. 2021. The Swedish Winogender dataset. In *Proceedings of the 23rd Nordic Conference on Computational Linguistics (NoDaLiDa)*, pages 452–459, Reykjavik, Iceland (Online). Linköping University Electronic Press, Sweden.

Christine Herlihy and Rachel Rudinger. 2021. MedNLI is not immune: Natural language inference artifacts in the clinical domain. In *Proceedings of the 59th Annual Meeting of the Association for Computational Linguistics and the 11th International Joint Conference on Natural Language Processing (Volume 2: Short Papers)*, pages 1020–1027, Online. Association for Computational Linguistics.

Tamanna Hossain, Sunipa Dev, and Sameer Singh. 2023. MISGENDERED: Limits of large language models in understanding pronouns. In *Proceedings of the 61st Annual Meeting of the Association for Computational Linguistics (Volume 1: Long Papers)*, pages

5352–5367, Toronto, Canada. Association for Computational Linguistics.

Jennifer Hu and Michael Frank. 2024. Auxiliary task demands mask the capabilities of smaller language models. In *First Conference on Language Modeling*.

Paul Jaccard. 1912. The distribution of the flora in the alpine zone. *New Phytologist*, 11(2):37–50.

Alon Jacovi, Avi Caciularu, Omer Goldman, and Yoav Goldberg. 2023. Stop uploading test data in plain text: Practical strategies for mitigating data contamination by evaluation benchmarks. In *Proceedings of the 2023 Conference on Empirical Methods in Natural Language Processing*, pages 5075–5084, Singapore. Association for Computational Linguistics.

Mandar Joshi, Danqi Chen, Yinhan Liu, Daniel S. Weld, Luke Zettlemoyer, and Omer Levy. 2020. SpanBERT: Improving pre-training by representing and predicting spans. *Transactions of the Association for Computational Linguistics*, 8:64–77.

Keita Kurita, Nidhi Vyas, Ayush Pareek, Alan W Black, and Yulia Tsvetkov. 2019. Measuring bias in contextualized word representations. In *Proceedings of the First Workshop on Gender Bias in Natural Language Processing*, pages 166–172, Florence, Italy. Association for Computational Linguistics.

Anne Lauscher, Archie Crowley, and Dirk Hovy. 2022. Welcome to the modern world of pronouns: Identity-inclusive natural language processing beyond gender. In *Proceedings of the 29th International Conference on Computational Linguistics*, pages 1221–1232, Gyeongju, Republic of Korea. International Committee on Computational Linguistics.

Hector J. Levesque, Ernest Davis, and Leora Morgenstern. 2012. The winograd schema challenge. In *Proceedings of the Thirteenth International Conference on Principles of Knowledge Representation and Reasoning*, KR'12, page 552–561. AAAI Press.

Shahar Levy, Koren Lazar, and Gabriel Stanovsky. 2021. Collecting a large-scale gender bias dataset for coreference resolution and machine translation. In *Findings of the Association for Computational Linguistics: EMNLP 2021*, pages 2470–2480, Punta Cana, Dominican Republic. Association for Computational Linguistics.

Shayne Longpre, Le Hou, Tu Vu, Albert Webson, Hyung Won Chung, Yi Tay, Denny Zhou, Quoc V. Le, Barret Zoph, Jason Wei, and Adam Roberts. 2023. The flan collection: Designing data and methods for effective instruction tuning. In *International Conference on Machine Learning, ICML 2023, 23-29 July 2023, Honolulu, Hawaii, USA*, volume 202 of *Proceedings of Machine Learning Research*, pages 22631–22648. PMLR.

Robert Munro and Alex (Carmen) Morrison. 2020. Detecting independent pronoun bias with partially-synthetic data generation. In *Proceedings of the 2020 Conference on Empirical Methods in Natural Language Processing (EMNLP)*, pages 2011–2017, Online. Association for Computational Linguistics.

Animesh Nighojkar, Antonio Laverghetta Jr., and John Licato. 2023. No strong feelings one way or another: Re-operationalizing neutrality in natural language inference. In *Proceedings of the 17th Linguistic Annotation Workshop (LAW-XVII)*, pages 199–210, Toronto, Canada. Association for Computational Linguistics.

Shon Otmazgin, Arie Cattan, and Yoav Goldberg. 2023. LingMess: Linguistically informed multi expert scorers for coreference resolution. In *Proceedings of the 17th Conference of the European Chapter of the Association for Computational Linguistics*, pages 2752–2760, Dubrovnik, Croatia. Association for Computational Linguistics.

Anaelia Ovalle, Palash Goyal, Jwala Dhamala, Zachary Jaggers, Kai-Wei Chang, Aram Galstyan, Richard Zemel, and Rahul Gupta. 2023. "i'm fully who i am": Towards centering transgender and non-binary voices to measure biases in open language generation. In *Proceedings of the 2023 ACM Conference on Fairness, Accountability, and Transparency*, pages 1246–1266.

Adam Poliak, Aparajita Haldar, Rachel Rudinger, J. Edward Hu, Ellie Pavlick, Aaron Steven White, and Benjamin Van Durme. 2018. Collecting diverse natural language inference problems for sentence representation evaluation. In *Proceedings of the 2018 Conference on Empirical Methods in Natural Language Processing*, pages 67–81, Brussels, Belgium. Association for Computational Linguistics.

Abhilasha Ravichander, Matt Gardner, and Ana Marasović. 2022. CONDAQA: A contrastive reading comprehension dataset for reasoning about negation. In *Proceedings of the 2022 Conference on Empirical Methods in Natural Language Processing*, pages 8729–8755, Abu Dhabi, United Arab Emirates. Association for Computational Linguistics.

Rachel Rudinger, Jason Naradowsky, Brian Leonard, and Benjamin Van Durme. 2018. Gender bias in coreference resolution. In *Proceedings of the 2018 Conference of the North American Chapter of the Association for Computational Linguistics: Human Language Technologies, Volume 2 (Short Papers)*, pages 8–14, New Orleans, Louisiana. Association for Computational Linguistics.

Nithya Sambasivan, Shivani Kapania, Hannah Highfill, Diana Akrong, Praveen Paritosh, and Lora M Aroyo. 2021. "everyone wants to do the model work, not the data work": Data cascades in high-stakes ai. In *Proceedings of the 2021 CHI Conference on Human Factors in Computing Systems*, CHI '21, New York, NY, USA. Association for Computing Machinery.

Nikil Selvam, Sunipa Dev, Daniel Khashabi, Tushar Khot, and Kai-Wei Chang. 2023. The tail wagging the dog: Dataset construction biases of social bias benchmarks. In *Proceedings of the 61st Annual Meeting of the Association for Computational Linguistics (Volume 2: Short Papers)*, pages 1373–1386, Toronto, Canada. Association for Computational Linguistics.

Preethi Seshadri, Pouya Pezeshkpour, and Sameer Singh. 2022. Quantifying social biases using templates is unreliable. *CoRR*, abs/2210.04337.

Vered Shwartz, Rachel Rudinger, and Oyvind Tafjord. 2020. "you are grounded!": Latent name artifacts in pre-trained language models. In *Proceedings of the 2020 Conference on Empirical Methods in Natural Language Processing (EMNLP)*, pages 6850–6861, Online. Association for Computational Linguistics.

Gabriel Stanovsky, Noah A. Smith, and Luke Zettlemoyer. 2019. Evaluating gender bias in machine translation. In *Proceedings of the 57th Annual Meeting of the Association for Computational Linguistics*, pages 1679–1684, Florence, Italy. Association for Computational Linguistics.

Arjun Subramonian, Xingdi Yuan, Hal Daumé III, and Su Lin Blodgett. 2023. It takes two to tango: Navigating conceptualizations of NLP tasks and measurements of performance. In *Findings of the Association for Computational Linguistics: ACL 2023*, pages 3234–3279, Toronto, Canada. Association for Computational Linguistics.

Kellie Webster, Marta Recasens, Vera Axelrod, and Jason Baldridge. 2018. Mind the GAP: A Balanced Corpus of Gendered Ambiguous Pronouns. *Transactions of the Association for Computational Linguistics*, 6:605–617.

Jieyu Zhao, Tianlu Wang, Mark Yatskar, Vicente Ordonez, and Kai-Wei Chang. 2018. Gender bias in coreference resolution: Evaluation and debiasing methods. In *Proceedings of the 2018 Conference of the North American Chapter of the Association for Computational Linguistics: Human Language Technologies, Volume 2 (Short Papers)*, pages 15–20, New Orleans, Louisiana. Association for Computational Linguistics.

A List of Occupations

The occupations along with their respective participants in parentheses are listed below in alphabetical order. This list is identical to the occupations and participants in Rudinger et al. (2018), except that we pair examiner with intern rather than victim:

accountant (taxpayer), administrator (undergraduate), advisor (advisee), appraiser (buyer), architect (student), auditor (taxpayer), baker (customer), bartender (customer), broker (client), carpenter (onlooker), cashier (customer), chef (guest), chemist (visitor), clerk (customer), counselor (patient), dietitian (client), dispatcher (bystander), doctor (patient), educator (student), electrician (homeowner), engineer (client), examiner (intern), firefighter (child), hairdresser (client), hygienist (patient), inspector (homeowner), instructor (student), investigator (witness), janitor (child), lawyer (witness), librarian (child), machinist (child), manager (customer), mechanic (customer) nurse (patient), nutritionist (patient), officer (protester), painter (customer), paralegal (client), paramedic (passenger), pathologist (victim), pharmacist (patient), physician (patient), planner (resident), plumber (homeowner), practitioner (patient), programmer (student), psychologist (patient), receptionist (visitor), salesperson (customer), scientist (undergraduate), secretary (visitor), specialist (patient), supervisor (employee), surgeon (child), teacher (student), technician (customer), therapist (teenager), veterinarian (owner), worker (pedestrian)

B Annotator Demographics

All three annotators (two authors and an additional annotator) are fluent English speakers. The two authors who create and validate templates have linguistic training at the undergraduate level. One author and one annotator have experience with using singular *they* and neopronouns, while the other author has prior exposure to singular *they* but not the neopronoun *xe*.

C Annotation Instructions

C.1 Task 1 Description

Together with this annotation protocol, you have received a link to a Google Sheet. The sheet contains 2 data columns and 2 task columns of randomized data. The data columns consist of

- Sentences which you are asked to annotate for grammaticality; and
- Questions about pronouns in the sentence, which you are asked to answer

Please be precise in your assignments and do not reorder the data. The columns have built-in data validation and we will perform further tests to check for consistent annotation.

C.1.1 Grammaticality

In the "Grammatical?" column, please enter your grammaticality judgments of the sentence, according to Standard English. The annotation options are:

- **grammatical** (for fluent, syntactically valid and semantically plausible sentences)
- **ungrammatical** (for sentences that have any typos, grammatical issues, or if the sentence describes a situation that don't make sense, or just sounds weird)
- **not sure** (if you are not sure whether it is clearly grammatical or ungrammatical)

Examples:

- *The driver told the passenger that he could pay for the ride with cash.*
  => grammatical
- *The driver said the passenger that he could pay for the ride with cash.*
  => ungrammatical (because 'said' is intransitive in Standard English)

C.1.2 Questions about pronouns

Every sentence contains a pronoun, and the "Question" column asks whether it refers to a person mentioned in the sentence or not. The annotation options are:

- **yes** (if the pronoun refers to the person)
- **no** (if the pronoun does not refer to the person)
- **not sure** (if you are not sure about whether the pronoun refers to the person)

Examples:

- *The driver told the passenger that he could pay for the ride with cash.*
  Does the pronoun he refer to the driver?
  => no
- *The driver told the passenger that he could pay for the ride with cash.*
  Does the pronoun he refer to the passenger?
  => yes

C.2 Task 2 Description

Together with this annotation protocol, you have received a link to a Google Sheet. The sheet contains 1 randomized data column and 1 task column. Each row in the data column consists of multiple sentences, of which precisely one sentence contains a blank. Your task is to determine the appropriate pronoun to fill in the blank, and enter it in the "Pronoun" column. Here, appropriate means correct in both form and case.
The tasks are designed to be unambiguous, so please provide only one solution and do not reorder the data.

Example:

- *The driver felt unhappy because he did not make enough money. The driver wondered whether ___ should take out a loan.*
  => he

D Prompting

Table 7 shows all 10 prompt templates we use to present our task instances to FLAN-T5. Each template is presented in three variants to the model, where the options are changed:

1. No options
2. The occupation is presented first and the participant second
3. The participant is presented first and the occupation second

E Additional Results

We report additional results on double- and single-entity sentences in WINOPRON: F_1 scores in Table 8, precision in Table 9, and recall in Table 10. Note that FLAN-T5 models generally perform worse on single-entity sentences compared to double-entity sentences because some of our prompts include options (see Section D for details) that confuse the model in this setting, despite being necessary to resolve double-entity sentences.

ID	Template
0	{task}\n\n{options}\nWho is {pronoun} referring to?
1	{task}\n\nWho is "{pronoun}" in this prior sentence (see options)?\n{options}
2	{task}\n\nWho is {pronoun} referring to in this sentence?\n{options}
3	Choose your answer: {task}\nTell me who {pronoun} is.\n{options}
4	{task}\nBased on this sentence, who is {pronoun}?\n\n{options}
5	Choose your answer: Who is {pronoun} in the following sentence?\n\n{task} \n\n{options}
6	Multi-choice problem: Which entity is {pronoun} this sentence?\n\n{task} \n\n{options}
7	Who is {pronoun} referring to in the following sentence?\n{task} \n\n{options}
8	Note that this question lists possible answers. Which person is {pronoun} referring to in the following sentence?\n{task} \n\n{options}
9	{task}\nWho is "{pronoun}"\n{options}

Table 7: Prompting templates, where "task" is filled with each dataset instance, "pronoun" is the unique third person singular pronoun in that dataset instance, and "options" are the occupation and the participant.

Data	LingMess	CAW-coref	SpanBERT		FLAN-T5				
			base	large	small	base	large	xl	xxl
			Double-entity sentences						
All	64.4	67.3	61.6	70.1	51.6	62.4	78.0	**89.0**	88.8
Nominative	73.5	77.6	67.2	77.2	51.9	65.4	85.1	94.7	**96.7**
Accusative	52.2	57.5	54.6	59.5	50.4	58.4	69.9	**82.5**	79.1
Possessive	67.4	66.5	62.9	73.6	52.3	63.4	79.1	89.7	**90.7**
he/him/his	79.2	79.6	62.8	71.5	51.5	64.1	81.5	88.8	**90.2**
she/her/her	76.3	76.6	62.1	71.6	51.5	66.1	83.3	**90.6**	89.9
they/them/their	67.5	63.7	61.2	68.9	51.8	60.5	77.0	**88.6**	88.0
xe/xem/xyr	*8.5*	*38.6*	60.4	68.5	51.4	58.7	70.3	**88.0**	87.3
			Single-entity sentences						
All	73.2	75.6	**95.5**	88.0	77.3	76.3	81.5	83.1	84.3
Nominative	80.0	82.5	**99.5**	99.3	78.3	80.8	89.8	93.3	97.0
Accusative	61.1	65.0	**87.3**	67.5	76.2	69.6	69.8	70.1	66.5
Possessive	77.1	78.0	**99.8**	97.1	77.5	78.5	84.7	85.7	89.2
he/him/his	92.7	94.3	**94.7**	85.6	77.6	81.3	86.8	88.2	88.6
she/her/her	90.9	91.6	**96.2**	88.9	77.4	81.1	87.6	88.8	87.1
they/them/their	75.2	69.8	**96.0**	88.7	79.3	76.1	84.3	85.7	86.8
xe/xem/xyr	2.2	27.3	**95.2**	88.7	75.0	66.3	67.0	69.4	74.6

Table 8: F_1 of coreference resolution systems on double- and single-entity sentences in WINOPRON. We report F_1 overall, and split by grammatical case and pronoun set. *Red, italicized numbers* are worse than chance (50.0 for double-entity sentences and not applicable for single-entity sentences).

Data	LingMess	CAW-coref	SpanBERT base	SpanBERT large	FLAN-T5 small	FLAN-T5 base	FLAN-T5 large	FLAN-T5 xl	FLAN-T5 xxl
Double-entity sentences									
All	79.1	80.1	62.1	70.6	51.9	62.9	78.4	**89.5**	89.4
Nominative	88.3	88.7	67.4	77.4	52.1	65.7	85.4	95.1	**97.1**
Accusative	63.4	67.9	55.3	59.9	50.7	58.8	70.2	**83.2**	79.5
Possessive	86.1	83.6	63.5	74.3	52.8	64.3	79.6	90.2	**91.5**
he/him/his	79.7	80.1	63.0	71.6	51.7	64.3	81.8	89.3	**90.6**
she/her/her	77.6	77.9	62.3	71.8	51.7	66.3	83.6	**91.1**	90.3
they/them/their	79.1	80.2	61.8	69.5	52.0	60.8	77.3	**89.0**	88.5
xe/xem/xyr	**100.0**	88.1	61.3	69.3	52.1	60.1	70.7	88.6	88.0
Single-entity sentences									
All	**100.0**	**100.0**	96.0	88.4	78.9	77.6	82.4	84.0	85.6
Nominative	**100.0**	**100.0**	**100.0**	**100.0**	79.3	81.6	90.4	93.9	97.4
Accusative	**100.0**	**100.0**	88.1	67.9	77.5	70.5	70.7	71.1	68.1
Possessive	**100.0**	**100.0**	99.8	97.1	79.8	80.7	85.9	86.8	90.8
he/him/his	**100.0**	**100.0**	95.0	86.0	78.6	81.9	87.5	88.9	89.5
she/her/her	**100.0**	**100.0**	96.4	89.1	78.5	81.7	88.1	89.4	87.9
they/them/their	**100.0**	**100.0**	96.4	89.1	80.3	76.9	85.2	86.5	87.9
xe/xem/xyr	**100.0**	**100.0**	96.3	89.3	77.9	69.2	68.3	70.9	76.7

Table 9: Precision on double- and single-entity sentences overall, and split by grammatical case and pronoun set. *Red, italicized numbers* are worse than chance (50.0 for double-entity sentences, N/A for single-entity sentences).

Data	LingMess	CAW-coref	SpanBERT base	SpanBERT large	FLAN-T5 small	FLAN-T5 base	FLAN-T5 large	FLAN-T5 xl	FLAN-T5 xxl
Double-entity sentences									
All	54.2	58.0	61.1	69.7	51.3	61.9	77.7	**88.5**	88.3
Nominative	62.9	69.0	67.1	77.1	51.8	65.2	84.8	94.3	**96.3**
Accusative	*44.4*	*49.8*	54.0	59.2	50.2	58.0	69.6	**81.9**	78.6
Possessive	55.4	55.2	62.3	72.9	51.9	62.5	78.7	89.3	**90.0**
he/him/his	78.6	79.2	62.5	71.4	51.4	63.9	81.1	88.3	**89.7**
she/her/her	75.0	75.3	61.9	71.4	51.4	65.9	83.0	**90.1**	89.5
they/them/their	58.9	52.8	60.6	68.3	51.6	60.2	76.8	**88.1**	87.5
xe/xem/xyr	*4.4*	*24.7*	59.4	67.8	50.8	57.4	69.9	**87.5**	86.6
Single-entity sentences									
All	57.8	60.8	**95.1**	87.6	75.9	75.0	80.6	82.1	83.1
Nominative	66.7	70.2	**99.0**	98.5	77.3	80.0	89.2	92.7	96.6
Accusative	44.0	48.1	**86.5**	67.1	74.9	68.7	69.0	69.1	65.0
Possessive	62.7	64.0	**99.8**	97.1	75.4	76.4	83.5	84.6	87.6
he/him/his	86.4	89.2	**94.4**	85.3	76.5	80.8	86.1	87.4	87.8
she/her/her	83.3	84.4	**96.1**	88.6	76.2	80.5	87.1	88.2	86.2
they/them/their	60.3	53.6	**95.6**	88.3	78.3	75.3	83.5	85.0	85.8
xe/xem/xyr	1.1	15.8	**94.2**	88.1	72.4	63.7	65.7	68.0	72.5

Table 10: Recall on double- and single-entity sentences overall, and split by grammatical case and pronoun set. *Red, italicized numbers* are worse than chance (50.0 for double-entity sentences, N/A for single-entity sentences)

DeepHCoref: A Deep Neural Coreference Resolution for Hindi Text

Kusum Lata[1], **Pardeep Singh**[2], **Kamlesh Dutta**[2], **Abhishek Kanwar**[2]
[1]Sharda University, Greater Noida, India
ranapoo@gmail.com, kusumlata.10@sharda.ac.in
[2]Department of Computer Science Engineering,
National Institute of Technology, Hamirpur, Himachal Pradesh, India
{pardeep,kd,20dcs013}@nith.ac.in

Abstract

Coreference Resolution is the process of detecting a cluster of mentions that point to the same entity. This paper presents the Coreference Resolution system for Hindi based on Bi-GRU-CNN and Biaffine classifier with IndicBERT and MuRIL BERT. The motivation behind this work is the scarcity of resources available for Hindi and to diminish the dependency on the external parser and hand-crafted feature used by the previous Coreference resolution model in the Hindi language. The coreference annotated dataset is used for the Hindi language, containing 3.6K verbalizations and 78K tokens from the news article domain. The experimental results received are promising in the form of Precision, Recall, and F-measure.

1 Introduction

Coreference Resolution (CR) is the task of creating a link between the referring expression and the referent entity. The Coreference Resolution will enhance the performance of numerous Natural Language Processing (NLP) applications viz. Machine Translation, Question Answering, Chatbots, Text Summarization, etc. The existing Coreference Resolution system (Haghighi and Klein, 2009; Lee et al., 2011; Björkelund and Kuhn, 2014; Durrett and Klein, 2013; Aloraini et al., 2020) divided the Coreference Resolution process into two steps: Mention detection that find out all the mentions such as named entities, pronominal, and nominal entities available in the text, and second step, creating a cluster of mentions that point to same real-world entities. We explain the concept of the CR with the help of the following example SH1:

SH1[1]: फिल्म महोत्सव में प्रकाश झा की नई फिल्म अपहरण का भी प्रीमियर होना है। गंगाजल के बाद उसकी यह किसी अलग विषय पर बनी दूसरी फिल्म है।

SE1[2]: *Prakash Jha's new film Apaharan is also to premiere at the film festival. This is his second film on a different subject after Gangajal.*

SHI1[3]: *Prakash Jha kee naee film apaharan ka bhee film mahotsav mein preemiyar hona hai. Gangaajal ke baad usakee yah kisee alag vishay par banee doosaree film hai.*

In this example of the sentence (in Hindi), **SH1**, the available mentions in this sentence after applying the mention detection step are:

फिल्म महोत्सव *(film festival /film Mahotsav)*, प्रकाश झा *(Prakash Jha)*, नई फिल्म *(naee film /new film)*, अपहरण *(apaharan)*, उसकी *(his /usakee)*, यह *(this /yah)*, दूसरी फिल्म *(second film /doosaree film)*, गंगाजल *(Gangaajal)* .

The mentions फिल्म महोत्सव *(film Mahotsav)*, नई फिल्म *(naee film)*, and दूसरी फिल्म *(doosaree film)* are nominal mentions. The mentions प्रकाश झा *(Prakash Jha)*, अपहरण *(apaharan)*, and गंगाजल *(Gangaajal)* are named mentions. The mentions उसकी *(usakee)* and यह *(yah)* are pronominal mentions.

The step of coreference resolution process for sentence SH1, is shown in Figure 1a and 1b. प्रकाश झा *(Prakash Jha)*, उसकी *(his /usakee)* are in one cluster. And similarly, नई फिल्म *(naee film)*,यह *(yah)*, and दूसरी फिल्म *(doosaree film)* are in the same cluster.

There are many shared task datasets such as ONTONOTES, CoNLL-2011/2012 exist for the English language prominently as discussed by authors Sukthanker et al. (2020); Stylianou and Vlahavas (2021); Lata et al. (2021). In addition, the CRAC shared tasks Žabokrtský et al. (2022, 2023) have made substantial contributions to recent work in multilingual Coreference Resolution. The CRAC 2023 shared task for several languages, including Catalan, Czech, English, French, Ger-

[1]SH: Sentence in Hindi

[2]SE: Sentence in English

[3]SHI: Sentence in Hinglish (Roman Gloss for Hindi)

Proceedings of the Seventh Workshop on Computational Models of Reference, Anaphora and Coreference (CRAC 2024), pages 67–77
November 15, 2024. ©2024 Association for Computational Linguistics

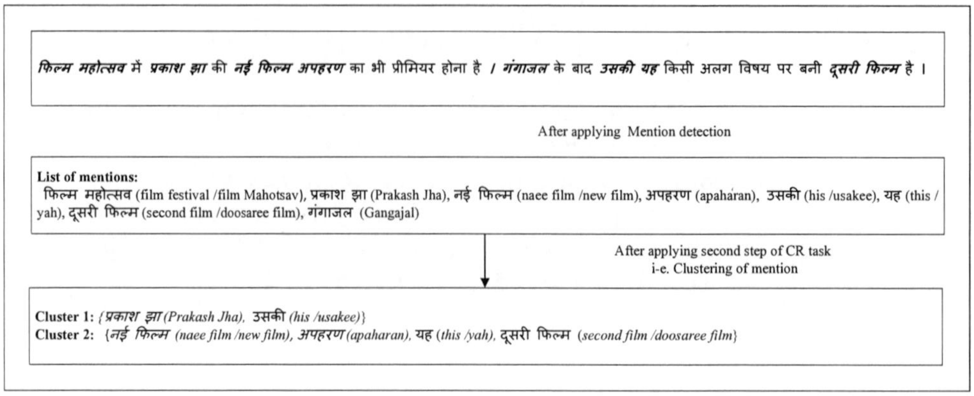

(a)

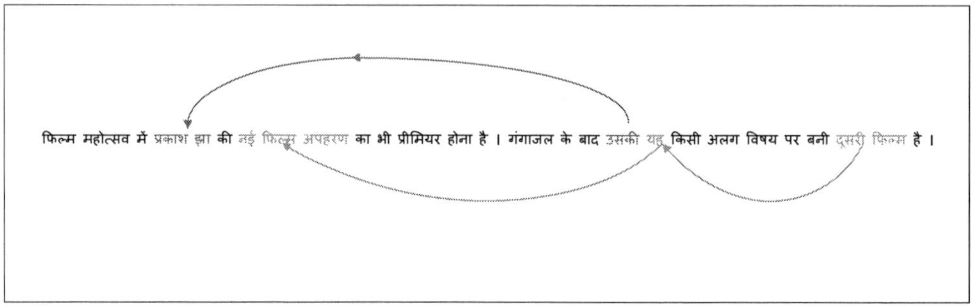

(b)

Figure 1: Coreference Resolution Process for sentence SH1

man, Hungarian, Lithuanian, Norwegian, Polish, Russian, Spanish, and Turkish, is available. There exists significant work on the deep learning-based Coreference Resolution model that has recently shown state-of-the-art performance for the English language. On the other hand, hardly little study has been done on the Coreference Resolution system for the Hindi Language such as Vasantlal (2017); Mishra et al. (2024)

Challenges in Hindi Language: One of the main reasons behind the lack of research in this area could be that numerous hurdles exist in Hindi language viz. no capitalization, free word order, lack of labeled data, being morphologically rich, ambiguity in proper nouns, and insufficiency of linguistic resources which need to be acknowledged while developing Coreference Resolution model.

1. Because Hindi has a flexible word order, it is possible to change the Subject-Object-Verb (SOV) structure without affecting the meaning. Due to this variety, it may be challenging for neural models to develop consistent patterns for coreference resolution because of the wide variations in how entities are positioned in relation to pronouns. When attempting to resolve coreferences in Hindi, neural models must be more flexible than English, where they can frequently rely on more rigid syntactic patterns. In place of spatial clues, this calls for a greater dependence on context-based learning. Attention-based models such as transformers are more appropriate for this task, however they still have issues with word order diversity.

2. As a pro-drop language, Hindi allows subject pronouns to be removed when circumstances suggest they should. It can be challenging for neural models to infer dropped pronouns from the surrounding context in the absence of explicit markers. Implicit references that aren't explicitly stated in the text must be understood by the model. Since neural networks usually rely on explicit tokens for prediction, they may find it difficult to resolve references effectively in sentences when subjects or objects are absent. In order to capture latent references, models must possess a high contextual awareness, which necessitates the integration of mechanisms such as attention. Hindi language displays intricate morphological variations according to case, gender, and number. This results in a vast range of surface forms for verbs, pronouns, and nouns. Given the diversity of forms, it might be dif-

ficult for neural models to learn to link several morphological variations of the same coreferent entity.

Hindi pronouns like वह *(vaha)*, which might signify "he","she," "it," or "that," are sometimes unclear. Depending on the context, a pronoun can be used to refer to several genders, numbers, or even inanimate objects. It is necessary for neural models to precisely distinguish between these allusions based on context, which is frequently more intricate in Hindi. For example:

SH2: लालू की पत्नी पूर्व मुख्यमंत्री राबड़ी देवी के सबसे छोटे भाई सुभाष ने राजद के वरिष्ठ नेता और पूर्व मंत्री जगदानंद सिंह पर आरोप लगाया कि वह पार्टी हितों के खिलाफ काम कर रहे हैं।

SHI2:*laaloo kee patnee poorv mukhyamantree raabadee devee ke sabase chhote bhaee subhaash ne raajad ke varishth neta aur poorv mantree jagadaanand sinh par aarop lagaaya ki vah paartee hiton ke khilaaph kaam kar rahe hain.*

SE2: *Subhash, the youngest brother of Lalu's wife and former chief minister Rabri Devi, accused senior RJD leader and former minister Jagadanand Singh that he is working against the interests of the party.*

In this example, वह *(vaha)*, refers to वरिष्ठ नेता *(varishth neta)*, पूर्व मंत्री जगदानंद सिंह *(poorv mantree jagadaanand singh)*, which is masculine. The pronoun वह *(vaha)* needs to match the gender of its antecedent. Even if the antecedent पूर्व मुख्यमंत्री राबड़ी देवी *(poorv mukhyamantree raabadee devee)* is feminine, the pronoun would still be वह *(vaha)*, however the context would specify the right referent. The gender agreement makes it more difficult to resolve coreferences because the algorithm has to accurately identify the antecedent's gender.

3. The other reason could be the restricted availability of training data in the appropriate format which is required for the specific task.

Contribution of the paper: The key contributions of the paper are as follows: We propose a neural network-based Coreference Resolution system to create clustering of mentions in Hindi text by utilizing Bi-GRU along with transformer-based IndicBERT and MuRIL BERT model and character-level embedding.

We compare the performance of Coreference Resolution system by employing language model with mBERT.

In this paper, our model aims to diminish the need for hand-crafted features and external dependency parsers. We compare the performance of Rule-based Coreference Resolution, a neural-based state-of-the-art Coreference Resolution model for the Hindi language with our model.

The rest of the paper is organized into the following sections. Section 2 contains a comprehensive background of models for Coreference Resolution that have been created or the Related Work done in the area. Section 3 describes the Proposed Approach for the work. Section 4 will expound on the Experimental Evaluation, and Section 5 verbalizes the Conclusion and Future Scope of our work.

2 Related Work

The Coreference Resolution task has been exhaustively researched in literature prominently for the English language. Firstly, we discuss the work related to Coreference Resolution for the English language followed by work for the Hindi Language.

2.1 Coreference Resolution for English

Recently, many researchers (Sukthanker et al., 2020; Lata et al., 2021; Stylianou and Vlahavas, 2021) have conducted in-depth surveys for Coreference Resolution. Various approaches are utilized for Coreference Resolution tasks, and Sukthanker et al. (2020) classified these approaches into three categories: Rule-based, Statistical and machine learning-based, and Deep learning-based. The author also analyzed resolution algorithms on different datasets. Stylianou and Vlahavas (2021) reviewed the most recent neural Coreference Resolution approaches, specifically those involving deep learning techniques. The neural Coreference Resolution approach was prominently employed and analyzed in the English language by different authorsWiseman et al. (2015); Clark and Manning (2016b,a); Lee et al. (2017, 2018). The coreference resolution task can be performed in a pipeline manner (Clark and Manning, 2016a) or a joint manner (Daumé III and Marcu, 2009).

Lee et al. (2017) proposed an end-to-end neural Coreference Resolution system that achieved state-of-the-art performance by combining two tasks: mention detection and Coreference Resolution. Their system automatically learned features for detecting mentions using Bi-directional LSTM and did not rely on hand-crafted features. They employed Glove embeddings and character embeddings to represent words and evaluated their system's performance on the CoNLL-2012 shared task for English coreference resolution, reporting F1-measures of 77.20% (MUC), 66.60% (B3), 62.60% (CEAF), and an overall F1 of 68.80%.

Building on this, Lee et al. (2018) extended their work by using ELMO embeddings Peters et al. (2018) and second-order inference, improving performance by 0.4 percentage points. Kantor and Globerson (2019) further modified Lee et al.'s model to provide entity-level representation by summing mention representations within a cluster and employed BERT embeddings (Devlin, 2018) instead of ELMO. Joshi et al. (2019) introduced BERT-large, improving the model's performance, while Joshi et al. (2020) later introduced SpanBERT to better represent and predict text spans, resulting in a 2.7% improvement over their previous model. Wu et al. (2020) developed CorefQA with SpanBERT, recasting coreference resolution as a query-based span prediction problem in question answering. They pre-trained the model using question-answering corpora and evaluated it on the CoNLL English shared task dataset, surpassing previous state-of-the-art models(Joshi et al., 2019, 2020) by 0.3% and 3.5%, respectively.

2.2 Coreference Resolution for Hindi

Several researchers have adapted approaches for pronominal resolution in Hindi text from the methods used in English. Prasad and Strube (2000) implemented the centering theory for resolving pronominal references in Hindi, while Dutta et al. (2008) adapted Hobbs Algorithm Hobbs (1978) to handle Hindi's free word order and grammatical nuances. Uppalapu and Sharma (2009) extended the centering theory-based algorithm by managing entities in present and prior utterances through distinct lists.

Devi et al. (2014) presented a generic anaphora resolution engine for Indian languages, employing Conditional Random Fields (CRF). However, most approaches for Hindi focus solely on pronominal resolution. Dakwale (2014) developed the first model to resolve nominal references, including pronominal ones, using a Rule-based approach, with reported MUC Precision, Recall, and F1-scores of 64%, 50%, and 56%, respectively. Sachan et al. (2015) developed a coreference resolution system for Hindi text based on an an active learning approach. The authors developed a method for resolving the in-document coreferences resolution that reduces the amount of human interference in this process. The performance of the coreference resolution system is better than Dakwale (2014) approach

Vasantlal (2017) recently proposed a hybrid sieve-based strategy for resolving pronouns and nominal references in Hindi, incorporating Paninian Dependency Grammar, POS labels, morphology, and linguistic resources like Hindi WordNet, DBpedia, Word2Vec, and GloVe. This method, however, relies on labeled datasets, with reported MUC Precision, Recall, and F1-scores of 79.53%, 63.7%, and 70%, respectively.

Ramrakhiyani et al. (2018) developed a Coreference Resolution system using Markov Logic Networks (MLN) to resolve actor mentions in Hindi narrative text. They evaluated their system on multiple datasets (Sardar, Plassey, Shivaji, Emergency, IIIT-H), reporting an average F1-measure of 70.46%, 64.91%, 68.98%, 63.12%, and 55.04%, respectively.

Mishra et al. (2024) presented TransMuCoRes, a translated dataset made with off-the-shelf tool for translation and word-alignment that is intended for Multilingual Coreference Resolution across 31 South Asian languages. On a test split of a manually annotated Hindi golden corpus, the top-performing model obtained LEA F1 64% and CoNLL F1 68%.

3 Coreference Resolution Model

This section explains how to resolve coreferences in Hindi text using the proposed approach. We employed the English Coreference Resolution approach outlined by Lee et al. (2018) for Coreference Resolution in Hindi text. We utilize a pre-trained Transformer-based Indic BERT (Kakwani et al., 2020) and MuRIL model (Khanuja et al., 2021; Devlin, 2018). The Coreference Resolution model for Hindi (DeepHCoref) consists of mention's span representation and a clustering step. The block diagram for DeepHCoref is shown in Figure 2.

3.1 Mention's Span Representation

We must create vector representations of words and spans. The following characteristics are used to construct word representations: (1) Word vectors derived from a pre-trained language model. (2) Word vectors regarding sentence context derived from a pre-trained language model. (3) Character-based word vectors. The vector representations of spans are created by combining all

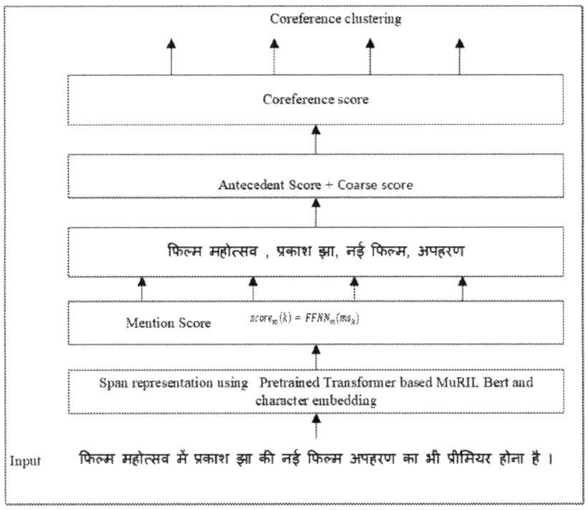

Figure 2: Block diagram of DeepHCoref.

these properties of words through concatenation operations, which are processed by recurrent layers with the help of the attention mechanism.

In our model, the span representation is created by employing pre-trained Indic BERT and MuRIL, whereas Lee et al. (2018) utilized ELMO embeddings. The authors used Bi-LSTM to get span representation, but we have utilized Bi-GRU for this purpose because we have a smaller training dataset, as described by Yang et al. (2020). They demonstrated that GRU is 29.29% faster than LSTM for small datasets and long texts in terms of training speed and performance.

First, we find the word embedding $\mathbf{vec}_i$ for each word w_i in a sentence from pre-trained Indic BERT, and then find the character embedding of the word through a Convolutional Neural Network (CNN). The concatenation of the word embedding with the character embedding is represented by $\mathbf{embed}_i$ for each word w_i, where $i = 1, 2, \ldots, W$, as shown in Figure 3. After this step, concatenated embedding $\mathbf{embed}_i$ is considered as input and given to a Bi-directional GRU (Bi-GRU) to generate word representations $\mathbf{x}_i$, where $i = 1, 2, \ldots, W$. The head-finding attention vector $\mathbf{hd}_k$ of a mention span is calculated as the weighted average of the mention's word representations as shown in equation 1.

$$\left.\begin{aligned} o_i &= FFNN_0(x_i) \\ att_{k,i} &= \frac{e^{o_i}}{\sum_{l=beg_k}^{end_k} e^{o_l}} \\ h_{dk} &= \sum_{l=beg_k}^{end_k} att_{k,i} \cdot x_i \end{aligned}\right\} \quad (1)$$

Where $\text{att}_{k,i}$ is the word-level attention parameter for the i-th word in the k-th mention, beg_k indicates the position of the starting word in the k-th mention, and end_k represents the ending position of a word. The mention's span representations ms_k are formed by combining $\mathbf{x}_i$ with head representations $\mathbf{hd}_k$, as shown in equation 2 and represented in Figure 4.

$$ms_k = [x_{beg_k}, x_{end_k}, h_{d_k}, \phi(k)] \quad (2)$$

Where $\phi(k)$ represents the mention feature embeddings. A feedforward neural network (FFNN) calculates the score of mention (sm_k) to identify the relevance of a candidate mention, as shown in equation 3.

$$score_m(k) = FFNN_m(ms_k) \quad (3)$$

3.2 Clustering Step

The next step is to link an antecedent for each possible mention. We calculate a lightweight mention pair score $\text{score}_{coarse}(k, n)$ between all relevant mention pairs (relevant mentions paired with all prior mentions) using a bilinear function, as shown in equation 4.

$$score_{coarse}(k, n) = ms_k^T W_{coarse} ms_n \quad (4)$$

These coarse scores are then used to select the best candidate antecedents. Next, we calculate a more accurate mention pair score, $\text{score}_{ant}(k, n)$, between the mention and its best antecedent candidate, as shown in equation 5.

$$\begin{aligned} \text{score}_{ant}(k, n) = \text{FFNN}_{ant}\,([&ms_k, ms_n, \\ &ms_k \odot ms_n, \phi(k, n)]) \end{aligned} \quad (5)$$

Where ms_k, ms_n are the antecedent and anaphora representations, and $\phi(k, n)$ is the feature vector of the distance between the mention pair. Finally, we compute the mention pairwise score $\text{score}(k, n)$, as shown in equation 6.

$$\text{score}(k, n) = \begin{cases} \text{score}_m(k) + \text{score}_m(n) \\ \quad + \text{score}_{ant}(k, n) \\ \quad + \text{score}_{coarse}(k, n), & k \neq \epsilon \\ 0, \quad k = \epsilon \end{cases} \quad (6)$$

Here, ϵ represents a fictitious antecedent in cases where the span is not a mention or when no antecedent exists in the candidate list. The antecedent with the highest $\text{score}(k, n)$ is predicted as the antecedent for each mention.

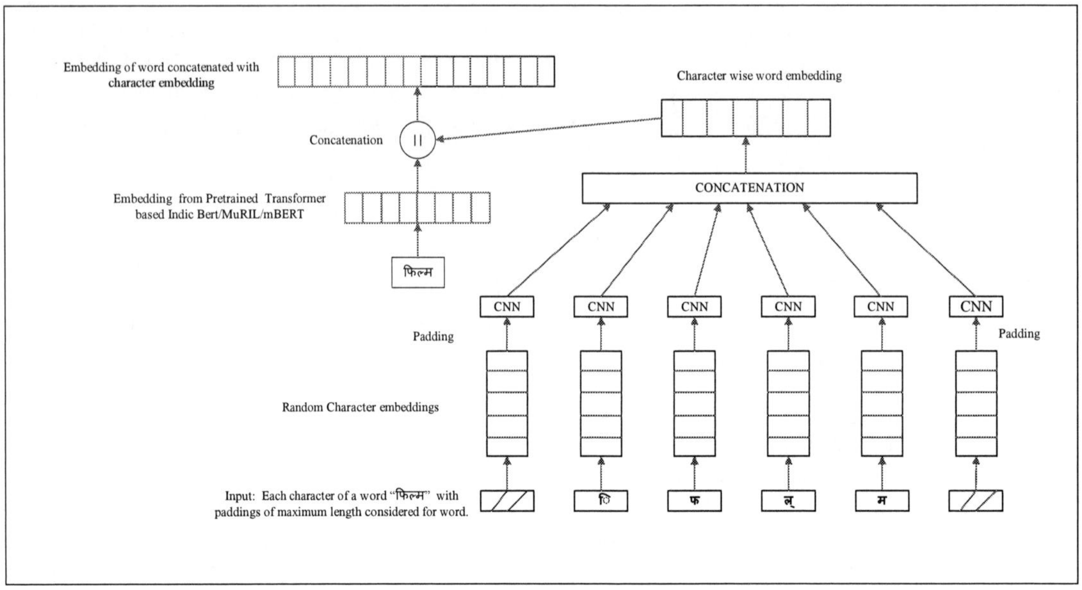

Figure 3: Concatenation of character embedding with Indic BERT /MuRIL/mBERT embedding.

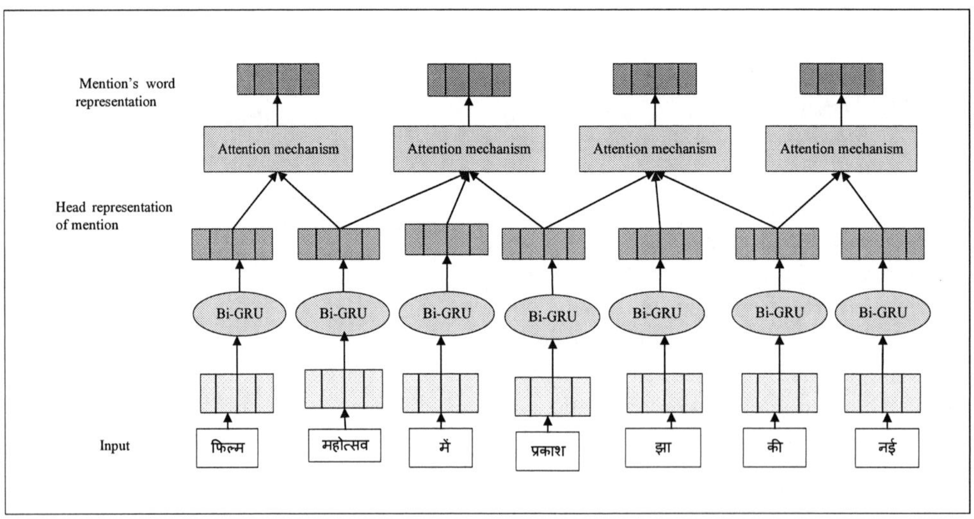

Figure 4: Mention span representation.

3.3 Data Preparation

Hindi, being a low-resource language, has limited training data available. We used coreference annotated data for the Hindi language Mujadia et al. (2016), which consists of 3.6K sentences and 78K tokens from news articles in the Hindi newspaper Amar Ujala, including news related to sports, politics, films, etc. The coreference annotated dataset created by the authors contains grammatical features such as number, gender, animacy features, dependency relations information, and chain of coreference and coreference relation types such as Part-of', 'Function-value pair' etc. Table 1 shows the corpus statistics. This dataset contains coreference chain which is created semi-automatically. We have assumed that the mentions and coreference chain annotated in this dataset are true. manual corrections were made as needed. We wrote a Python script to convert the dataset from SSF format Bharati et al. (2007) into JSON lines format, as shown in Figure 5.

Hindi Dataset	Size
# Documents	275
# Sentences	3.6K
# Tokens	78K

Table 1: Corpus statistics for Hindi dataset


```
{"clusters": [[[3,4],[18,18]], [[6,7],[8,8],[19,19], [25,26]]
"doc_key": "(nw/fullnews_id_250.txt); part 250",
"sentences": [["फिल्म", "महोत्सव", "में", "प्रकाश", "झा", "की", "नई", "फिल्म", "अपहरण", "का", "भी", "प्रीमियर" "होना", "है", "।"]
["गंगाजल", "के", "बाद", "उसकी", "यह", "किसी", "अलग", "विषय", "पर", "बनी", "दूसरी", "फिल्म", "है", "।"]],
"speakers": [illegible]
}
```


Figure 5: Sample of text data in JSON lines format.

3.4 Mention Detection

We used an external mention detection system to detect mentions. Lata et al. (2022) reviewed mention detection algorithms and highlighted their importance in coreference resolution tasks. Aloraini et al. (2020) demonstrated that separate mention detection modules perform better than joint systems for coreference resolution. We used their approach for the detection of mentions, which trains the system end-to-end initially and gradually transitions to a pipeline-based approach. This technique mitigates the impact of false positive mentions and improves the performance of coreference resolution.

4 Experimental Setup and Evaluation

4.1 Experimental Setup

We used an NVIDIA 970GTX GPU and a 4.00 GHz Intel i7-4790 processor with 64GB RAM and TensorFlow backend support to train our models. In all experiments, the dataset is randomly split into training, development, and test sets. The training set is used for training the model, the development set for optimizing settings, and the test set for evaluating model performance.

Hyperparameters

The hyperparameter settings for the presented work are shown in Table 2. We used the default settings employed by Lee et al. Lee et al. (2018), and employed 300-dimensional fastText (IndicFT)[4] embeddings instead of GloVe/ELMo embeddings.

Parameter	Value	Parameter	Value
Word Embedding Dimension	300	Bi-GRU Dropout	0.5
Bi-GRU Size	200	Bi-GRU Layers	3
FFNN Layers	2	CNN Filter Widths	3,4,5
FFNN Layer Size	150	CNN Filter Size	50
FFNN Dropout	0.2	BERT Embedding Size	1024
Learning Rate	0.001	Decay Rate	0.999
Max Span Width	30	Max Antecedents	50
Mention Ratio	0.4	Optimizer	Adam

Table 2: Hyperparameter settings

Additionally, we employed three transformer-based BERT language models: MuRIL(Khanuja et al., 2021), Multilingual-BERT (mBERT) (Devlin et al., 2019), and IndicBERT (Kakwani et al., 2020).

4.2 Experimental Results

The system predicts mentions and coreferential mentions using the proposed approach. Results are evaluated using metrics such as MUC (Vilain et al., 1995), B-CUBE (Bagga and Baldwin, 1998), and CEAFϕ4 (Luo, 2005). The CoNLL-2012 scoring script (v8.01) (Pradhan et al., 2014) was used to evaluate the performance of our DeepHCoref system. As discussed in Section 3.4, We have applied an external mention detection module to detect the mentions. Table 3 shows the performance of the mention detection model with MuRIL, IndicBERT, and mBERT in both joint and separate settings in high recall setting. We have compared the joint model(in which we train both mention detection and Coreference Resolution simultaneously), and the separate model(in which we train mention

[4]https://indicnlp.ai4bharat.org/fasttext/

detection and Coreference Resolution separately) with different variants: Hindi Mention Detection with MuRIL (HMD – MuRIL), Hindi Mention Detection with IndicBERT (HMD – IndicBERT), and Hindi Mention Detection with mBERT (HMD-mBERT). The observation from the table is that the mention detection module, which is trained separately is consistently outperformed as compared to joint HMD. Table 4 shows the results of the Hindi Mention Detection (HMD) models which are not in the High Recall setting. It is observed that HMD-mBERT performed better than other variants.

Model	Joint model			Separate model		
	Recall	Precision	F-measure	Recall	Precision	F-measure
HMD - MuRIL	71.68	27.61	39.86	**74.18**	28.41	41.02
HMD - IndicBERT	74.53	28.71	41.45	**76.63**	29.31	42.40
HMD - mBERT	86.38	33.27	48.04	**89.38**	34.07	49.33

Table 3: Comparison of joint and separate Hindi Mention Detection (HMD) models

Model	Recall	Precision	F-measure
HMD - MuRIL	30.51	76.96	43.70
HMD - IndicBERT	36.23	80.74	50.01
HMD - mBERT	61.90	83.55	71.11

Table 4: Hindi Mention Detection (HMD) experimental results on test data

Table 5 shows the performance of the Coreference Resolution system on test data, which utilizes different BERT models (MuRIL, IndicBERT, and mBERT). We observe that the the best model variant combines mBERT (DeepHCoref + mBERT + HMD) with mBERT performs significantly better than those with IndicBERT and MuRIL.

We observed that IndicBERT's performance is limited, likely due to its smaller sequence length (128) and smaller training dataset compared to mBERT, which was trained with a sequence length of 512. However, the MuRIl was also trained on the sequence length, i-e., 512, same as mBERT, and trained explicitly for the Indian language. Surprisingly, the MuRIL model on our task performed lower than the IndicBERT and mBERT model on test set. The overall performance of our DeepHCoref + mBERT + HMD model is lower than the baseline rule-based model, likely due to the small dataset size.

Despite having a higher average CoNLL F1 measure score (67 vs. 55.47) than our model(DeepHCoref + mBERT + HMD), the wl-coref-xlmr model (Mishra et al., 2024) depends on a dependency parsing mechanism through the Stanza library(Qi et al., 2020). In certain languages or contexts where there is a dearth of training data or complex syntax, dependency parsers such as Stanza may parse sentences incorrectly due to their imperfection. The Coreference Resolution task may encounter difficulties if the dependency parse tree incorrectly recognizes heads or other syntactic relationships. On the other hand, our model does not rely on external syntactic parsers, which provides a simpler pipeline and eliminates the possibility of errors introduced by dependency parsers, especially in languages with limited resources. Further improvements could be achieved by training the model on a larger dataset. Moreover, creating a gold-standard Coreference Resolution dataset for Hindi would significantly enhance model performance. Currently, the available dataset is semi-automatically generated and does not explicitly label singleton mentions.

5 Conclusion and Future Scope

Coreference resolution is a crucial yet challenging problem in Natural Language Processing. In this research, we applied a state-of-the-art English coreference system to the Hindi language to enhance the Coreference Resolution task for Hindi. We presented a Hindi Coreference Resolution model, developed by integrating the multilingual language model MuRIL, which is specifically pre-trained for Indian languages/mBERT, along with CNN and Bi-GRU.

In this study, we also investigated the performance of the proposed system using IndicBERT and mBERT language models on the same dataset. The results show that the mBERT language model performs significantly better than both IndicBERT and MuRIL for the Hindi Coreference Resolution task. In future work, we will analyze the reasons behind the lower performance of our model with MuRIL-large.

The performance of the suggested model also demonstrates that the Hindi Coreference Resolution system, DeepHCoref, can be further improved by using a more extensive training dataset and a larger language model. Future research will explore in depth how the removal of singletons affects the Coreference Resolution system. Additionally, in this work, coreference is resolved within a single document; future studies can investigate the resolution of coreference problems

Model	MUC			B-CUBE			CEAFϕ4			Avg. (CoNLL)	
	R	P	F1	R	P	F1	R	P	F1	R	F1
Rule-based CR (Vasantlal, 2017)	63.7	79.53	70.00	-	-	-	-	-	-	-	-
wl-coref-xlmr (Mishra et al., 2024)	-	74	-	-	-	-	-	66	-	62	67
fast-coref-xlmr (Mishra et al., 2024)	-	45	-	-	-	-	-	35	-	33	38
DeepHCoref + MuRIL	23.79	63.57	34.62	16.33	59.17	25.60	17.61	44.86	25.29	28.50	28.50
DeepHCoref + IndicBERT	29.06	67.43	40.61	20.57	62.31	30.90	21.11	49.59	29.80	33.58	33.77
DeepHCoref + mBERT	53.39	72.74	61.85	43.04	66.86	52.37	40.67	61.75	48.56	54.17	54.17
DeepHCoref + mBERT + HMD	54.50	72.84	62.34	43.84	67.36	53.11	42.82	61.15	49.86	55.47	55.47

Table 5: Hindi Coreference Resolution results on the test set

across documents.

In this work, our model does not explicitly handle the zero mentions (pro-drop), Because there are no annotations for zero mentions (pro-drop) in the dataset we used. However for languages like Hindi, pro-drop must be addressed if Coreference Resolution is to be improved. We intend to investigate strategies for dealing with zero mentions in future work, such as utilizing syntactic features to infer implicit pronouns or adding pro-drop annotations to datasets. These modifications may improve the model's performance even more in low-resource languages As, Hindi dataset is not currently available in the CorefUD collection, despite notable progress in multilingual coreference resolution. Consequently, the Hindi coreference corpus made accessible byMujadia et al. (2016) is the foundation of our work. Our future research endeavors to investigate the integration of Hindi into multilingual datasets such as CorefUD.

Acknowledgements

The authors would like to thank all reviewers for reviewing this work, and providing very insightful comments which helped us to improve the quality of manuscript. The authors also would like to thank the authors Juntao Yu and Mujadia Vandan Vasantlal for providing support to understand after direct contact.

References

Abdulrahman Aloraini, Juntao Yu, and Massimo Poesio. 2020. Neural coreference resolution for arabic. In *Proceedings of the Third Workshop on Computational Models of Reference, Anaphora and Coreference*, pages 99–110.

Amit Bagga and Breck Baldwin. 1998. Algorithms for scoring coreference chains. In *The first international conference on language resources and evaluation workshop on linguistics coreference*, volume 1, pages 563–566. Citeseer.

Akshar Bharati, Rajeev Sangal, and Dipti M Sharma. 2007. Ssf: Shakti standard format guide. *Language Technologies Research Centre, International Institute of Information Technology, Hyderabad, India*, pages 1–25.

Anders Björkelund and Jonas Kuhn. 2014. Learning structured perceptrons for coreference resolution with latent antecedents and non-local features. In *Proceedings of the 52nd Annual Meeting of the Association for Computational Linguistics (Volume 1: Long Papers)*, pages 47–57.

Kevin Clark and Christopher D Manning. 2016a. Deep reinforcement learning for mention-ranking coreference models. In *Proceedings of the 2016 Conference on Empirical Methods in Natural Language Processing*, pages 2256–2262.

Kevin Clark and Christopher D Manning. 2016b. Improving coreference resolution by learning entity-level distributed representations. In *Proceedings of the 54th Annual Meeting of the Association for Computational Linguistics (Volume 1: Long Papers)*, pages 643–653.

Praveen Dakwale. 2014. *Anaphora resolution in hindi*. Ph.D. thesis, PhD thesis, International Institute of Information Technology Hyderabad.

Hal Daumé III and Daniel Marcu. 2009. A large-scale exploration of effective global features for a joint entity detection and tracking model. *arXiv preprint arXiv:0907.0807*.

Sobha Lalitha Devi, Vijay Sundar Ram, and Pattabhi RK Rao. 2014. A generic anaphora resolution engine for indian languages. In *Proceedings of COLING 2014, the 25th International Conference on Computational Linguistics: Technical Papers*, pages 1824–1833.

Jacob Devlin. 2018. Bert: Pre-training of deep bidirectional transformers for language understanding. *arXiv preprint arXiv:1810.04805*.

Jacob Devlin, Ming-Wei Chang, Kenton Lee, and Kristina Toutanova. 2019. BERT: Pre-training of deep bidirectional transformers for language understanding. In *Proceedings of the 2019 Conference of the North American Chapter of the Association for Computational Linguistics: Human Language*

Technologies, Volume 1 (Long and Short Papers), pages 4171–4186, Minneapolis, Minnesota. Association for Computational Linguistics.

Greg Durrett and Dan Klein. 2013. Easy victories and uphill battles in coreference resolution. In *Proceedings of the 2013 conference on empirical methods in natural language processing*, pages 1971–1982.

Kamlesh Dutta, Nupur Prakash, and Saroj Kaushik. 2008. Resolving pronominal anaphora in hindi using hobbs algorithm. *Web Journal of Formal Computation and Cognitive Linguistics*, 1(10):5607–11.

Aria Haghighi and Dan Klein. 2009. Simple coreference resolution with rich syntactic and semantic features. In *Proceedings of the 2009 conference on empirical methods in natural language processing*, pages 1152–1161.

Jerry R Hobbs. 1978. Resolving pronoun references. *Lingua*, 44(4):311–338.

Mandar Joshi, Danqi Chen, Yinhan Liu, Daniel S Weld, Luke Zettlemoyer, and Omer Levy. 2020. Spanbert: Improving pre-training by representing and predicting spans. *Transactions of the association for computational linguistics*, 8:64–77.

Mandar Joshi, Omer Levy, Luke Zettlemoyer, and Daniel S Weld. 2019. Bert for coreference resolution: Baselines and analysis. In *Proceedings of the 2019 Conference on Empirical Methods in Natural Language Processing and the 9th International Joint Conference on Natural Language Processing (EMNLP-IJCNLP)*, pages 5803–5808.

Divyanshu Kakwani, Anoop Kunchukuttan, Satish Golla, NC Gokul, Avik Bhattacharyya, Mitesh M Khapra, and Pratyush Kumar. 2020. Indicnlpsuite: Monolingual corpora, evaluation benchmarks and pre-trained multilingual language models for indian languages. In *Findings of the Association for Computational Linguistics: EMNLP 2020*, pages 4948–4961.

Ben Kantor and Amir Globerson. 2019. Coreference resolution with entity equalization. In *Proceedings of the 57th Annual Meeting of the Association for Computational Linguistics*, pages 673–677.

Simran Khanuja, Diksha Bansal, Sarvesh Mehtani, Savya Khosla, Atreyee Dey, Balaji Gopalan, Dilip Kumar Margam, Pooja Aggarwal, Rajiv Teja Nagipogu, Shachi Dave, et al. 2021. Muril: Multilingual representations for indian languages. *arXiv preprint arXiv:2103.10730*.

Kusum Lata, Pardeep Singh, and Kamlesh Dutta. 2021. A comprehensive review on feature set used for anaphora resolution. *Artificial Intelligence Review*, 54:2917–3006.

Kusum Lata, Pardeep Singh, and Kamlesh Dutta. 2022. Mention detection in coreference resolution: survey. *Applied Intelligence*, 52(9):9816–9860.

Heeyoung Lee, Yves Peirsman, Angel Chang, Nathanael Chambers, Mihai Surdeanu, and Dan Jurafsky. 2011. Stanford's multi-pass sieve coreference resolution system at the conll-2011 shared task. In *Proceedings of the fifteenth conference on computational natural language learning: Shared task*, pages 28–34.

Kenton Lee, Luheng He, Mike Lewis, and Luke Zettlemoyer. 2017. End-to-end neural coreference resolution. *arXiv preprint arXiv:1707.07045*.

Kenton Lee, Luheng He, and Luke Zettlemoyer. 2018. Higher-order coreference resolution with coarse-to-fine inference. In *Proceedings of the 2018 Conference of the North American Chapter of the Association for Computational Linguistics: Human Language Technologies, Volume 2 (Short Papers)*, pages 687–692.

Xiaoqiang Luo. 2005. On coreference resolution performance metrics. In *Proceedings of human language technology conference and conference on empirical methods in natural language processing*, pages 25–32.

Ritwik Mishra, Pooja Desur, Rajiv Shah, and Ponnurangam Kumaraguru. 2024. Multilingual coreference resolution in low-resource south asian languages. In *Proceedings of the 2024 Joint International Conference on Computational Linguistics, Language Resources and Evaluation (LREC-COLING 2024)*, pages 11813–11826.

Vandan Mujadia, Palash Gupta, and Dipti Misra Sharma. 2016. Coreference annotation scheme and relation types for hindi. In *Proceedings of the Tenth International Conference on Language Resources and Evaluation (LREC'16)*, pages 161–168.

Matthew E. Peters, Mark Neumann, Mohit Iyyer, Matt Gardner, Christopher Clark, Kenton Lee, and Luke Zettlemoyer. 2018. Deep contextualized word representations. In *Proceedings of the 2018 Conference of the North American Chapter of the Association for Computational Linguistics: Human Language Technologies, Volume 1 (Long Papers)*, pages 2227–2237, New Orleans, Louisiana. Association for Computational Linguistics.

Sameer Pradhan, Xiaoqiang Luo, Marta Recasens, Eduard Hovy, Vincent Ng, and Michael Strube. 2014. Scoring coreference partitions of predicted mentions: A reference implementation. In *Proceedings of the conference. Association for Computational Linguistics. Meeting*, volume 2014, page 30. NIH Public Access.

Rashrni Prasad and Michael Strube. 2000. Discourse salience and pronoun resolution in hindi.

Peng Qi, Yuhao Zhang, Yuhui Zhang, Jason Bolton, and Christopher D Manning. 2020. Stanza: A python natural language processing toolkit for many human languages. *arXiv preprint arXiv:2003.07082*.

Nitin Ramrakhiyani, Swapnil Hingmire, Sachin Pawar, Sangameshwar Patil, Girish Palshikar, Pushpak Bhattacharyya, and Vasudeva Verma. 2018. Resolving actor coreferences in hindi narrative text. In *Proceedings of the 15th International Conference on Natural Language Processing*, pages 50–58.

Mrinmaya Sachan, Eduard Hovy, and Eric P Xing. 2015. An active learning approach to coreference resolution. In *Twenty-Fourth International Joint Conference on Artificial Intelligence*.

Nikolaos Stylianou and Ioannis Vlahavas. 2021. A neural entity coreference resolution review. *Expert Systems with Applications*, 168:114466.

Rhea Sukthanker, Soujanya Poria, Erik Cambria, and Ramkumar Thirunavukarasu. 2020. Anaphora and coreference resolution: A review. *Information Fusion*, 59:139–162.

Bhargav Uppalapu and Dipti Misra Sharma. 2009. Pronoun resolution for hindi. In *7th Discourse Anaphora and Anaphor Resolution Colloquium (DAARC 2009)*, pages 123–134.

Mujadia Vandan Vasantlal. 2017. *Capturing and resolving entities and their mentions in discourse*. Ph.D. thesis, Doctoral dissertation, International Institute of Information Technology ....

Marc Vilain, John D Burger, John Aberdeen, Dennis Connolly, and Lynette Hirschman. 1995. A model-theoretic coreference scoring scheme. In *Sixth Message Understanding Conference (MUC-6): Proceedings of a Conference Held in Columbia, Maryland, November 6-8, 1995*.

Sam Joshua Wiseman, Alexander Matthew Rush, Stuart Merrill Shieber, and Jason Weston. 2015. Learning anaphoricity and antecedent ranking features for coreference resolution. In *Proceedings of the 53rd Annual Meeting of the Association for Computational Linguistics and the 7th International Joint Conference on Natural Language Processing (Volume 1: Long Papers)*. Association for Computational Linguistics.

Wei Wu, Fei Wang, Arianna Yuan, Fei Wu, and Jiwei Li. 2020. Corefqa: Coreference resolution as query-based span prediction. In *Proceedings of the 58th annual meeting of the association for computational linguistics*, pages 6953–6963.

Shudong Yang, Xueying Yu, and Ying Zhou. 2020. Lstm and gru neural network performance comparison study: Taking yelp review dataset as an example. In *2020 International workshop on electronic communication and artificial intelligence (IWECAI)*, pages 98–101. IEEE.

Zdeněk Žabokrtský, Miloslav Konopík, Anna Nedoluzhko, Michal Novák, Maciej Ogrodniczuk, Martin Popel, Ondřej Pražák, Jakub Sido, and Daniel Zeman. 2023. Findings of the second shared task on multilingual coreference resolution. In *Proceedings of the CRAC 2023 Shared Task on Multilingual Coreference Resolution*, pages 1–18.

Zdeněk Žabokrtský, Miloslav Konopík, Anna Nedoluzhko, Michal Novák, Maciej Ogrodniczuk, Martin Popel, Ondřej Pražák, Jakub Sido, Daniel Zeman, and Yilun Zhu. 2022. Findings of the shared task on multilingual coreference resolution. In *Proceedings of the CRAC 2022 Shared Task on Multilingual Coreference Resolution*, pages 1–17.

Findings of the Third Shared Task on Multilingual Coreference Resolution

Michal Novák[1], Barbora Dohnalová[1], Miloslav Konopík[2], Anna Nedoluzhko[1], Martin Popel[1], Ondřej Pražák[2], Jakub Sido[2], Milan Straka[1], Zdeněk Žabokrtský[1], Daniel Zeman[1]

[1] Charles University, Faculty of Mathematics and Physics,
Institute of Formal and Applied Linguistics, Prague, Czechia
{mnovak,nedoluzko,popel,straka,zabokrtsky,zeman}@ufal.mff.cuni.cz
bdohnalova@matfyz.cz

[2] University of West Bohemia, Faculty of Applied Sciences,
Department of Computer Science and Engineering, Pilsen, Czechia
{konopik,ondfa,sidoj}@kiv.zcu.cz

Abstract

The paper presents an overview of the third edition of the shared task on multilingual coreference resolution, held as part of the CRAC 2024 workshop. Similarly to the previous two editions, the participants were challenged to develop systems capable of identifying mentions and clustering them based on identity coreference.

This year's edition took another step towards real-world application by not providing participants with gold slots for zero anaphora, increasing the task's complexity and realism. In addition, the shared task was expanded to include a more diverse set of languages, with a particular focus on historical languages. The training and evaluation data were drawn from version 1.2 of the multilingual collection of harmonized coreference resources CorefUD, encompassing 21 datasets across 15 languages. 6 systems competed in this shared task.

1 Introduction

The concept of a shared task dedicated to multilingual coreference resolution began with SemEval-2010 (Recasens et al., 2010), which included seven languages, and CoNLL-2012 (Pradhan et al., 2012), which featured three languages. In the Multilingual Coreference Resolution Shared Task at CRAC 2022 (Žabokrtský et al., 2022), the scope was expanded to 10 languages, with multiple datasets for some, using the CorefUD 1.0 collection (Nedoluzhko et al., 2022). In the second edition of this shared task, held with CRAC 2023, 12 languages were involved (Žabokrtský et al., 2023). The present paper details the third edition of this shared task, organized in 2024, once again in collaboration with CRAC.

This year's shared task introduces two significant changes compared to the previous edition. First, there is an increased focus on zero mentions. These zero mentions appear in 10 datasets for the following languages: Ancient Greek, Catalan, Czech, Hungarian, Old Church Slavonic, Polish, Spanish, and Turkish. In the previous two editions of the shared task, zero mentions were technically present in the input (like any other mentions), which made the shared task's setting a bit artificial. Now, requiring the participants not only to identify coreference relations but also to generate zeros in places relevant for coreference, makes the task closer to real-world scenarios (and harder).

Second, this year's shared task uses a newer version of CorefUD. Compared to the previous version 1.1, CorefUD 1.2 comprises new languages and corpora. Ancient Greek, Ancient Hebrew, and Old Church Slavonic have been added, further broadening the task's scope beyond Latin-script languages and toward those with significantly fewer resources. Additionally, the introduction of LitBank for English extends the range of available domains by including novels with substantially longer documents. These expansions aim to develop more robust solutions that are better suited for real-world applications. Furthermore, updated versions of previously included resources, such as English-GUM and Turkish-ITCC, have been used. The conversion of zeros in Polish-PCC has been considerably improved, and the conversion pipelines for multiple other datasets have been refined too.

Proceedings of the Seventh Workshop on Computational Models of Reference, Anaphora and Coreference (CRAC 2024), pages 78–96
November 15, 2024.

The rest of the paper is organized as follows. Section 2 discusses the changes in the shared task's data compared to the previous edition. Section 3 outlines the evaluation metrics used in the task, including both the primary and supplementary scores. Section 4 details the baseline system and other participating systems. Section 5 presents a summary of the results and Section 6 provides the conclusion.

2 Datasets

As in the previous years, the shared task takes its training and evaluation data from the public part of the CorefUD collection (Nedoluzhko et al., 2022),[1] now in its latest release (1.2).[2] The public edition of CorefUD 1.2 consists of 21 datasets for 15 languages (4 language families). Compared to CorefUD 1.1, which was used last year (Žabokrtský et al., 2023), there are 4 new datasets and 3 new languages including one language (Ancient Hebrew) from a new language family. The new datasets are Ancient Greek PROIEL, Old Church Slavonic PROIEL, Ancient Hebrew PTNK, and English LitBank. Beside adding these new datasets, most of the "old" datasets from CorefUD 1.1 were updated in various ways. Table 1 gives an overview of the datasets and their sizes.

2.1 New Resources

Ancient Greek PROIEL (grc_proiel; Haug and Jøhndal, 2008) is a collection of New Testament gospels from the PROIEL treebank. The main goal of the PROIEL coreference annotation is to catch *givenness*, i.e. how readers determine the reference of nominal phrases. As a result, referential noun phrases are annotated for identity coreference and bridging relations, except relative pronouns and appositions. In addition to noun phrases, zero anaphora for pro-dropped arguments is annotated, most often unexpressed subjects. Due to the texts domain, special attention is paid to the annotation of generic and other non-specific references. The original annotation marks only mention heads, so the mention spans were determined based on syntactic dependencies. Where possible, consecutive Bible chapters were kept in the same document to preserve occasional cross-chapter coreference links; however, coreference crossing training/dev/test boundaries is lost. Manual morphosyntactic annotation from PROIEL was converted to the UD scheme.

Old Church Slavonic PROIEL (cu_proiel; Haug and Jøhndal, 2008) includes Codex Marianus and selected chapters of Suprasliensis from the PROIEL and TOROT treebanks. Coreference annotation follows the PROIEL annotation guidelines, same as for Ancient Greek (see above). Manual morphosyntactic annotation from PROIEL was converted to the UD scheme.

Ancient Hebrew PTNK (hbo_ptnk; Swanson et al., 2024) contains portions of the Hebrew Bible as digitized and annotated in the Biblia Hebraica Stuttgartensia. Entity and coreference annotation follows guidelines similar to those of the English GUM corpus. Several high-frequency entities have hundreds of mentions throughout the Bible (e.g., God, Abraham, Isaac or Jacob); however, since the CorefUD 1.2 version of the resource uses chapters as documents (which are then distributed between training/dev/test parts of the data), coreference between chapters is not preserved. The current version of the dataset also lacks annotation of zero mentions (their addition is planned in the future, as Hebrew is a pro-drop language). Manual morphosyntactic annotation was done natively in the UD scheme.

English LitBank (en_litbank; Bamman et al., 2019) contains texts from 100 literary novels of English-language fiction in LitBank. Compared to other English corpora, the dataset contains longer texts with an average length over 2000 words. Coreference annotation is close to the OntoNotes coreference annotation style (BBN Technologies, 2006) with several significant changes such as explicit annotation of singletons and applying coreference annotation to only the ACE categories (people, locations, organizations, facilities, geopolitical entities, and vehicles, see Walker and Consortium, 2005). Annotation of literary texts also demands for more detailed insight into the identity phenomenon, thus near-identity or the revelation of identity is paid more attention in the dataset. Morphosyntactic annotation was predicted by UDPipe, as it was not part of the original resource. A coreference entity has on average 10.8 mentions, which is the highest number in CorefUD 1.2 (see Table 1).

2.2 Updated Resources

More data The English GUM corpus (en_gum) is now in its version 10, which has approximately

[1] https://ufal.mff.cuni.cz/corefud
[2] http://hdl.handle.net/11234/1-5478

document	total number of				entities				mentions			
					total	per 1k	length		total	per 1k	length	
	docs	sents	words	empty n.	count	words	max	avg.	count	words	max	avg.
Ancient_Greek-PROIEL	19	6,475	64,111	6,283	3,215	50	332	6.6	21,354	333	52	1.7
Ancient_Hebrew-PTNK	40	1,161	28,485	0	870	31	102	7.2	6,247	219	22	1.5
Catalan-AnCora	1,298	13,613	429,313	6,377	17,558	41	101	3.6	62,417	145	141	4.8
Czech-PCEDT	2,312	49,208	1,155,755	35,654	49,225	43	236	3.4	168,055	145	79	3.6
Czech-PDT	3,165	49,428	834,720	21,808	46,628	56	172	3.3	154,905	186	99	3.1
English-GUM	217	12,147	211,920	115	8,270	39	131	4.4	36,733	173	95	2.6
English-LitBank	100	8,560	210,530	0	2,164	10	261	10.8	23,340	111	129	1.6
English-ParCorFull	19	543	10,798	0	188	17	38	4.4	835	77	37	2.1
French-Democrat	126	13,057	284,883	0	7,162	25	895	6.5	46,487	163	71	1.7
German-ParCorFull	19	543	10,602	0	243	23	43	3.7	896	85	30	2.0
German-PotsdamCC	176	2,238	33,222	0	880	26	15	2.9	2,519	76	34	2.6
Hungarian-KorKor	94	1,351	24,568	1,988	1,124	46	41	3.7	4,103	167	42	2.2
Hungarian-SzegedKoref	400	8,820	123,968	4,857	4,769	38	36	3.2	15,165	122	36	1.6
Lithuanian-LCC	100	1,714	37,014	0	1,087	29	23	4.0	4,337	117	19	1.5
Norwegian-BokmaalNARC	346	15,742	245,515	0	5,658	23	298	4.7	26,611	108	51	1.9
Norwegian-NynorskNARC	394	12,481	206,660	0	5,079	25	84	4.3	21,847	106	57	2.1
Old_Church_Slavonic-PROIEL	26	6,832	61,759	6,289	3,396	55	134	6.5	22,116	358	52	1.5
Polish-PCC	1,828	35,874	538,885	18,615	22,143	41	135	3.7	82,706	153	108	1.9
Russian-RuCor	181	9,035	156,636	0	3,515	22	141	4.6	16,193	103	18	1.7
Spanish-AnCora	1,356	14,159	458,418	8,112	19,445	42	110	3.6	70,663	154	101	4.8
Turkish-ITCC	24	4,732	55,358	11,584	4,019	73	369	5.4	21,569	390	31	1.1

Table 1: CorefUD 1.2 data sizes in terms of the total number of documents, sentences, words (i.e. non-empty nodes), empty nodes (empty words), coreference entities (total count, relative count per 1000 words, average and maximal length in number of mentions) and coreference mentions (total count, relative count per 1000 words, average and maximal length in number of words). All the counts are excluding singletons and for the concatenation of train+dev+test. Train/dev/test splits of these datasets roughly follow the 8/1/1 ratio. See Table **??** for details.

10% more data. All the other datasets are the same size as before (except for a few minor changes resulting from annotation corrections).

Substantial changes Re-implementation of conversion from non-CorefUD formats and/or major revision of the annotation was applied to French Democrat (fr_democrat), Polish PCC (pl_pcc), and Turkish ITCC (tr_itcc). Besides improved basic coreference annotation, in Polish and Turkish this also involved a significant boost in annotation of zero mentions (empty nodes), which are the theme of the present edition of the shared task. Many changes were also applied to Czech (cs_pdt, cs_pcedt), Catalan (ca_ancora) and Spanish (es_ancora); here the changes affected both the conversion of coreference and the manual morphosyntactic annotation in UD.[3]

New prediction of morphosyntax Finally, for datasets that do not come with manual morphosyntactic annotation, the UD relations, tags and features were predicted with newer models for UDPipe (based on UD release 2.12). This involves all the remaining corpora except for the two Norwegian ones, which did not change and have manual UD annotation.

[3]More details on the changes can be found in the README files of the individual corpora.

2.3 Zero mentions

Zero mention refers to instances where a referent (typically the subject or object of a sentence) is implied but not explicitly mentioned in the text. Zero mention is common in pro-drop languages, where subject pronouns can be omitted because the verb conjugation often provides enough information to infer the subject.

In CorefUD, zero mentions are technically represented by *empty nodes*, artificially inserted into the UD trees in places where zero mentions are needed. Using this representation, a zero mention can be grouped with other mentions in a coreference chain to express coreference relations, fully analogously to overt (non-zero) mentions.

Languages differ substantially in what may be unexpressed. For example, Czech is considered a strongly pro-drop language and Russian is a partially pro-drop language, while English is not considered a pro-drop language. In addition, not only a subject pronoun but also an object or possessive pronoun can be dropped in some languages such as

Hungarian. Another level of variability is caused by different design choices of authors of the original coreference resources; for example, some do annotate nominal ellipsis, while some do not. At this moment, harmonization of zero mentions is limited in CorefUD, and zero mentions from the original data resources are mostly preserved (i.e., captured by empty nodes).

In the previous two editions of this shared task, gold empty nodes (i.e., the slots for zero mentions) represented as empty nodes were available to participants both in the training and test data. That, however, was rather artificial, as zero mentions are by definition not overt in input texts. Hence their presence should be predicted too, as is the case in the current shared task.

2.4 Data preprocessing and starting points

Compared to the public edition of CorefUD 1.2, the data provided for the shared task participants underwent slight adjustments.

Gold data used for training and evaluation received a minor technical modification: the forms of empty nodes were removed. This change was made to align the data more closely with the output of the baseline empty node prediction, which does not predict these forms (see Section 4.1). Apart from this, the data remained consistent with the CorefUD 1.2 release, retaining manually annotated morpho-syntactic features (for datasets that originally included them), gold empty nodes, and gold coreference annotations. While we made the gold train and dev sets available for download, the gold test set was kept secret and used exclusively within CodaLab for submissions evaluation.

Input data were intended for processing by participants' systems and subsequent submission. To better simulate a real-world scenario where no manual linguistic annotation is available, we removed the forms of empty nodes and replaced the original morpho-syntactic features with the outputs of UD 2.12 models across all datasets, including those with originally human-annotated features. Additionally, the gold empty nodes and coreference annotations were removed.

Nevertheless, participants could choose from different *starting points* for entering the shared task, with varying degrees of work required. Depending on the chosen starting point, participants were provided with different levels of empty nodes' and coreference predictions from the baseline systems (see Section 4.1). The three available starting points were:

1. *Coreference and zeros from scratch.* Participants were required to develop a system that resolves both coreference and predicts empty nodes potentially involved in zero anaphora. While this starting point is more challenging, it offers significant potential for gains.

2. *Coreference from scratch.* In this scenario, empty nodes were provided by the baseline system, allowing participants to focus solely on developing a coreference resolution system. Systems submitted in last year's edition could be applied to this starting point with some retraining.

3. *Refine the baseline.* Participants were given both empty nodes and coreference relations, as predicted by the baseline systems. This starting point is the simplest yet less flexible option.

The input data preprocessing was performed on the dev and test sets.

3 Evaluation Metrics

The systems participating in the shared task are evaluated with the CorefUD scorer. Similarly to the last year's edition, the primary evaluation score is the CoNLL F1 score with head mention matching and singletons excluded. As gold and predicted zero mentions are no longer guaranteed to match one-to-one, we introduce the dependency-based method to align them. Furthermore, we calculate several other supplementary scores to compare the shared task submissions.

Official scorer We use the CorefUD scorer[4] in its version from May 2024 to evaluate the submissions of the participants. It has been upgraded to build on the Universal Anaphora (UA) scorer 2.0 (Yu et al., 2023) instead of the UA scorer 1.0 (Yu et al., 2022). Besides the features that had been an integral part of the older CorefUD scorer and were newly introduced to the UA scorer 2.0, e.g., Mention Overlap Ratio (MOR; Žabokrtský et al., 2022), anaphor-level evaluation of zeros, support for discontinuous mentions and the CorefUD 1.0 file format, the upgrade fixed a bug in partial matching method and

[4]https://github.com/ufal/corefud-scorer

introduced the linear method of matching zero mentions. Naturally, it still allows to take advantage of the implementations of all generally used coreferential measures with no modifications. Unlike the UA scorer, the CorefUD scorer provides support for head match and newly for dependency-based method of matching zero mentions.

Mention matching Due to shortcomings of using *exact* and *partial* mention matching (see Žabokrtský et al. (2023) for details), we arrived at the decision to use the *head match* method in the primary metrics last year. Gold and predicted mentions are considered matching if their heads[5] correspond to identical tokens. Full spans are ignored, except for the case of multiple mentions with the same head in order to disambiguate between them.

Matching of zeros However, none of the matching methods can be any longer applied to empty nodes. As in this year the participants are expected to predict empty nodes involved in zero anaphora, they are not guaranteed to align one-to-one with the gold empty nodes. They can be missing, spurious, or predicted at different surface positions within the sentence, yet playing the same role.

We thus introduce the *dependency-based method of matching zero mentions*. It looks for the matching of zeros within the same sentence that maximizes the F-score of predicting dependencies of zeros in the enhanced dependency graph.[6] Specifically, the task is cast as searching for a one-to-one matching in a weighted bipartite graph (with gold and predicted mentions as the two partitions) to maximize the total sum of weights in the matching. Each candidate pair (gold zero mention – predicted zero mention) is weighed with a non-zero score only if the two mentions belong to the same sentence. The score is then calculated as a weighted sum of two features:

- the F-score of the gold zero dependencies recognized in the predicted zero, considering both parent and dependency type assignments (weighted by a factor of 10);
- the F-score of the gold zero dependencies recognized in the predicted zero, considering only parent assignments (weighed by a factor of 1).

The scoring mechanism prioritizes the exact assignment of both parents and types. Nevertheless, it is ensured to sufficiently work even if the predictions contain no dependency type assignments.

This matching strategy differs to the linear matching of zeros presented by Yu et al. (2023), which aligns the zeros only if their word indices[7] are identical. Such matching may thus fail if the zero is predicted at different surface position or if only one of the multiple zeros with the same parent is predicted.

Primary score Following the best practices for coreference resolution, we utilize the CoNLL F_1 score (Denis and Baldridge, 2009; Pradhan et al., 2014) as the primary evaluation score. It is an unweighted average of the F_1 scores of three coreference metrics: MUC (Vilain et al., 1995), B^3 (Bagga and Baldwin, 1998) and CEAF-e (Luo, 2005). The final ranking of participating submissions is then based on a macro-average of CoNLL F_1 scores over all datasets in the CorefUD test collection.

Supplementary scores Besides the primary CoNLL F_1 score, we report alternative versions of this score using different ways of mention matching: partial match[8] and exact match. Furthermore, we calculate the primary metrics using the head-match for all mentions including singletons.

We also report the systems' performance in terms of the coreference metrics that contribute to the CoNLL score as well as other standard measures, e.g. BLANC (Recasens and Hovy, 2011) and LEA (Moosavi and Strube, 2016). We employ the MOR score to evaluate the quality of mention matching, while ignoring the assignment of mentions to coreferential entities. Moreover, this year, it is particularly interesting to analyze the performance of the systems on zero anaphora. To this end, we use the anaphor-decomposable score for zeros (Žabokrtský et al., 2022), which is an application of the scoring schema proposed by Tuggener (2014).

[5] Note that gold mention heads in the CorefUD data were determined from the dependency tree using the Udapi block `corefud.MoveHead`.

[6] Stored in the DEPS field of the CoNLL-U format.

[7] Stored in the ID field of the CoNLL-U format.

[8] The partial-match setup was used in the primary metrics in the first edition of the shared task (Žabokrtský et al., 2022).

4 Participating Systems

4.1 Baseline

This year, two baseline systems are provided: one for predicting empty nodes as slots for zero anaphora, and another for coreference resolution.

Empty Nodes Prediction Baseline Predicting empty nodes is a novel task in this year's shared task. To accommodate participants who want to focus solely on coreference resolution, we provide a baseline for predicting empty nodes. We release the source code,[9] the trained multilingual model,[10] and development and testing data with predicted empty nodes.

The baseline model architecture is as follows. Every sentence is processed independently, and its words are split into subwords by the XLM-RoBERTa tokenizer (Conneau et al., 2020). The subwords are passed through the XLM-RoBERTa large pretrained model, and the embeddings of the first subword of every word are utilized as the word representations. Then, two candidate representations for every word are generated, by (1) passing the word representations through a ReLU-activated 2k-unit dense layer, a dropout layer and a 768-unit dense layer; (2) concatenating the described outputs with the original word representations and passed through an analogous dense-dropout-dense module. Each candidate representation might generate an empty node, whose dependency head would be the word generating the candidate. The candidate representations are processed by three heads, each first applying a 2k-unit dense layer, ReLU, and dropout: (1) a binary classification head predicting whether the candidate is an empty node or not, (2) word-order prediction head implemented using self-attention selecting the word after which the empty node should be added, and (3) dependency relation prediction head, which first concatenates the candidate representation and the representation of the word most probable according to the word-order prediction head, and then predicts the dependency relation.

The model was trained on a combination of all languages containing empty nodes, sampling every language proportionally to the square root of its size. Further details and used hyperparameters are available in the source code repository.[9]

Language	Recall	Precision	F1
ca_ancora	91.01	92.32	91.66
cs_pcedt	59.84	78.22	67.81
cs_pdt	71.56	81.47	76.19
cu_proiel	78.76	81.61	80.16
es_ancora	91.92	92.04	91.98
grc_proiel	86.58	90.29	88.39
hu_korkor	60.21	74.68	66.67
hu_szeged	89.52	91.93	90.71
pl_pcc	91.61	87.50	89.51
tr_itcc	93.81	79.05	85.80

Table 2: Empty nodes prediction baseline performance on the development sets of CorefUD 1.2 languages containing empty nodes. An empty node is considered correct if it has the correct dependency head, dependency relation, and word order.

The performance of the empty nodes prediction baseline is quantified in Table 2 using precision, recall, and F1 score, where a predicted empty node is considered correct if its dependency head, dependency relation, and word order are all correct.

Coreference Resolution Baseline The baseline for coreference resolution is the same as in the two previous years. It is a multilingual end-to-end neural coreference resolution by (Pražák et al., 2021). The model is the adaptation of the standard end-to-end neural coreference resolution system originally proposed by Lee et al. (2017). The model iterates over all possible spans up to the maximum length and predicts the antecedent for each potential span directly. Because it does not predict the mentions in the separate step, it should be sufficient for the datasets where singletons are not annotated. The baseline coreference model uses mBERT base as an encoder.

4.2 System Submissions

This year, six systems were submitted to the shared task by the following four teams: DFKI_TR,[11]

[9] https://github.com/ufal/crac2024_zero_nodes_baseline

[10] https://www.kaggle.com/models/ufal-mff/crac2024_zero_nodes_baseline/

[11] DFKI = Deutsches Forschungszentrum für Künstliche Intelligenz (German Research Center for Artificial Intelligence). The DFKI-CorefGen system was submitted to CodaLab by user "natalia_s".

ÚFAL CorPipe,[12] UWB[13] and Ritwikmishra.[14] Some of the files produced by the Ritwikmishra system were not valid CoNLL-U and the scorer failed, thus resulting in zero F1 for these datasets (see Table 6). We applied an automatic correction[15] and call the resulting system RitwikmishraFix. The tables with results in Section 5 also include the baseline system (BASELINE) as described in Section 4.1 and the same baseline system applied on gold empty nodes (BASELINE-GZ). The total number of systems compared is thus 9.

The following descriptions are based on the information provided by the respective participants in an online questionnaire. Basic properties of the systems are also summarized in Table 3.

DFKI-CorefGen The DFKI-CorefGen system performs mention identification and co-reference resolution jointly, treating both tasks as text generation. Given a piece of text, the system identifies all mentions and groups them into clusters by marking the mentions with square brackets accompanied by cluster identifiers. The approach resolves co-reference incrementally, processing each new sentence to find mentions and cluster them, while also correcting cluster assignments in the previous context if needed.

To train the model, DFKI-CorefGen applies prefix tuning using OpenPrompt (Ding et al., 2021). The system utilizes multilingual T5 base (Xue et al., 2021) as the foundation model. During training, the pre-trained model is kept frozen, and only the prefix component is tuned.

CorPipe-2stage CorPipe-2stage is a minor evolution of the system implemented in the previous year (Straka and Straková, 2022). It combines the baseline provided by the shared task organizers for the prediction of zeros, followed by the last year's version of CorPipe, which first predicts the mentions and then the links among them using a single pre-trained Transformer encoder. Three model variants are trained, based on either mT5-large, InfoXLM-large, or mT5-xl. For every variant, 7 multilingual models are trained on a combination of all the treebanks, differing only in random initialization. The treebanks are sampled proportionally to the square root of their size, and most hyperparameters are taken from the last year's CorPipe. Then, for each treebank, the best-performing checkpoints are selected from the shared pool of checkpoints and ensembled.

CorPipe Contrary to the CorPipe-2stage submission using two Transformer encoders, the submission CorPipe predicts the zero mentions directly from the words, jointly with the nonzero mention prediction and the link prediction. It uses the same approach of 3 Transformer encoder variants, 7 multilingual models per variant, and ensemble selection for each treebank.

CorPipe-single CorPipe-single uses the same checkpoint pool as the CorPipe system, but it chooses a single mT5-large-based model for prediction on all treebanks.

Ondfa The Ondfa system extends the baseline system and participant systems from previous years (Pražák and Konopik, 2022). The approach involves initially training a joint cross-lingual model (XLM-R-large, mT5-xxl) for all datasets. Subsequently, the model is fine-tuned for each dataset separately, using LORA in the case of mT5.

Mentions are newly represented only with their headwords (except for cs_pcedt and lt_lcc, where multiword mentions were allowed), which has been shown to improve the primary metric (head-match) results on the dev sets. Syntax trees are also incorporated as features into the model. The UWB team also modified their model to handle singletons.

Ritwikmishra This submission reuses the TransMuCoRes system from (Mishra et al., 2024), which is a fine-tuned *wl-coref* architecture (Dobrovolskii, 2021) built on top of the XLM-R-base model. This system is applied in a zero-shot manner on both the development and test sets.

4.3 System Comparison

Most of the systems, including DFKI-CorefGen and the CorPipe variants, developed their approaches completely from scratch. However, CorPipe-2stage, Ritwikmishra, and Ondfa utilized the provided baseline predictions of empty nodes (the *Coreference from scratch* starting point). Additionally, Ondfa built upon the baseline coreference

[12]ÚFAL = Ústav formální a aplikované lingvistiky (Institute of Formal and Applied Linguistics). The ÚFAL CorPipe team submitted 3 systems: CorPipe, CorPipe-2stage and CorPipe-single, by CodaLab users "straka", "straka-twostage" and "straka-single-multilingual-model", respectively.

[13]UWB = University of West Bohemia. The Ondfa system was submitted to CodaLab by user "ondfa".

[14]The Ritwikmishra system was submitted to CodaLab by user "ritwikmishra".

[15]Mostly moving Entity annotations from multi-word tokens (where they are forbidden) to the words.

Name	Baseline	Starting point	Official data
DFKI-TR	No	From scratch	Yes
CorPipe	No	From scratch	Yes
CorPipe-single	No	From scratch	Yes
CorPipe-2stage	Prediction of zeros	Coreference from scratch	Yes
Ondfa	Coref. resolution	Coreference from scratch	Yes
Ritwikmishra	No	Coreference from scratch	No (TransMuCoRes)

Name	Pretrained model	Model size	Seq. length
DFKI-TR	mT5-base	580M + 3.4M	512 subwords
CorPipe	mT5-large, mT5-xl, InfoXLM-large	3.7B+280M (3-model ensemble, average)	2560 for mT5, 512 for InfoXLM, 512 during training
CorPipe-single	mT5-large	538M+57M	2560 during prediction, 512 during training
CorPipe-2stage	mT5-large, mT5-xl, InfoXLM-large	5.1B+400M (5-model ensemble, average)	2560 for mT5, 512 for InfoXLM, 512 during training
Ondfa	XLM-R-large, mT5-xxl	550M + 20M (xlmr), 5.7B + 70-400M (mt5)	512, 2048, 4096 2048, 4096
Ritwikmishra	XLM-R-base	270M + 4.3M	variable

Name	Tuned per lang.?	Batch size	Tuned hyperparameters
DFKI-TR	No	1	Not specified
CorPipe	Yes (21 models)	8, 12	Model variant (rest taken from 2023)
CorPipe-single	No	8	Taken from 2023
CorPipe-2stage	Yes (21 models)	8, 12	Model variant (rest taken from 2023)
Ondfa	Yes	1 doc	LORA rank (rest taken from 2023)
Ritwikmishra	No	8	None

Table 3: The table compares properties of systems participating in the task. The systems are ordered alphabetically. The shortcuts in the headings are defined as follows: **Name** is the name of the submission, **Baseline**: what type of baseline the system builds on (see Section 4.1). **Starting point**: the chosen starting level out of the three possible ones as listed in Section 2.4, *From scratch* denotes the *Coreference and zeros from scratch* starting point. **Official data**: Use of CorefUD 1.2 public edition for training, **Tuned per lang.?** indicates whether participants tuned their model for each language or not. **Model size**: The model size is split between the Pretrained model size and the size of the added head. **variable** means various settings depending on features and architecture.

resolution system, but no submission was based solely on the baseline predictions (the *Refine the baseline* starting point).

The systems leveraged various pre-trained models: DFKI-CorefGen employed mT5-base (Xue et al., 2021); the CorPipe variants used combinations of encoder blocks from mT5-large, mT5-xl (Xue et al., 2021), and InfoXLM-large (Chi et al., 2021); Ondfa utilized XLM-R-large (Conneau et al., 2020) and mT5-xxl (Xue et al., 2021); and Ritwikmishra opted for XLM-R-base (Conneau et al., 2020).

Model sizes varied significantly, ranging from around 600M parameters for DFKI-CorefGen and Ritwikmishra to 6.1B for Ondfa's mT5-xxl model. The CorPipe systems distinguished themselves by employing ensemble methods with multiple models. Language-specific tuning was another point of differentiation: CorPipe, CorPipe-2stage, and Ondfa fine-tuned their models for individual languages, while DFKI-CorefGen, CorPipe-single, and Ritwikmishra maintained a single multilingual model approach.

Regarding training data, most systems utilized the official CorefUD 1.2 public edition. Ritwikmishra, however, diverged from this trend by using the TransMuCoRes dataset (Mishra et al., 2024).

5 Results and Comparison

5.1 Main Results

The main results are summarized in Table 4. The CorPipe-2stage system is the best one according to the official primary metric (head-match excluding singletons) as well as according to three alternative metrics: partial-match excluding singletons (which was the primary metric in 2022), exact-match excluding singletons and head-match including singletons. All four metrics result in the same ordering of systems with a single exception of the Ondfa system, which is the sixth best according to exact-match, but the fourth best according to other metrics. This is caused by the fact that for all but two datasets (cf. description of Ondfa in Section 4.2), Ondfa predicted only the head word and the span was always just this single word.

The third edition of the shared task is also a good time to look into how the state of the art in multilingual coreference resolution develops. However, the results are not directly comparable across the years as the CorefUD collection has grown and some details of the shared task have changed over the years. The baseline system has not fundamentally changed, set aside that it has been trained on slightly different data. We can thus compare the relative improvement of the best system over the baseline. As shown in Table 4, while the gain over the baseline was 31% last year, this year it is 39%.

Table 5 shows recall, precision, and F1 for six metrics. The F1 scores of the first five metrics (MUC. B^3, BLANC, and LEA) result in the same ordering of systems (same as the primary metric) except for RitwikmishraFix, which is slightly better than DFKI-CorefGen in BLANC and LEA. Most of the systems have higher precision than recall for all the metrics, but the highest disbalance is in the BASELINE system. CorPipe* are the only systems that have higher recall than precision at least for CEAF-e (but other metrics have similar precision and recall).

The MOR metric (mention overlap ratio) measures only the mention matching quality, while ignoring the coreference, but even then the ordering of systems is similar to the primary metric (Ondfa is the fourth worst according to MOR, again because it does not predict full spans for most datasets).

Table 6 shows the primary metric (CoNLL F1 head-match) for individual datasets. The winner (CorPipe-2stage) is the best system for 15 out of 21 datasets, so the results are more diverse than last year, when the winner (CorPipe) was the best system across all datasets and languages. Interestingly, there is a substantial improvement of all systems on tr_itcc relative to the last year (BASELINE-GZ 51.16% this year vs. BASELINE-2023=22.75% last year; the winner has 68.18 this year vs. 55.63 last year). This is due to the fixes in the dataset and possibly because zero anaphora was newly introduced in the source corpus (Pamay and Eryiğit, 2024).

5.2 Evaluation of Zeros

Table 7 shows the performance of the systems on zero anaphora resolution on datasets with annotated zeros. Let us start with a comparison of the BASELINE and BASELINE-GZ systems, which differ only in the nature of the empty nodes (predicted vs. gold).[16] It confirms that by moving to the realistic setup for zeros the task became much more challenging, illustrated by the performance drop in the F1 score by 5-19 points for most of the datasets. Note that for some datasets (cs_pdt, cs_pcedt, pl_pcc) the task is so challenging that none of the systems was able to outperform BASELINE-GZ.

If we ignore the results of BASELINE-GZ, the winning CorPipe-2stage system dominates the performance on zeros across most of the languages, being outperformed by the Ondfa systems on 4 datasets. This correlates with the CoNLL scores across languages observed in Table 6. Interestingly, we observe huge disproportion in the performance changes between the winning system and the BASELINE-GZ across the datasets of the same language. Whereas the BASELINE-GZ is better by 3 points on cs_pdt, it is better by 14 points on cs_pcedt. Similarly, while the BASELINE-GZ is worse by 2 points on hu_korkor, it is better by 19 points on hu_szeged. It suggests significant differences in the guidelines for zero annotation across the datasets, even of the same language.

Annual comparison of the results performed by baselines run in the gold zero setup (BASELINE-GZ and BASELINE-2023) shows similar scores on zeros, which confirms that these baselines are comparable. The only exception is pl_pcc, on which BASELINE-GZ improved by 25 percentage points. This can be explained by the fixes in the CorefUD conversion pipeline from the source corpus that fo-

[16]The gold empty nodes in the testset were not available to the participants, thus BASELINE-GZ is not directly comparable with the other systems; it serves as a comparison with the previous year, when all empty nodes were gold.

system	excluding singletons			with singletons
	head-match	**partial-match**	**exact-match**	**head-match**
CorPipe-2stage	**73.90**	**72.19** (-1.71)	**69.86** (-4.04)	**75.65** (+1.75)
CorPipe	72.75	70.30 (-2.45)	68.36 (-4.39)	74.65 (+1.90)
CorPipe-single	70.18	68.02 (-2.16)	66.07 (-4.11)	71.96 (+1.78)
Ondfa	69.97	69.82 (-0.15)	40.25 (-29.72)	70.67 (+0.69)
BASELINE-GZ	54.60	53.95 (-0.65)	52.63 (-1.97)	47.89 (-6.71)
BASELINE	53.16	52.48 (-0.68)	51.26 (-1.90)	46.45 (-6.71)
DFKI-CorefGen	33.38	32.36 (-1.02)	30.71 (-2.68)	38.65 (+5.26)
RitwikmishraFix	30.63	32.21 (+1.58)	28.27 (-2.35)	27.05 (-3.58)
Ritwikmishra	16.47	16.65 (+0.17)	14.16 (-2.31)	15.42 (-1.06)
WINNER-2023	74.90	73.33 (-1.57)	71.46 (-3.44)	76.82 (+1.91)
BASELINE-2023	56.96	56.28 (-0.68)	54.75 (-2.21)	49.32 (-7.64)

Table 4: Main results: the CoNLL metric macro-averaged over all datasets. The table shows the primary metric (head-match excluding singletons) and three alternative metrics: partial-match excluding singletons, exact-match excluding singletons and head-match with singletons. A difference relative to the primary metric is reported in parenthesis. The best score in each column is in bold. The systems are ordered by the primary metric. The last two rows showing the winner and baseline results from CRAC 2023 are copied from the last year Findings (Žabokrtský et al., 2023), and thus are not directly comparable with the rest of the table because both the test and training data have been changed (CorefUD 1.1 vs. 1.2). Similar notes apply to the following tables.

system	MUC	B^3	CEAF-e	BLANC	LEA	MOR
CorPipe-2stage	**79 / 81 / 80**	**69 / 74 / 71**	**71 / 70 / 70**	**67 / 73 / 70**	**66 / 71 / 68**	78 / 82 / **80**
CorPipe	79 / 80 / 79	69 / 72 / 70	71 / 68 / 69	67 / 72 / 69	65 / 69 / 67	78 / 80 / 79
CorPipe-single	77 / 76 / 77	68 / 67 / 67	69 / 66 / 67	66 / 66 / 66	64 / 63 / 64	**79** / 77 / 77
Ondfa	75 / 81 / 78	64 / 72 / 67	64 / 67 / 65	62 / 71 / 65	61 / 69 / 64	41 / **87** / 54
BASELINE-GZ	56 / 75 / 63	43 / 63 / 50	46 / 57 / 50	41 / 63 / 48	39 / 58 / 46	49 / 86 / 61
BASELINE	54 / 73 / 62	41 / 62 / 49	44 / 56 / 49	39 / 62 / 46	37 / 57 / 44	48 / 85 / 60
DFKI-CorefGen	37 / 52 / 41	26 / 38 / 29	25 / 42 / 30	21 / 39 / 23	21 / 31 / 23	43 / 71 / 50
RitwikmishraFix	33 / 50 / 36	26 / 43 / 28	27 / 37 / 29	24 / 39 / 24	24 / 39 / 25	30 / 65 / 36
Ritwikmishra	18 / 31 / 18	15 / 27 / 15	15 / 22 / 16	13 / 23 / 12	13 / 25 / 13	17 / 38 / 20

Table 5: Recall / Precision / F1 for individual secondary metrics. All scores macro-averaged over all datasets.

system	ca_ancora	cs_pcedt	cs_pdt	cu_proiel	de_parcorfull	de_potsdam	en_gum	en_litbank	en_parcorfull	es_ancora	fr_democrat	grc_proiel	hbo_ptnk	hu_korkor	hu_szeged	lt_lcc	no_bokmaalnarc	no_nynorsknarc	pl_pcc	ru_rucor	tr_itcc
CorPipe-2stage	82.22	**74.85**	**77.18**	**61.58**	69.53	71.79	**75.66**	**79.60**	68.89	**82.46**	68.16	**71.34**	**72.02**	63.17	**69.97**	**75.79**	**79.81**	**78.01**	**78.50**	**83.22**	**68.18**
CorPipe	81.02	73.71	75.84	60.72	**71.68**	71.45	74.61	79.10	**69.75**	80.98	**68.77**	68.53	70.86	60.32	68.12	75.78	79.55	77.52	77.03	83.09	59.37
CorPipe-single	80.42	72.82	74.82	57.11	61.62	67.02	74.39	78.08	58.61	79.75	67.89	66.01	67.18	60.09	67.32	75.19	78.92	76.60	75.20	81.21	53.43
Ondfa	**82.46**	70.82	75.80	54.97	71.40	**71.91**	70.53	74.15	55.58	81.94	62.69	61.64	61.56	**64.86**	69.26	71.97	74.51	72.07	76.34	80.47	64.49
BASELINE-GZ	69.59	68.93	66.15	27.56	47.21	55.65	63.18	63.54	33.08	70.64	53.62	31.87	24.60	41.65	54.64	62.00	64.96	63.70	67.00	65.83	51.16
BASELINE	68.32	64.06	63.83	24.51	47.21	55.65	63.19	63.54	33.08	69.58	53.62	28.76	24.60	35.14	54.51	62.00	64.96	63.70	66.24	65.83	44.05
DFKI-CorefGen	34.77	32.89	30.88	22.52	23.07	45.85	35.49	46.59	32.69	37.76	36.34	25.87	37.96	23.53	33.85	42.73	37.92	35.69	27.19	47.79	9.65
RitwikmishraFix	27.05	0.00	0.00	6.79	25.35	48.90	48.64	61.47	53.12	30.04	43.63	5.60	0.12	33.40	30.28	44.31	56.41	53.17	0.00	53.89	20.97
Ritwikmishra	0.00	0.00	0.00	6.79	25.35	48.90	0.00	0.00	53.12	0.00	43.72	5.60	0.09	33.40	30.32	44.78	0.00	0.00	0.00	53.88	0.00
BASELINE-2023	65.26	67.72	65.22	–	44.11	57.13	63.08	–	35.19	66.93	55.31	–	–	40.71	55.32	63.57	65.10	65.78	66.08	69.03	22.75

Table 6: Results for individual languages in the primary metric (CoNLL).

system	ca_ancora	cs_pdt	cs_pcedt	cu_proiel	es_ancora	grc_proiel	hu_korkor	hu_szeged	pl_pcc	tr_itcc
CorPipe-2stage	88 / 85 / 86	77 / 82 / 80	59 / 74 / 66	**75** / **78** / **76**	**90** / **92** / **91**	**84** / **88** / **86**	56 / 75 / 64	**83** / 68 / 75	**90** / 84 / 87	**83** / 80 / 82
CorPipe	83 / 78 / 81	71 / 76 / 74	62 / 63 / 62	**75** / 74 / 75	84 / 84 / 84	79 / 83 / 81	55 / 74 / 63	71 / 68 / 70	85 / 78 / 82	70 / 68 / 69
CorPipe-single	81 / 77 / 79	72 / 72 / 72	63 / 58 / 60	75 / 72 / 73	83 / 83 / 83	80 / 77 / 78	52 / 71 / 60	72 / 65 / 68	83 / 75 / 79	66 / 60 / 63
Ondfa	**88** / **86** / **87**	75 / **84** / 79	55 / 81 / 66	71 / 74 / 72	90 / 91 / 90	78 / 85 / 81	57 / **78** / **66**	**83** / **72** / **77**	90 / 83 / 86	82 / **82** / **82**
BASELINE-GZ	82 / 82 / 82	**82** / 84 / **83**	**78** / **82** / **80**	60 / 72 / 66	87 / 87 / 87	64 / 66 / 65	**60** / 65 / 62	53 / 59 / 56	89 / **86** / **87**	75 / 82 / 78
BASELINE	79 / 76 / 77	70 / 74 / 72	55 / 69 / 61	52 / 62 / 56	83 / 83 / 83	63 / 70 / 66	41 / 61 / 49	49 / 57 / 53	85 / 78 / 82	68 / 71 / 70
DFKI-CorefGen	0 / 0 / 0	0 / 0 / 0	0 / 0 / 0	0 / 0 / 0	0 / 0 / 0	0 / 0 / 0	0 / 0 / 0	0 / 0 / 0	0 / 0 / 0	0 / 0 / 0
RitwikmishraFix	0 / 50 / 0	0 / 0 / 0	0 / 0 / 0	0 / 0 / 0	0 / 0 / 0	0 / 0 / 0	0 / 0 / 0	0 / 0 / 0	0 / 0 / 0	0 / 0 / 0
Ritwikmishra	0 / 0 / 0	0 / 0 / 0	0 / 0 / 0	0 / 0 / 0	0 / 0 / 0	0 / 0 / 0	0 / 0 / 0	0 / 0 / 0	0 / 0 / 0	0 / 0 / 0
WINNER-2023	93 / 92 / 92	91 / 92 / 92	87 / 88 / 87	–	94 / 95 / 95	–	82 / 89 / 85	88 / 70 / 78	75 / 69 / 72	–
BASELINE-2023	82 / 82 / 82	81 / 84 / 82	77 / 81 / 79	–	87 / 88 / 87	–	60 / 68 / 64	61 / 57 / 59	50 / 80 / 62	–

Table 7: Recall / Precision / F1 for anaphor-decomposable score of coreference resolution on zero anaphors across individual languages. Only datasets containing anaphoric zeros are listed (en_gum excluded as all zeros in its test set are non-anaphoric). Note that these scores are directly comparable to neither the CoNLL score nor the supplementary scores calculated with respect to whole entities in Table 5.

cused on zeros. The annual comparison of relative improvements of the best systems over these baselines in terms of the zero anaphora score reveals that the improvements are much lower than they were last year, again confirming the more difficult nature of this year's setup for zeros.

5.3 Further analysis

Similarly to previous years, we provide several additional tables in the appendices to shed more light on the differences between the submitted systems.

Tables 8–9 show results factorized according to the different universal part of speech tags (UPOS) in the mention heads. Table 8 contains results on datasets where all entities without any mention with a given UPOS as head were deleted. Table 9 contains results on datasets where all mentions without a given UPOS as head were deleted, so these results may be a bit misleading because e.g. the PRON column does not consider all pronominal coreference, but only pronoun-to-pronoun coreference. An entity with one pronoun and one noun mention is excluded from this table (because it becomes a singleton after deleting noun or pronoun mentions and singletons are excluded from the evaluation in these tables).

Tables 10–13 show various statistics on the entities and mentions in a concatenation of all the test sets. Note that such statistics are mostly influenced by larger datasets.

Table 14 shows the distribution of error types based on the methodology of Kummerfeld and Klein (2013) and reveals that even systems with similar final F1 scores have different strengths and weaknesses.

6 Conclusions and Future Work

The paper summarizes the 2024 edition of the shared task on multilingual coreference resolution. Given that it is the third edition already, let us explore some generalizations.

First, the set of covered languages keeps growing: 11 languages in 2022, 13 languages in 2023, and 16 languages in 2024. Maintaining the pace of adding a few new languages each year seems realistic in the near future.

Second, in terms of the number of participating systems, the picture is mixed: 8 systems (5 teams) in 2022, 9 systems (7 teams) in 2023, and 6 systems (4 teams) in 2024. The relatively limited amount of participating teams can be partially attributed to the fact that the coreference resolution community is much smaller than e.g. the dependency parsing community. But still, it is an open question why the shared task has not attracted more coreference research teams.

Third, although there is a great variance in performance both among individual systems and across languages, the ordering of the systems remains relatively stable. However, it is not straightforward to quantify the growth of the state of the art along the individual shared task's editions; comparing simply the absolute values of the primary score would not make sense. The main reason is that the data collection gradually became bigger and more diverse (e.g., by including typologically different languages, with different scripts and different data sizes). At the same time, the task itself differed slightly too, moving closer to real-world scenarios (by not providing the participants with gold morphosyntactic annotation and gold zero mentions in the input), which makes the task harder too.

One of the possible approaches to isolating the state-of-the-art growth trend is to use the baseline system's performance as the point of reference because the baseline's architecture remained unchanged throughout the three years. The winner system outperformed the baseline's primary score by 21 % relative in 2022, by 31 % relative in 2023, and by 39 % relative in 2024. This indicates that the task of multilingual coreference resolution is still in a quickly progressing phase. We believe that the existence of this shared task series was one of the most influential factors behind this growth.

For future iterations of this shared task, we plan to provide a sequence-to-sequence (text-to-text) format for the training, evaluation and testing data. This new format will be designed to simplify the use of large language models (LLMs) like GPT, LLaMA, or Claude for the coreference resolution task.

The text-to-text format is particularly well suited for prompting approaches, which have shown significant promise in various NLP tasks. By offering data in this format, we aim to encourage more diverse approaches to the problem, potentially leading to novel solutions and improved performance.

We will release this new data format alongside the existing CoNLL-U format, giving participants the flexibility to choose the most suitable format for their systems.

Acknowledgements

This work has been supported by Charles University Research Centre program No. 24/SSH/009, Ministry of Education, Youth, and Sports of the Czech Republic, Project No. LM2023062 LINDAT/CLARIAH-CZ, Grant No. SGS-2022-016 Advanced methods of data processing and analysis, and the Grant 20-16819X (LUSyD) of the Czech Science Foundation (GAČR). We thank all the participants of the shared task for participating and for providing brief descriptions of their systems. We also thank anonymous reviewers for very useful remarks.

References

Amit Bagga and Breck Baldwin. 1998. Algorithms for scoring coreference chains. In *Proceedings of The First International Conference on Language Resources and Evaluation Workshop on Linguistics Coreference*, pages 563–566.

David Bamman, Olivia Lewke, and Anya Mansoor. 2019. An annotated dataset of coreference in english literature. *ArXiv*, abs/1912.01140.

BBN Technologies. 2006. *Co-reference Guidelines for English OntoNotes*.

Peter Bourgonje and Manfred Stede. 2020. The Potsdam Commentary Corpus 2.2: Extending Annotations for Shallow Discourse Parsing. In *Proceedings of the 12th Language Resources and Evaluation Conference*, pages 1061–1066, Marseille, France. European Language Resources Association.

Zewen Chi, Li Dong, Furu Wei, Nan Yang, Saksham Singhal, Wenhui Wang, Xia Song, Xian-Ling Mao, Heyan Huang, and Ming Zhou. 2021. InfoXLM: An information-theoretic framework for cross-lingual language model pre-training. In *Proceedings of the 2021 Conference of the North American Chapter of the Association for Computational Linguistics: Human Language Technologies*, pages 3576–3588, Online. Association for Computational Linguistics.

Alexis Conneau, Kartikay Khandelwal, Naman Goyal, Vishrav Chaudhary, Guillaume Wenzek, Francisco Guzmán, Edouard Grave, Myle Ott, Luke Zettlemoyer, and Veselin Stoyanov. 2020. Unsupervised cross-lingual representation learning at scale. In *Proceedings of the 58th Annual Meeting of the Association for Computational Linguistics*, pages 8440–8451, Online. Association for Computational Linguistics.

Pascal Denis and Jason Baldridge. 2009. Global joint models for coreference resolution and named entity classification. *Procesamiento del lenguaje natural*, 42.

Ning Ding, Shengding Hu, Weilin Zhao, Yulin Chen, Zhiyuan Liu, Hai-Tao Zheng, and Maosong Sun. 2021. Openprompt: An open-source framework for prompt-learning. *arXiv preprint arXiv:2111.01998*.

Vladimir Dobrovolskii. 2021. Word-level coreference resolution. In *Proceedings of the 2021 Conference on Empirical Methods in Natural Language Processing*, pages 7670–7675, Online and Punta Cana, Dominican Republic. Association for Computational Linguistics.

Jan Hajič, Eduard Bejček, Jaroslava Hlaváčová, Marie Mikulová, Milan Straka, Jan Štěpánek, and Barbora Štěpánková. 2020. Prague Dependency Treebank - Consolidated 1.0. In *Proceedings of the 12th International Conference on Language Resources and Evaluation (LREC 2020)*, pages 5208–5218, Marseille, France. European Language Resources Association.

Dag Trygve Truslew Haug and Marius L. Jøhndal. 2008. Creating a Parallel Treebank of the Old Indo-European Bible Translations. In *Proceedings of the second workshop on language technology for cultural heritage data (LaTeCH 2008)*.

Jonathan K. Kummerfeld and Dan Klein. 2013. Error-driven analysis of challenges in coreference resolution. In *Proceedings of the 2013 Conference on Empirical Methods in Natural Language Processing*, pages 265–277, Seattle, Washington, USA. Association for Computational Linguistics.

Frédéric Landragin. 2021. Le corpus Democrat et son exploitation. Présentation. *Langages*, 224:11–24.

Ekaterina Lapshinova-Koltunski, Christian Hardmeier, and Pauline Krielke. 2018. ParCorFull: a Parallel Corpus Annotated with Full Coreference. In *Proceedings of the Eleventh International Conference on Language Resources and Evaluation (LREC 2018)*, Miyazaki, Japan. European Language Resources Association.

Kenton Lee, Luheng He, Mike Lewis, and Luke Zettlemoyer. 2017. End-to-end neural coreference resolution. In *Proceedings of the 2017 Conference on Empirical Methods in Natural Language Processing*, pages 188–197, Copenhagen, Denmark. Association for Computational Linguistics.

Xiaoqiang Luo. 2005. On coreference resolution performance metrics. In *Proceedings of the Conference on Human Language Technology and Empirical Methods in Natural Language Processing*, HLT 2005, pages 25–32. Association for Computational Linguistics.

Petter Mæhlum, Dag Haug, Tollef Jørgensen, Andre Kåsen, Anders Nøklestad, Egil Rønningstad, Per Erik Solberg, Erik Velldal, and Lilja Øvrelid. 2022. NARC–Norwegian anaphora resolution corpus. In *Proceedings of the Fifth Workshop on Computational Models of Reference, Anaphora and Coreference*, pages 48–60, Gyeongju, Korea. Association for Computational Linguistics.

Ritwik Mishra, Pooja Desur, Rajiv Ratn Shah, and Ponnurangam Kumaraguru. 2024. Multilingual coreference resolution in low-resource South Asian languages. In *Proceedings of the 2024 Joint International Conference on Computational Linguistics, Language Resources and Evaluation (LREC-COLING 2024)*, pages 11813–11826, Torino, Italia. ELRA and ICCL.

Nafise Sadat Moosavi and Michael Strube. 2016. Which Coreference Evaluation Metric Do You Trust? A Proposal for a Link-based Entity Aware Metric. In *Proceedings of the 54th Annual Meeting of the Association for Computational Linguistics (Volume 1: Long Papers)*, pages 632–642, Berlin, Germany. Association for Computational Linguistics.

Anna Nedoluzhko, Michal Novák, Silvie Cinková, Marie Mikulová, and Jiří Mírovský. 2016. Coreference in Prague Czech-English Dependency Treebank. In *Proceedings of the Tenth International Conference on Language Resources and Evaluation (LREC 2016)*, pages 169–176, Portorož, Slovenia. European Language Resources Association.

Anna Nedoluzhko, Michal Novák, Martin Popel, Zdeněk Žabokrtský, Amir Zeldes, and Daniel Zeman. 2022. CorefUD 1.0: Coreference meets Universal Dependencies. In *Proceedings of the Thirteenth Language Resources and Evaluation Conference*, pages 4859–4872, Marseille, France. European Language Resources Association.

Maciej Ogrodniczuk, Katarzyna Glowińska, Mateusz Kopeć, Agata Savary, and Magdalena Zawisławska. 2013. Polish Coreference Corpus. In *Human Language Technology. Challenges for Computer Science and Linguistics — 6th Language and Technology Conference (LTC 2013), Revised Selected Papers*, volume 9561 of *Lecture Notes in Computer Science*, pages 215–226. Springer.

Maciej Ogrodniczuk, Katarzyna Głowińska, Mateusz Kopeć, Agata Savary, and Magdalena Zawisławska. 2015. *Coreference in Polish: Annotation, Resolution and Evaluation*. Walter De Gruyter.

Tuğba Pamay and Gülşen Eryiğit. 2018. Turkish Coreference Resolution. In *2018 Innovations in Intelligent Systems and Applications (INISTA)*, pages 1–7.

Tuğba Pamay and Gülşen Eryiğit. 2024. Enhancing Turkish Coreference Resolution: Insights from deep learning, dropped pronouns, and multilingual transfer learning. *Computer Speech & Language*, 89.

Sameer Pradhan, Xiaoqiang Luo, Marta Recasens, Eduard Hovy, Vincent Ng, and Michael Strube. 2014. Scoring Coreference Partitions of Predicted Mentions: A Reference Implementation. In *Proceedings of the 52nd Annual Meeting of the Association for Computational Linguistics (Volume 2: Short Papers)*, pages 30–35, Baltimore, Maryland. Association for Computational Linguistics.

Sameer Pradhan, Alessandro Moschitti, Nianwen Xue, Olga Uryupina, and Yuchen Zhang. 2012. CoNLL-2012 Shared Task: Modeling Multilingual Unrestricted Coreference in OntoNotes. In *Joint Conference on EMNLP and CoNLL - Shared Task*, pages 1–40, Jeju Island, Korea. Association for Computational Linguistics.

Ondřej Pražák and Miloslav Konopik. 2022. End-to-end multilingual coreference resolution with mention head prediction. In *Proceedings of the CRAC 2022 Shared Task on Multilingual Coreference Resolution*, pages 23–27, Gyeongju, Republic of Korea. Association for Computational Linguistics.

Ondřej Pražák, Miloslav Konopík, and Jakub Sido. 2021. Multilingual coreference resolution with harmonized annotations. In *Proceedings of the International Conference on Recent Advances in Natural Language Processing (RANLP 2021)*, pages 1119–1123, Held Online. INCOMA Ltd.

Marta Recasens and Eduard H. Hovy. 2011. BLANC: Implementing the Rand index for coreference evaluation. *Natural Language Engineering*, 17(4):485–510.

Marta Recasens, Lluís Màrquez, Emili Sapena, M. Antònia Martí, Mariona Taulé, Véronique Hoste, Massimo Poesio, and Yannick Versley. 2010. SemEval-2010 task 1: Coreference resolution in multiple languages. In *Proceedings of the 5th International Workshop on Semantic Evaluation*, pages 1–8, Uppsala, Sweden. Association for Computational Linguistics.

Marta Recasens and M. Antònia Martí. 2010. AnCora-CO: Coreferentially Annotated Corpora for Spanish and Catalan. *Language Resources and Evaluation*, 44(4):315–345.

Milan Straka and Jana Straková. 2022. ÚFAL CorPipe at CRAC 2022: Effectivity of Multilingual Models for Coreference Resolution. In *Proceedings of the CRAC 2022 Shared Task on Multilingual Coreference Resolution*, pages 28–37. Association for Computational Linguistics.

Daniel G. Swanson, Bryce D. Bussert, and Francis Tyers. 2024. Towards named-entity and coreference annotation of the Hebrew Bible. In *Proceedings of the Third Workshop on Language Technologies for Historical and Ancient Languages (LT4HALA) @ LREC-COLING-2024*, pages 36–40, Torino, Italia. ELRA and ICCL.

Mariona Taulé, M. Antònia Martí, and Marta Recasens. 2008. AnCora: Multilevel Annotated Corpora for Catalan and Spanish. In *Proceedings of the Sixth International Conference on Language Resources and Evaluation (LREC 2008)*, Marrakech, Morocco. European Language Resources Association.

Svetlana Toldova, Anna Roytberg, Alina Ladygina, Maria Vasilyeva, Ilya Azerkovich, Matvei Kurzukov, G. Sim, D.V. Gorshkov, A. Ivanova, Anna Nedoluzhko, and Yulia Grishina. 2014. Evaluating Anaphora and Coreference Resolution for Russian. In *Komp'juternaja lingvistika i intellektual'nye tehnologii. Po materialam ezhegodnoj Mezhdunarodnoj konferencii Dialog*, pages 681–695.

Don Tuggener. 2014. Coreference resolution evaluation for higher level applications. In *Proceedings of the 14th Conference of the European Chapter of the Association for Computational Linguistics, volume 2: Short Papers*, pages 231–235, Gothenburg, Sweden. Association for Computational Linguistics.

Noémi Vadász. 2022. Building a Manually Annotated Hungarian Coreference Corpus: Workflow and Tools. In *Proceedings of the Fifth Workshop on Computational Models of Reference, Anaphora and Coreference*, pages 38–47, Gyeongju, Korea. Association for Computational Linguistics.

Marc Vilain, John Burger, John Aberdeen, Dennis Connolly, and Lynette Hirschman. 1995. A Model-Theoretic Coreference Scoring Scheme. In *Sixth Message Understanding Conference (MUC-6): Proceedings of a Conference Held in Columbia, Maryland, November 6-8, 1995.*

Veronika Vincze, Klára Hegedűs, Alex Sliz-Nagy, and Richárd Farkas. 2018. SzegedKoref: A Hungarian Coreference Corpus. In *Proceedings of the Eleventh International Conference on Language Resources and Evaluation (LREC 2018)*, Miyazaki, Japan. European Language Resources Association.

C. Walker and Linguistic Data Consortium. 2005. *ACE 2005 Multilingual Training Corpus*. LDC corpora. Linguistic Data Consortium.

Linting Xue, Noah Constant, Adam Roberts, Mihir Kale, Rami Al-Rfou, Aditya Siddhant, Aditya Barua, and Colin Raffel. 2021. mT5: A massively multilingual pre-trained text-to-text transformer. In *Proceedings of the 2021 Conference of the North American Chapter of the Association for Computational Linguistics: Human Language Technologies*, pages 483–498, Online. Association for Computational Linguistics.

Juntao Yu, Sopan Khosla, Nafise Sadat Moosavi, Silviu Paun, Sameer Pradhan, and Massimo Poesio. 2022. The Universal Anaphora Scorer. In *Proceedings of the Language Resources and Evaluation Conference*, pages 4873–4883, Marseille, France. European Language Resources Association.

Juntao Yu, Michal Novák, Abdulrahman Aloraini, Nafise Sadat Moosavi, Silviu Paun, Sameer Pradhan, and Massimo Poesio. 2023. The Universal Anaphora Scorer 2.0. In *Proceedings of the 15th International Conference on Computational Semantics*, pages 183–194, Nancy, France. Association for Computational Linguistics.

Zdeněk Žabokrtský, Miloslav Konopík, Anna Nedoluzhko, Michal Novák, Maciej Ogrodniczuk, Martin Popel, Ondřej Pražák, Jakub Sido, and Daniel Zeman. 2023. Findings of the second shared task on multilingual coreference resolution. In *Proceedings of the CRAC 2023 Shared Task on Multilingual Coreference Resolution*, pages 1–18, Singapore. Association for Computational Linguistics.

Amir Zeldes. 2017. The GUM Corpus: Creating Multilayer Resources in the Classroom. *Language Resources and Evaluation*, 51(3):581–612.

Voldemaras Žitkus and Rita Butkienė. 2018. Coreference Annotation Scheme and Corpus for Lithuanian Language. In *Fifth International Conference on Social Networks Analysis, Management and Security, SNAMS 2018, Valencia, Spain, October 15-18, 2018*, pages 243–250. IEEE.

Zdeněk Žabokrtský, Miloslav Konopík, Anna Nedoluzhko, Michal Novák, Maciej Ogrodniczuk, Martin Popel, Ondřej Pražák, Jakub Sido, Daniel

Zeman, and Yilun Zhu. 2022. Findings of the Shared Task on Multilingual Coreference Resolution. In *Proceedings of the CRAC 2022 Shared Task on Multilingual Coreference Resolution*, pages 1–17, Gyeongju, Korea. Association for Computational Linguistics.

A CorefUD 1.2 Details

Ancient Greek	PROIEL	grc_proiel	(Haug and Jøhndal, 2008)
Ancient Hebrew	PTNK	hbo_ptnk	(Swanson et al., 2024)
Catalan	AnCora	ca_ancora	(Taulé et al., 2008; Recasens and Martí, 2010)
Czech	PCEDT	cs_pcedt	(Nedoluzhko et al., 2016)
Czech	PDT	cs_pdt	(Hajič et al., 2020)
English	GUM	en_gum	(Zeldes, 2017)
English	ParCorFull	en_parcorfull	(Lapshinova-Koltunski et al., 2018)
English	LitBank	en_litbank	(Bamman et al., 2019)
French	Democrat	fr_democrat	(Landragin, 2021)
German	ParCorFull	de_parcorfull	(Lapshinova-Koltunski et al., 2018)
German	PotsdamCC	de_potsdam	(Bourgonje and Stede, 2020)
Hungarian	KorKor	hu_korkor	(Vadász, 2022)
Hungarian	SzegedKoref	hu_szeged	(Vincze et al., 2018)
Lithuanian	LCC	lt_lcc	(Žitkus and Butkienė, 2018)
Norwegian	Bokmål NARC	no_bokmaalnarc	(Mæhlum et al., 2022)
Norwegian	Nynorsk NARC	no_nynorsknarc	(Mæhlum et al., 2022)
Old Church Slavonic	PROIEL	cu_proiel	(Haug and Jøhndal, 2008)
Polish	PCC	pl_pcc	(Ogrodniczuk et al., 2013, 2015)
Russian	RuCor	ru_rucor	(Toldova et al., 2014)
Spanish	AnCora	es_ancora	(Taulé et al., 2008; Recasens and Martí, 2010)
Turkish	ITCC	tr_itcc	(Pamay and Eryiğit, 2018)

B CoNLL results by head UPOS

system	NOUN	PRON	PROPN	DET	ADJ	VERB	ADV	NUM
CorPipe-2stage	**70.23**	**69.93**	**76.23**	49.20	42.45	33.64	28.70	**38.39**
CorPipe	69.06	69.66	75.07	52.35	**42.99**	**35.02**	**33.04**	37.49
CorPipe-single	66.69	66.90	71.72	**53.18**	36.57	30.95	27.74	37.06
Ondfa	66.79	66.54	69.18	49.08	33.61	26.90	29.98	34.18
BASELINE-GZ	48.49	55.58	52.18	32.39	25.05	11.34	17.67	28.09
BASELINE	46.77	49.73	51.51	33.08	23.65	10.83	16.89	26.66
DFKI-CorefGen	30.49	33.97	31.54	18.50	10.11	2.72	8.56	10.57
RitwikmishraFix	27.31	29.17	31.28	17.76	12.07	7.59	6.25	8.57
Ritwikmishra	15.92	16.67	16.64	12.97	8.41	5.49	4.81	6.48

Table 8: CoNLL F1 score (head-match) evaluated only on entities with heads of a given UPOS. In both the gold and prediction files we deleted some entities before running the evaluation. We kept only entities with at least one mention with a given head UPOS (universal part of speech tag). For the purpose of this analysis, if the head node had deprel=flat children, their UPOS tags were considered as well, so for example in "Mr./NOUN Brown/PROPN" both NOUN and PROPN were taken as head UPOS, so the entity with this mention will be reported in both columns NOUN and PROPN. Otherwise, the CoNLL F1 scores are the same as in the primary metric, i.e. an unweighted average over all datasets, head-match, without singletons. Note that when distinguishing entities into events and nominal entities, the VERB column can be considered as an approximation of the performance on events. One of the limitations of this approach is that copula is not treated as head in the Universal Dependencies, so, e.g., phrase *She is nice* is not considered for the VERB column, but for the ADJ column (head of the phrase is *nice*).

system	NOUN	PRON	PROPN	DET	ADJ	VERB	ADV	NUM
CorPipe-2stage	**60.43**	**60.00**	**61.33**	**49.58**	**47.09**	**47.07**	**48.05**	**46.82**
CorPipe	59.37	58.26	60.22	47.00	44.31	43.99	44.53	44.31
CorPipe-single	55.50	55.25	54.64	43.08	40.28	39.77	39.77	39.91
Ondfa	57.22	54.58	56.04	44.21	41.65	41.28	41.34	41.42
BASELINE-GZ	38.50	45.45	39.85	28.88	26.23	26.06	26.29	26.06
BASELINE	37.30	39.46	39.46	27.84	25.52	25.12	25.56	25.30
DFKI-CorefGen	20.99	26.05	22.71	16.68	14.24	14.04	14.46	14.20
RitwikmishraFix	25.26	26.08	25.53	18.06	17.01	16.27	16.43	16.49
Ritwikmishra	14.29	14.05	12.74	10.38	9.56	8.89	9.12	9.13

Table 9: CoNLL F1 score (head-match) evaluated only on mentions with heads of a given UPOS. In both the gold and prediction files we deleted some mentions before running the evaluation. We kept only mentions with a given head UPOS (again considering also deprel=flat children).

C Statistics of the submitted systems on concatenation of all test sets

The systems are sorted alphabetically in tables in this section. The predictions of the Ritwikmishra system were not valid CoNLL-U and thus are excluded in these tables (the script collecting the statistics failed), see the numbers of the RitwikmishraFix system instead.

	entities				distribution of lengths				
system	total	per 1k	length		1	2	3	4	5+
	count	words	max	avg.	[%]	[%]	[%]	[%]	[%]
gold	47,680	102	509	2.2	61.0	21.9	6.8	3.3	7.0
BASELINE	15,168	33	154	3.9	0.0	57.4	17.0	7.7	17.9
BASELINE-GZ	15,534	33	154	3.9	0.0	57.4	17.1	7.8	17.7
CorPipe	49,943	107	288	2.1	62.1	20.5	7.1	3.3	7.0
CorPipe-2stage	49,980	107	299	2.1	62.4	20.7	6.9	3.2	6.8
CorPipe-single	50,179	108	573	2.1	62.4	20.2	7.0	3.4	7.1
DFKI-CorefGen	33,188	71	191	2.1	70.3	14.9	5.7	2.6	6.4
Ondfa	48,739	105	203	2.1	63.5	20.1	6.4	3.1	6.9
RitwikmishraFix	6,703	14	637	3.5	29.2	37.3	13.0	6.0	14.5

Table 10: Statistics on coreference entities. The total number of entities and the average number of entities per 1000 tokens in the running text. The maximum and average entity "length", i.e., the number of mentions in the entity. Distribution of entity lengths (singletons have length = 1). The four best systems (CorPipe* and Ondfa) have the statistics similar to the gold data (although they all slightly overgenerate, i.e. predicts more entities than in the gold data). The remaining systems undergenerate and the two baselines and RitwikmishraFix also predict on average longer entities (i.e. with more mentions) than in the gold data.

system	mentions				distribution of lengths					
	total	per 1k	length		0	1	2	3	4	5+
	count	words	max	avg.	[%]	[%]	[%]	[%]	[%]	[%]
gold	74,305	159	100	2.9	12.6	44.0	18.1	7.3	3.6	14.3
BASELINE	59,859	128	27	2.1	14.8	47.4	17.8	6.6	3.1	10.2
BASELINE-GZ	61,277	131	27	2.1	14.8	47.0	17.9	6.8	3.1	10.5
CorPipe	74,076	159	100	2.9	12.5	44.6	18.1	7.3	3.5	14.0
CorPipe-2stage	73,239	157	116	2.8	12.4	44.9	18.1	7.3	3.5	13.7
CorPipe-single	75,350	162	145	2.8	12.9	44.3	18.1	7.4	3.5	13.8
DFKI-CorefGen	44,731	96	65	2.6	0.0	57.4	20.5	7.0	3.3	11.8
Ondfa	71,531	153	22	1.1	12.3	82.1	2.1	1.1	0.5	2.0
RitwikmishraFix	21,458	46	16	1.5	0.0	66.5	22.6	7.0	2.1	1.8

Table 11: Statistics on non-singleton mentions. The total number of mentions and the average number of mentions per 1000 words of running text. The maximum and average mention length, i.e., the number of nonempty nodes (words) in the mention. Distribution of mention lengths (zeros have length = 0). The four best systems (CorPipe* and Ondfa) generate a similar number of non-singleton mentions as in the gold data (although last year, the three best systems overgenerated mentions). The average length of mentions predicted by Ondfa is notably lower than in the gold data because Ondfa predicted single-word mentions only in all datasets except for cs_pcedt and lt_lcc. No system predicts long mentions (4 and 5+ words) more frequently than in the gold data, although CorPipe is near to the gold distribution.

system	mentions				distribution of lengths					
	total	per 1k	length		0	1	2	3	4	5+
	count	words	max	avg.	[%]	[%]	[%]	[%]	[%]	[%]
gold	29,087	62	81	3.4	1.8	30.8	24.7	13.7	7.5	21.6
BASELINE	0	0	0	0.0	0.0	0.0	0.0	0.0	0.0	0.0
BASELINE-GZ	0	0	0	0.0	0.0	0.0	0.0	0.0	0.0	0.0
CorPipe	31,030	67	163	3.5	2.0	29.7	25.7	13.8	7.6	21.4
CorPipe-2stage	31,164	67	163	3.5	2.1	29.9	25.9	13.9	7.5	20.7
CorPipe-single	31,309	67	93	3.5	1.7	29.8	25.6	13.9	7.6	21.4
DFKI-CorefGen	23,342	50	71	2.9	0.0	35.5	28.5	13.4	6.7	15.9
Ondfa	30,971	66	19	1.0	2.1	96.3	0.5	0.3	0.2	0.5
RitwikmishraFix	1,959	4	13	1.8	0.0	45.6	40.0	10.4	2.6	1.4

Table 12: Statistics on singleton mentions. See the caption of Table 11 for details. The two baseline systems do not attempt to predict singletons at all. Interestingly, last year all systems predicted 7–9 times less singletons than in the gold data. This year, the four best systems (CorPipe* and Ondfa) predict slightly more singletons than in the gold data. Note that singletons are not annotated in all the (gold) datasets.

system	mention type [%]			distribution of head UPOS [%]									
	w/empty	w/gap	non-tree	NOUN	PRON	PROPN	DET	ADJ	VERB	ADV	NUM	_	other
gold	14.7	0.7	1.6	40.2	28.6	14.7	6.7	2.5	2.2	1.1	0.5	2.8	0.6
BASELINE	15.9	0.0	1.6	36.6	20.3	15.6	7.5	2.3	0.9	1.1	0.3	14.9	0.5
BASELINE-GZ	16.0	0.0	1.7	37.1	31.4	15.4	7.5	2.2	1.0	1.1	0.4	3.4	0.5
CorPipe	14.0	0.0	1.8	40.4	19.0	14.9	6.9	2.3	1.8	1.1	0.4	12.5	0.7
CorPipe-2stage	13.8	0.0	1.9	40.3	19.1	15.0	6.9	2.4	1.6	1.1	0.5	12.5	0.6
CorPipe-single	14.4	0.0	1.8	40.5	18.8	14.7	6.8	2.3	1.7	1.1	0.5	12.9	0.6
DFKI-CorefGen	0.0	0.0	3.9	40.7	27.8	16.3	10.0	1.4	1.0	1.2	0.4	0.0	1.2
Ondfa	12.6	0.0	0.2	40.6	19.2	14.8	6.9	2.5	1.6	1.2	0.5	12.3	0.5
RitwikmishraFix	0.1	0.0	0.8	28.9	31.3	27.7	5.7	1.8	2.3	0.8	0.8	0.0	0.6

Table 13: Detailed statistics on non-singleton mentions. The left part of the table shows the percentage of: mentions with at least one empty node (w/empty); mentions with at least one gap, i.e. discontinuous mentions (w/gap); and non-treelet mentions, i.e. mentions not forming a connected subgraph (catena) in the dependency tree (non-tree). Note that these three types of mentions may be overlapping. We can see that none of the systems attempts to predict discontinuous mentions. DFKI-CorefGen has a notably higher percentage (3.9%) of non-treelet mention spans. The right part of the table shows the distribution of mentions based on the universal part-of-speech tag (UPOS) of the head word. Note that this distribution has to be interpreted with the total number of non-singleton mentions predicted (as reported in Table 11) in mind. For example, 31.4% of non-singleton mentions predicted by BASELINE-GZ are pronominal (head=PRON), while there are only 28.6% of pronominal non-singleton mentions in the gold data. However, BASELINE-GZ predicts actually less pronominal non-singleton mentions (61277*31.4%=19241) than in the gold data (74305*28.6%=21251). Note that the same word may be assigned a different UPOS tag in the predicted and gold data (in case of empty nodes or if the gold data includes manual annotation). The empty UPOS tag (_) is present only in the empty nodes and none of the systems attempts to predict the actual UPOS tag of empty nodes (they all keep the empty tag from the baseline predictor of empty nodes, although about 78% of the empty nodes in the gold devset are pronouns).

System	Span Errors	Extra Entity Errors	Extra Mention Errors	Conflated Entities Errors	Missing Entity Errors	Missing Mention Errors	Divided Entity Errors
BASELINE							
BASELINE-GZ							
CorPipe							
CorPipe-2stage							
CorPipe-single							
DFKI-CorefGen							
Ondfa							
RitwikmishraFix							
Most Errors	22120	2711	10709	3570	15095	20088	2493

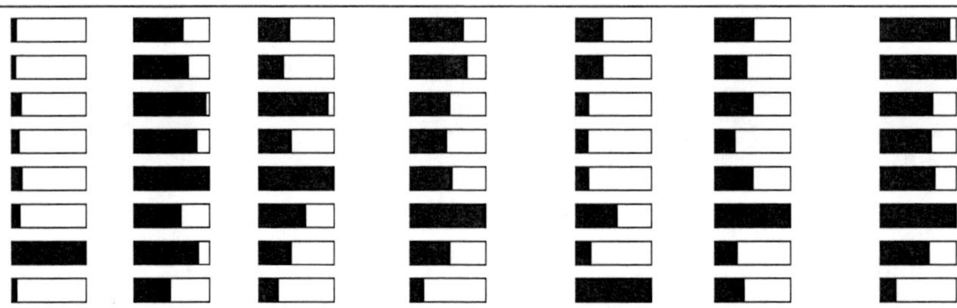

Table 14: Distribution of error types based on the methodology of Kummerfeld and Klein (2013). By gradually transforming the prediction files into gold data, we can classify several types of transformations, which then map to types of errors. The number in the last row is the maximal total number of errors (summed over all datasets) of the given type, that any of the predictions made. The partially filled bars display the percentage of the maximal number of errors in the given column. The table should be viewed column-wise to compare individual prediction systems. The Span Errors column shows once again that Ondfa does not attempt to predict the whole span (only the head). CorPipe-single and CorPipe are the two worst systems in the number of Extra Entity and Extra Mention errors. However, according to Table 5, these systems have recall as high as precision, while other systems (e.g. Ondfa) have recall much lower; thus the high number of extra entities and mentions seems to be a good trade-off. Interestingly, CorPipe-2stage has the same recall as CorPipe (in almost all metric), but a slightly higher precision in Table 5, which corresponds to the relatively lower number of Extra Entity and especially Extra Mention errors.

CorPipe at CRAC 2024: Predicting Zero Mentions from Raw Text

Milan Straka
Charles University, Faculty of Mathematics and Physics
Institute of Formal and Applied Linguistics
Malostranské nám. 25, Prague, Czech Republic
straka@ufal.mff.cuni.cz

Abstract

We present CorPipe 24, the winning entry to the CRAC 2024 Shared Task on Multilingual Coreference Resolution. In this third iteration of the shared task, a novel objective is to also predict empty nodes needed for zero coreference mentions (while the empty nodes were given on input in previous years). This way, coreference resolution can be performed on raw text. We evaluate two model variants: a two-stage approach (where the empty nodes are predicted first using a pretrained encoder model and then processed together with sentence words by another pretrained model) and a single-stage approach (where a single pretrained encoder model generates empty nodes, coreference mentions, and coreference links jointly). In both settings, CorPipe surpasses other participants by a large margin of 3.9 and 2.8 percent points, respectively. The source code and the trained model are available at https://github.com/ufal/crac2024-corpipe.

1 Introduction

The CRAC 2024 Shared Task on Multilingual Coreference Resolution (Novák et al., 2024) is a third iteration of a shared task, whose goal is to accelerate research in multilingual coreference resolution (Žabokrtský et al., 2023, 2022). This year, the shared task features 21 datasets in 15 languages from the CorefUD 1.2 collection (Popel et al., 2024).

Compared to the last year—apart from 4 new datasets in 3 languages—a novel task is to predict the so-called *empty nodes* (according to the Universal Dependencies terminology; Nivre et al. 2020). The empty nodes can be considered "slots" that can be part of coreference mentions even if not being present on the surface level of a sentence. The empty nodes are particularly useful in pro-drop languages (like Slavic and Romance languages), where pronouns are sometimes dropped from a sentence when they can be inferred, for example by verb morphology, like in the Czech example *"Řekl, že nepřijde"*, translated as *"(He) said that (he) won't come"*.

We present CorPipe 24, an improved version of our system submitted in last years (Straka, 2023; Straka and Straková, 2022). We evaluate two variants of the system. In a two-stage variant, the empty nodes are first predicted by a baseline system utilizing a pretrained language encoder model;[1] then, the predicted empty nodes are, together with the input words, processed by original CorPipe using another pretrained encoder. In comparison, a single-stage variant employs a single pretrained encoder model, which predicts the empty nodes, coreference mentions, and coreference links jointly.

Our contributions are as follows:

- We present the winning entry to the CRAC 2024 Shared Task on Multilingual Coreference Resolution, surpassing other participants by a large margin of 3.9 and 2.8 percent points with a two-stage and a single-stage variant, respectively.
- We compare the two-stage and the single-stage settings, showing that the two-stage system outperforms the single-stage system by circa one percent points, both in the regular and the ensembled setting.
- Apart from the CorefUD 1.2, we evaluate the CorPipe performance also on OntoNotes (Pradhan et al., 2013), a frequently used English dataset.
- The CorPipe 24 source code is available at https://github.com/ufal/crac2024-corpipe under an open-source license. The two-stage and the single-stage models are also released, under the CC BY-NC-SA license.

[1] Our implementation of the baseline system was available to all shared task participants in case they do not want to predict the empty nodes themselves.

Proceedings of the Seventh Workshop on Computational Models of Reference, Anaphora and Coreference (CRAC 2024), pages 97–106
November 15, 2024. ©2024 Association for Computational Linguistics

2 Related Work

Traditionally, coreference resolution was solved by first predicting the coreference mentions and subsequently performing coreference linking (clustering) of the predicted mentions. However, in recent years, the end-to-end approach (Lee et al., 2017, 2018; Joshi et al., 2019, 2020) has become more popular. Indeed, the baseline of the CRAC 2022, 2023, and 2024 shared tasks (Pražák et al., 2021) follow this approach, as well as the second-best solution of CRAC 2022 (Pražák and Konopik, 2022) and the third-best solution of CRAC 2023.

The end-to-end approach has been improved by Kirstain et al. (2021) not to explicitly construct the span representations, and by Dobrovolskii (2021) to consider only the word level, ignoring the span level altogether during coreference linking. Simultaneously, Wu et al. (2020) formulated coreference resolution in a question answering setting, reaching superior results at the expense of substantially more model predictions and additional question-answering data.

The current state-of-the-art results on OntoNotes (Pradhan et al., 2013), a frequently used English coreference resolution dataset, are achieved by autoregressive models with billions of parameters: Liu et al. (2022) propose a specialized autoregressive system, while Bohnet et al. (2023) employ a text-to-text paradigm. However, both these architectures must call the trained model repeatedly to process a single sentence.

3 Two-stage CorPipe

The two-stage variant of CorPipe processes input in two steps: first, empty nodes are predicted using the baseline system available to all shared task participants; then, the coreference resolution is performed using CorPipe. This approach is very similar to the last year's edition of the CRAC Shared Task, where the empty nodes were already given on input. Therefore, the last year's version CorPipe 23 (Straka, 2023) can be used.

3.1 Empty Nodes Baseline

The baseline for predicting empty nodes generates for each empty node only the minimum amount of information needed: the word order position defined by an input word that the empty node should follow (the word order position determines the position of the empty node in coreference mentions) and the dependency head and the dependency re-

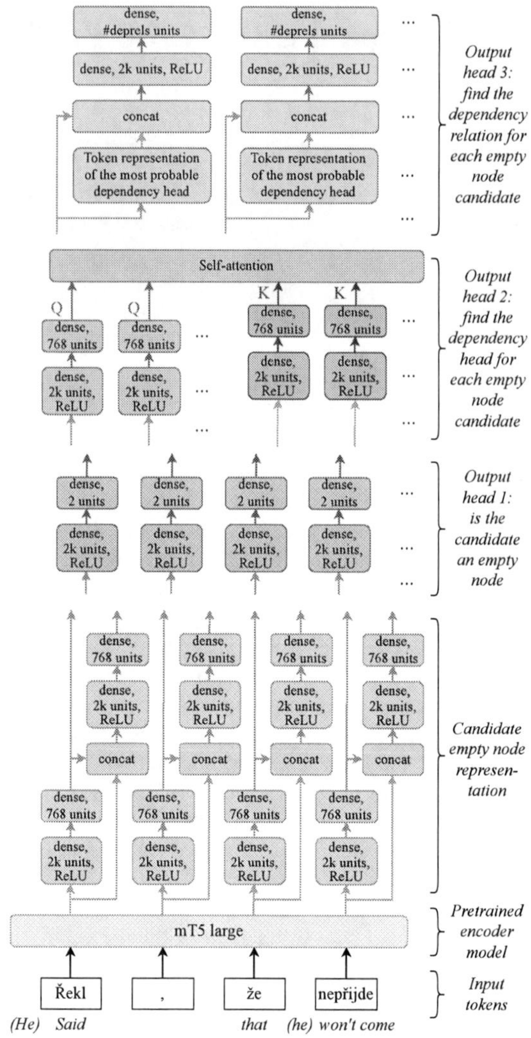

Figure 1: The system architecture of the empty node prediction baseline. Every ReLU activation is followed by a dropout layer layer with a dropout rate of 50%.

lation of the empty node (required by the empty node matching during evaluation); no forms or lemmas are predicted even if provided in the training data. The baseline predicts the empty nodes non-autoregressively, generating at most two empty nodes for every input word; the input word becomes the dependency head of the predicted empty node.

The overview of the architecture is displayed in Figure 1. The input words of a single sentence are first tokenized, passed through a pretrained mT5-large encoder (Conneau et al., 2020), and each input word is represented by the embedding of its first subword. Then, the candidate for empty nodes are generated, two per word. The first candidate is generated by passing the input word representations through a 2k-unit dense layer with ReLU activation, a dropout layer, and a 768-unit dense layer. The second candidate is generated by concatenating the first candidate representation with the input word representation and passing the result through an analogous dense-dropout-dense module. Then, three heads are attached, each first passing its input by a ReLU-activated 2k-unit dense layer and dropout: (1) a classification layer deciding whether a candidate actually generates an empty node, (2) a self-attention layer choosing the word order position (i.e., an input word to follow) for every candidate, and (3) a dependency relation classification layer, which processes the candidate representation concatenated with the representation of the word most likely according to the word-order prediction head. Please refer to the released source code for further details.

We train a single multilingual model using the AdaFactor optimizer (Shazeer and Stern, 2018) for 20 epochs, each epoch consisting of 5 000 batches containing 64 sentences each. The learning rate first linearly increases from zero to the peak learning rate of 1e-5 in the first epoch, and then decays to zero in the rest of the training according to a cosine schedule (Loshchilov and Hutter, 2017). Each sentence is sampled from the combination of all corpora containing empty nodes (see Table 1), proportionally to the square root of the word size of the corresponding corpus. The model is trained for 19 hours using a single L40 GPU with 48GB RAM.

The source code is released under the MPL license at `https://github.com/ufal/crac2024_zero_nodes_baseline`, together with the complete set of used hyperparameters. Furthermore, the trained model is available under the CC BY-SA-NC license at `https://www.kaggle.com/models/ufal-mff/crac2024_zero_nodes_baseline/`. Finally, the development sets and the test sets of the CorefUD 1.2 datasets with predicted empty nodes are available to all participants of the CRAC 2024 Shared Task.

The intrinsic performance of the baseline system on the development sets of CorefUD 1.2 is presented in Table 1. A predicted empty node is considered correct if it has correct dependency head, dependency relation, and also the word order.

Treebank	Precison	Recall	F_1-score
ca	92.32	91.01	91.66
cs_pcedt	78.22	59.84	67.81
cs_pdt	81.47	71.56	76.19
cu	81.61	78.76	80.16
es	92.04	91.92	91.98
grc	90.29	86.58	88.39
hu_korkor	74.68	60.21	66.67
hu_szegedkoref	91.93	89.52	90.71
pl	87.50	91.61	89.51
tr	79.05	93.81	85.80

Table 1: Empty nodes prediction baseline performance on the development sets of CorefUD 1.2 corpora containing empty nodes. An empty node is evaluated as correct if it has the correct dependency head, dependency relation, and word order.

3.2 Coreference Resolution

With the empty nodes predicted by the baseline, we can directly employ the CorPipe 23 from the last year of the shared task (Straka, 2023). The overview of the architecture is presented in Figure 2 and briefly described; for more details, please refer to the original paper.

CorPipe processes the document one sentence at a time; to provide as much context as possible, as many preceding and at most 50 following tokens are additionally added on input, to the limit of the maximum segment size (512 or 2 560). The words are first passed through a pretrained language encoder model. Then, coreference mentions are predicted using an extension of BIO encoding capable of representing possibly overlapping set of spans. Finally, each predicted mention is represented as a concatenation of its first and last word, and the most likely entity link (possibly to itself) of every mention is generated using a self-attention layer.

During training, the maximum segment size is always 512; however, during inference, we consider also larger segment size of 2 560 for the mT5 models, which support larger segment sizes due to their relative positional embeddings.

3.3 Training

We train the coreference resolution system analogously to the CorPipe 23 training procedure (Straka, 2023). Three model variants are trained, based on either mT5-large, mT5-xl (Xue et al., 2021), or InfoXLM-large (Chi et al., 2021). For every variant, 7 multilingual models are trained on a combination of all corpora, differing only in random initialization. The sentences are sampled proportionally to the square root of the word size of the corresponding corpora.

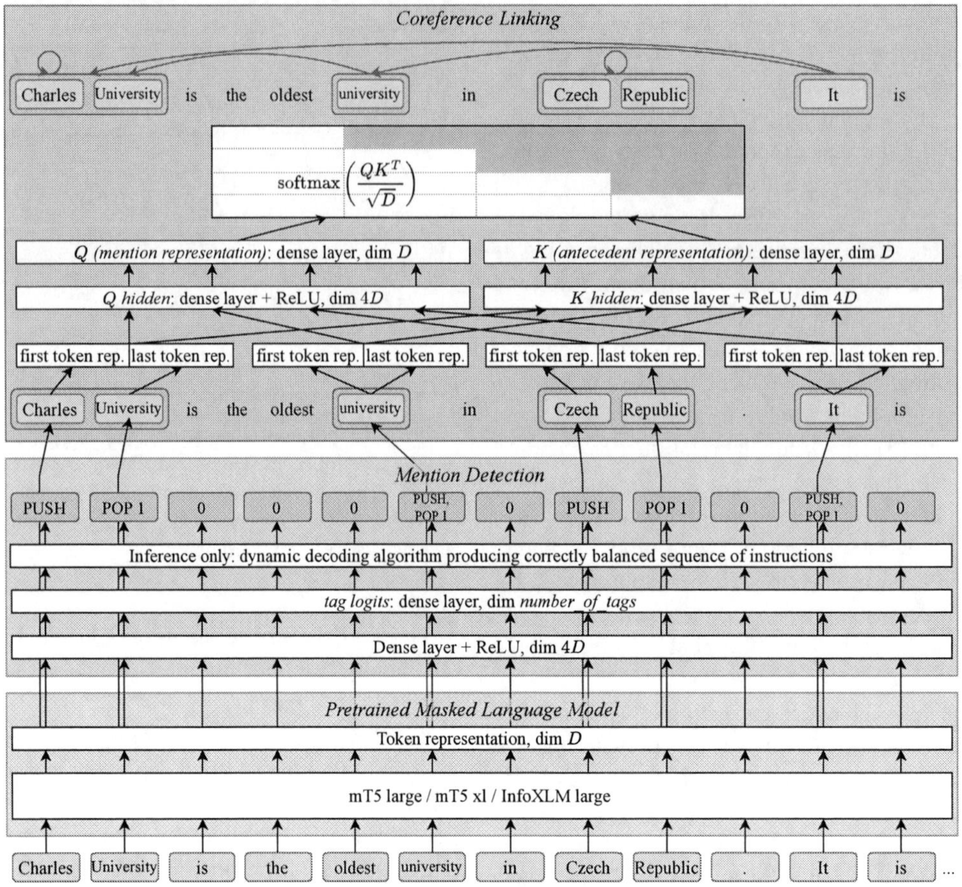

Figure 2: The CorPipe 23 model architecture introduced in Straka (2023).

Every model is trained for 15 epochs, each epoch consisting of 10k batches. The mT5-large and InfoXLM-large variants use the batch size of 8 and train for 14 hours on a single A100 with 40GB RAM; the mT5-xl variant employ the batch size of 12 and train for 17 hours on 4 A100s with 40GB RAM each. The mT5 variants are trained using the AdaFactor optimizer (Shazeer and Stern, 2018) and the InfoXLM-large is trained using Adam (Kingma and Ba, 2015). The learning rate is first increased from 0 to the peak learning rate in the first 10% of the training and then decayed according to the cosine schedule (Loshchilov and Hutter, 2017); we employ the peak learning rates of 6e-4, 5e-4, and 2e-5 for the mT5-large, mT5-xl, and InfoXLM-large encoders, respectively.

For each model, we keep the checkpoints after every epoch, obtaining a pool of $3 \cdot 7 \cdot 15$ checkpoints. From this pool, we select three configurations: (1) a single checkpoint reaching the highest development score on all the corpora, (2) a best-performing checkpoint for every corpus according to its development set, (3) an ensemble of 5 best-performing checkpoints for every corpus.

4 Single-stage CorPipe

While the two-stage variant is full-fledged, allowing coreference mention to be composed of any continual sequence of input words and empty nodes, it requires two large pretrained encoders, which makes the model about twice as big and twice as slow compared to a single model.

Therefore, we also propose a single-stage variant, with the goal of using just a single pretrained language encoder model. For simplicity's sake, we restrict the model in the following way: if a coreference mention contains an empty node, the whole mention must be just this single empty node. In other words, a coreference mention either does not contain empty nodes, or it is just a single empty node. Note that this restriction does not decrease the score under the head-match metric because only the mention head is used during score computation.

With the described restriction, we no longer need

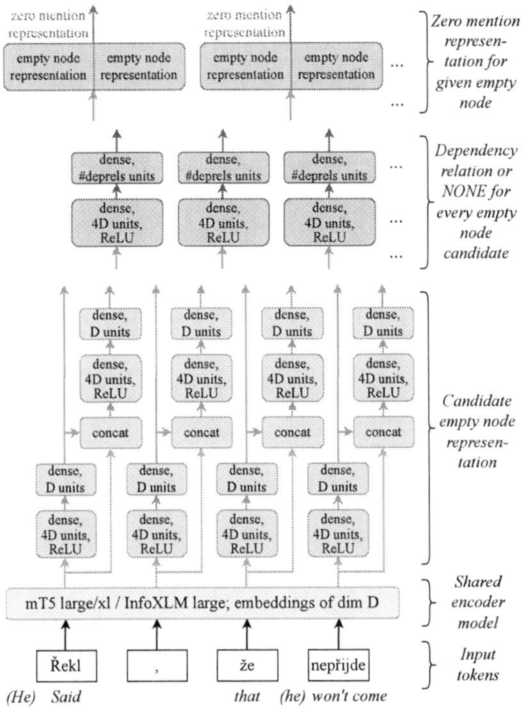

Figure 3: The changes in the CorPipe 23 architecture when empty nodes and zero mentions are generated jointly with mention detection and coreference linking.

to distinguish between empty nodes and zero coreference mentions; therefore, the single-stage model predicts only such empty nodes that are also zero coreference mentions. Finally, the word order of an empty node is no longer needed for evaluation; as a result, we no longer predict the word order explicitly and place the empty node after its dependency head in the word order.

In Figure 3, we visualize the proposed changes to the CorPipe architecture needed to support joint empty nodes/zero mentions prediction. Analogously to the empty nodes baseline described in Section 3.1, we start by generating two candidate empty nodes representations from every input word representation. We then run a classification head for every candidate, which either predicts `NONE` when the candidate should not generate an empty node, or it predicts the dependency relation of the generated empty node. Finally, to construct a representation of a zero coreference mention, we concatenate the empty node representation to itself because the empty node is both the first and the last word of the mention. The coreference linking then proceeds as before, just using a concatenation of surface mentions and zero mentions.

The single-stage model is trained analogously to the two-stage model. The only differences are that (1) we pass only the input words through the pretrained language encoder model, (2) we add the loss of the classifier predicting dependency relation or `NONE` to the other losses (using simple addition), and (3) we concatenate the zero mention representations to the surface mention representations before the coreference linking step.

We closely follow the training procedure of the two-stage model described in Section 3.3. Notably, we also consider the same three pretrained encoders, train the same number of models using the same optimizers and learning rates, and select the same three configurations (single best-performing checkpoint, per-corpus best checkpoint, and a per-corpus 3-model ensemble).[2]

5 Shared Task Results

In the shared task, each team was allowed to submit at most three systems. We submitted the following configurations:

- **CorPipe-single**, the large-sized single-stage model checkpoint achieving the best development performance across all corpora;
- **CorPipe**, the best-performing 3-model single-stage ensemble for every corpus;
- **CorPipe-2stage**, the best-performing 5-model two-stage ensemble for every corpus.

The first configuration corresponds to a real-world deployment scenario, where a single model would be used for all corpora; the latter configurations are the highest performing single-stage approach (**CorPipe**, Section 4) and two-stage approach (**CorPipe-2stage**, Section 3).

The official results of the shared task's primary metric are presented in Table 2. All our submissions outperform other participant systems, even if **CorPipe-single** only slightly. Overall, the ensembled single-stage variant outperforms other participants by 2.8 percent points, and the ensembled two-stage variant outperforms other participants by 3.9 percent points.

Table 3 shows the results of the submitted systems using four metrics. Apart from the primary head-match metric, our three submissions outperform all others also when evaluated using exact match and with singletons. When considering par-

[2]We only managed to use a 3-model ensemble before the shared task deadline, while we use a 5-model ensemble for the two-stage variant.

System	Avg	ca	cs pced	cs pdt	cu	de parc	de pots	en gum	en litb	en parc	es	fr	grc	hbo	hu kork	hu szeg	lt	no bokm	no nyno	pl	ru	tr
CorPipe-2stage	**73.90** **1**	82.2 2	**74.8** **1**	**77.2** **1**	**61.6** **1**	69.5 3	71.8 2	**75.7** **1**	**79.6** **1**	68.9 2	**82.5** **1**	68.2 2	**71.3** **1**	**72.0** **1**	63.2 2	**70.0** **1**	**75.8** **1**	**79.8** **1**	**78.0** **1**	**78.5** **1**	**83.2** **1**	**68.2** **1**
CorPipe	72.75 2	81.0 3	73.7 2	75.8 2	60.7 2	**71.7** **1**	71.5 3	74.6 2	79.1 2	**69.8** **1**	81.0 3	**68.8** **1**	68.5 2	70.9 2	60.3 3	68.1 3	75.8 2	79.5 2	77.5 2	77.0 2	83.1 2	59.4 3
CorPipe-single	70.18 3	80.4 4	72.8 3	74.8 4	57.1 3	61.6 4	67.0 4	74.4 3	78.1 3	58.6 3	79.8 4	67.9 3	66.0 3	67.2 3	60.1 4	67.3 4	75.2 3	78.9 3	76.6 3	75.2 4	81.2 3	53.4 4
Ondfa	69.97 4	**82.5** **1**	70.8 4	75.8 3	55.0 4	71.4 2	**71.9** **1**	70.5 4	74.2 4	55.6 4	81.9 2	62.7 4	61.6 4	61.6 4	**64.9** **1**	69.3 2	72.0 4	74.5 4	72.1 4	76.3 3	80.5 4	64.5 2
BASELINE†	53.16 5	68.3 5	64.1 5	63.8 5	24.5 5	47.2 5	55.6 5	63.2 5	63.5 5	33.1 6	69.6 5	53.6 5	28.8 5	24.6 6	35.1 5	54.5 5	62.0 5	65.0 5	63.7 5	66.2 5	65.8 5	44.0 5
DFKI-CorefGen	33.38 6	34.8 6	32.9 6	30.9 6	22.5 6	23.1 7	45.9 7	35.5 6	46.6 6	32.7 7	37.8 6	36.3 7	25.9 6	38.0 5	23.5 7	33.9 6	42.7 7	37.9 6	35.7 6	27.2 6	47.8 7	9.7 6
Ritwikmishra	16.47 7	0.0 7	0.0 7	0.0 7	6.8 7	25.4 6	48.9 6	0.0 7	0.0 7	53.1 5	0.0 7	43.7 6	5.6 7	0.1 7	33.4 6	30.3 7	44.8 6	0.0 7	0.0 7	0.0 7	53.9 6	0.0 7

Table 2: Official results of CRAC 2024 Shared Task on the test set (CoNLL score in %). The system † is described in Pražák et al. (2021); the rest in Novák et al. (2024).

System	Head-match	Partial-match	Exact-match	With Singletons
CorPipe-2stage	**73.90** **1**	**72.19** **1**	**69.86** **1**	**75.65** **1**
CorPipe	72.75 2	70.30 2	68.36 2	74.65 2
CorPipe-single	70.18 3	68.02 4	66.07 3	71.96 3
Ondfa	69.97 4	69.82 3	40.25 5	70.67 4
BASELINE	53.16 5	52.48 5	51.26 4	46.45 5
DFKI-CorefGen	33.38 6	32.36 6	30.71 6	38.65 6
Ritwikmishra	16.47 7	16.65 7	14.16 7	15.42 7

Table 3: Official results of CRAC 2024 Shared Task on the test set with various metrics in %.

tial match, the CorPipe-single is outperformed by the system Ondfa, assumingly because it limits the predicted mentions just to their heads, which slightly improves partial match but severely deteriorates exact match.

6 Ablations Experiments

6.1 CorefUD 1.2

Table 4 contains quantitative analysis of ablation experiments on the CorefUD 1.2 test set. In Table 4.A, we compare the three configurations of the single-stage model variant. Selecting the best-performing checkpoint for every corpus increases the overall score by 1.4 percent points, while making the model up to 21 times larger. Further addition of ensembling improves the score by another 1.2 percent points.

The same comparison is available also for the two-stage model variant in Table 4.B. We observe a similar trend of 1.2 percent points increase for the best per-corpus checkpoint approach and further 1.4 percent points increase during ensembling.

The sections C, D, and E of Table 4 compare the individual checkpoint configurations of the single-stage and the two-stage models. We observe that the effect of the two-stage model is 0.9–1.1 percent point increase in all checkpoint configuration. We hypothesize that two factors contribute to the better performance of the two-stage variant: first, the empty node representation is computed by a pretrained encoder, allowing better contextualization of the empty node representation. Second, the mentions with empty nodes are represented in the original form, i.e., the mentions can contain any sequence of input words and empty nodes, while the single-stage variant represent zero mentions always by a single empty node.

It would be interesting to evaluate the two-stage variant using the gold empty nodes instead of predicted empty nodes to quantify the decrease of the score caused by empty node prediction errors. Unfortunately, such an evaluation is not supported by the shared task evaluation platform. Nevertheless, Table 4.F at least shows that such a difference for the provided baseline coreference system (Pražák et al., 2021) is 1.4 percent points, as reported by the shared task organizers.

Finally, meaningful comparison of the shared task results between this year and the last year is very difficult to carry out. While many corpora have changed only marginally and the evaluation metric is the same (so the results are reasonably comparable), other corpora have changed substantially (especially Polish and Turkish). Even so, we provide numerical comparison of this year's and last year's best systems in Table 4.G. This year's results are slightly worse than in the last year, on

System	Avg	ca	cs pced	cs pdt	cu	de parc	de pots	en gum	en litb	en parc	es	fr	grc	hbo	hu kork	hu szeg	lt	no bokm	no nyno	pl	ru	tr
A) CorPipe Single-stage Variants																						
Single model	70.18	80.4	72.8	74.8	57.1	61.6	67.0	74.4	78.1	58.6	79.8	67.9	66.0	67.2	60.1	67.3	75.2	78.9	76.6	75.2	81.2	53.4
Per-corpus best	+1.42	−0.4	−0.6	−0.2	+2.5	+7.2	+2.7	−0.4	−0.6	+10.4	−0.0	−0.3	+1.0	+1.5	**+2.5**	−1.6	**+0.9**	−0.4	+0.9	−0.2	−0.2	+5.1
Per-corpus ensemble	**+2.62**	**+0.6**	**+0.9**	**+1.0**	**+3.6**	**+10.1**	**+4.5**	**+0.2**	**+1.0**	**+11.2**	**+1.2**	**+0.9**	**+2.5**	**+3.7**	+0.2	**+0.8**	+0.6	**+0.6**	**+0.9**	**+1.8**	**+1.9**	**+6.0**
B) CorPipe Two-stage Variants																						
Single model	71.32	81.0	74.2	75.9	56.7	64.7	66.4	74.7	78.2	57.9	81.2	67.2	67.6	64.2	61.6	67.9	**77.7**	77.6	77.3	77.4	81.3	67.0
Per-corpus best	+1.18	+0.1	+0.4	+0.3	+3.7	**+4.9**	+0.6	−1.2	+0.5	+10.2	+0.7	−0.2	+1.3	+5.6	−0.2	−0.6	−4.2	+2.2	+0.4	+0.5	−0.1	+0.2
Per-corpus ensemble	**+2.58**	**+1.2**	**+0.6**	**+1.3**	**+4.9**	+4.8	**+5.4**	**+1.0**	**+1.4**	**+11.1**	**+1.3**	**+1.0**	**+3.7**	**+7.8**	**+1.6**	**+2.1**	−1.9	**+2.2**	**+0.7**	**+1.1**	**+1.9**	**+1.2**
C) Comparison of Single-model Variants																						
Single-stage	70.18	80.4	72.8	74.8	**57.1**	61.6	**67.0**	74.4	78.1	**58.6**	79.8	**67.9**	66.0	**67.2**	60.1	67.3	75.2	**78.9**	76.6	75.2	81.2	53.4
Two-stage	**+1.12**	**+0.6**	**+1.4**	**+1.1**	−0.4	**+3.1**	−0.6	**+0.3**	**+0.1**	−0.7	**+1.5**	−0.7	**+1.6**	−3.0	**+1.5**	**+0.6**	**+2.5**	−1.3	**+0.7**	**+2.2**	**+0.1**	**+13.6**
D) Comparison of Per-corpus Best Variants																						
Single-stage	71.59	80.0	72.2	74.6	59.6	68.8	**69.7**	**74.0**	77.5	**69.0**	79.7	**67.6**	67.0	68.7	**62.6**	65.7	**76.1**	78.5	77.5	75.0	81.0	58.5
Two-stage	**+0.91**	**+1.1**	**+2.4**	**+1.6**	**+0.8**	**+0.8**	−2.7	−0.5	**+1.2**	−0.9	**+2.2**	−0.6	**+1.9**	**+1.1**	−1.2	**+1.6**	−2.6	**+1.3**	**+0.2**	**+2.9**	**+0.2**	**+8.8**
E) Comparison of Per-corpus Ensemble Variants																						
Single-stage	72.75	81.0	73.7	75.8	60.7	**71.7**	71.5	74.6	79.1	**69.8**	81.0	**68.8**	68.5	70.9	60.3	68.1	75.8	79.5	77.5	77.0	83.1	59.4
Two-stage	**+1.15**	**+1.2**	**+1.1**	**+1.4**	**+0.9**	−2.2	**+0.3**	**+1.1**	**+0.5**	−0.8	**+1.5**	−0.6	**+2.8**	**+1.1**	**+2.9**	**+1.9**	**+0.0**	**+0.2**	**+0.5**	**+1.5**	**+0.1**	**+8.8**
F) Comparison of the Baseline System with Gold and Predicted Empty Nodes																						
Predicted empty nodes	53.16	68.3	64.1	63.8	24.5	**47.2**	**55.6**	**63.2**	**63.5**	**33.1**	69.6	**53.6**	28.8	**24.6**	35.1	54.5	**62.0**	**65.0**	**63.7**	66.2	**65.8**	44.0
Gold empty nodes	**+1.44**	**+1.3**	**+4.8**	**+2.4**	**+3.1**	0.0	0.0	0.0	0.0	0.0	**+1.0**	0.0	**+3.1**	0.0	**+6.5**	**+0.1**	0.0	0.0	0.0	**+0.8**	0.0	**+7.2**
G) Comparison of the CorPipe-2stage Ensemble System and the CRAC23 Best Results																						
CorPipe-2stage, ensemble	74.55	82.2	74.8	77.2	—	69.5	71.8	75.7	—	68.9	82.5	68.2	—	—	63.2	70.0	75.8	**79.8**	78.0	78.5	**83.2**	**68.2**
CorPipe23, CRAC23	**+0.65**	**+1.0**	**+4.5**	**+2.3**	—	**+1.5**	**+0.0**	**+0.8**	—	**+2.1**	**+1.0**	**+0.4**	—	—	**+6.3**	**+0.8**	**+0.6**	−0.2	**+1.0**	**+1.3**	−0.6	−11.7

Table 4: Ablations experiments on the CorefUD 1.2 test set (CoNLL score in %).

Paper	Model	#model calls	∅, ELMO, base PLM	large PLM ~350M	xl PLM ~3B	xxl PLM ~11B
(Lee et al., 2017)	e2e	1	$67.2_{\varnothing}$			
(Lee et al., 2018)	e2e	1	70.4_{ELMO}			
(Lee et al., 2018)	c2f	1	73.0_{ELMO}			
(Joshi et al., 2019)	c2f	1	73.9_{BERT}	76.9_{BERT}		
(Joshi et al., 2020)	c2f	1		79.6_{SpanBERT}		
(Kirstain et al., 2021)	s2e	1		$80.3_{\mathrm{Longformer}}$		
(Otmazgin et al., 2023)	s2e/LingMess	1		$81.4^{\text{+additional annotations}}_{\mathrm{Longformer}}$		
(Dobrovolskii, 2021)	WL	1		81.0_{RoBERTa}		
(D'Oosterlinck et al., 2023)	WL/CAW	1		81.6_{RoBERTa}		
(Liu et al., 2022)	ASP	$\mathcal{O}(n)$	76.6_{T5}	79.3_{T5}	82.3_{T0}	82.5_{FlanT5}
(Bohnet et al., 2023)	seq2seq	$\mathcal{O}(n)$			$78.0^{\mathrm{dev}}_{\mathrm{mT5}}$	83.3_{mT5}
(Wu et al., 2020)	CorefQA	$\mathcal{O}(n)$	$79.9^{\text{+QA data}}_{\mathrm{SpanBERT}}$	$83.1^{\text{+QA data}}_{\mathrm{SpanBERT}}$		
This paper	CorPipe	1		80.7_{T5}	82.0_{FlanT5}	
This paper	CorPipe	1		77.2_{mT5}	78.9_{mT5}	

Table 5: Comparison of CorPipe and other models on OntoNotes, using pretrained models of various size.

average by 0.65 percent points, but the difference is quite comparable to the effect of predicted/gold empty nodes on the baseline system (cf. Table 4.F).

6.2 OntoNotes

To compare the performance of the CorPipe architecture to English state-of-the-art models, we train also models on the OntoNotes dataset (Pradhan et al., 2013). The dataset does not contain any empty nodes, so we use the last year's training setup, with the two exceptions: we also consider pretrained English-specific encoders T5 (Raffel et al., 2020) and Flan-T5 (Chung et al., 2024), and we consider larger segment size during training (up to 1 536 subwords).

The results are presented in Table 5. In the large-sized setting, CorPipe outperforms all models except models utilizing additional data (Otmazgin et al., 2023; Wu et al., 2020) and models utilizing the word-level approach (Dobrovolskii, 2021; D'Oosterlinck et al., 2023).[3] In the xl-sized settings, our model is 0.3 percent points below the state of the art of Liu et al. (2022); notably, CorPipe outperforms the state of the art system Bohnet et al. (2023) and all large-sized models not using additional training data. Unfortunately, we did not have the resources to train an xxl-sized model.

7 Conclusions

We presented CorPipe 24, the winning entry to the CRAC 2024 Shared Task on Multilingual Coreference Resolution (Novák et al., 2024). Our system has two variants, either first predicting empty nodes using a pretrained language encoder model and then performing coreference resolution employing another pretrained model, or predicting the empty nodes jointly with mention detection and coreference linking. Both variants surpass other participants by a large margin of 3.9 and 2.8 percent points, respectively. The source code and the trained model are available at `https://github.com/ufal/crac2024-corpipe`.

Acknowledgements

This work has been supported by the Grant Agency of the Czech Republic, project EXPRO LUSyD (GX20-16819X), and has been using data provided by the LINDAT/CLARIAH-CZ Research Infrastructure (`https://lindat.cz`) of the Ministry of Education, Youth and Sports of the Czech Republic (Project No. LM2023062).

Limitations

The presented system has demonstrated its performance only on a limited set of 15 languages, and heavily depends on a large pretrained model, transitively receiving its limitations and biases.

Training with the mT5-large pretrained model requires a 40GB GPU, which we consider affordable; however, training with the mT5-xl pretrained model needs nearly four times as much GPU memory.

[3]We are of course curious to find out how the word-level approach works on the CorefUD dataset. Nevertheless, we hypothesize that on some of the CorefUD corpora it might not work well because the mention heads in these corpora are considerably less unique than in OntoNotes.

References

Bernd Bohnet, Chris Alberti, and Michael Collins. 2023. Coreference resolution through a seq2seq transition-based system. *Transactions of the Association for Computational Linguistics*, 11:212–226.

Zewen Chi, Li Dong, Furu Wei, Nan Yang, Saksham Singhal, Wenhui Wang, Xia Song, Xian-Ling Mao, Heyan Huang, and Ming Zhou. 2021. InfoXLM: An information-theoretic framework for cross-lingual language model pre-training. In *Proceedings of the 2021 Conference of the North American Chapter of the Association for Computational Linguistics: Human Language Technologies*, pages 3576–3588, Online. Association for Computational Linguistics.

Hyung Won Chung, Le Hou, Shayne Longpre, Barret Zoph, Yi Tay, William Fedus, Yunxuan Li, Xuezhi Wang, Mostafa Dehghani, Siddhartha Brahma, Albert Webson, Shixiang Shane Gu, Zhuyun Dai, Mirac Suzgun, Xinyun Chen, Aakanksha Chowdhery, Alex Castro-Ros, Marie Pellat, Kevin Robinson, Dasha Valter, Sharan Narang, Gaurav Mishra, Adams Yu, Vincent Zhao, Yanping Huang, Andrew Dai, Hongkun Yu, Slav Petrov, Ed H. Chi, Jeff Dean, Jacob Devlin, Adam Roberts, Denny Zhou, Quoc V. Le, and Jason Wei. 2024. Scaling instruction-finetuned language models. *Journal of Machine Learning Research*, 25(70):1–53.

Alexis Conneau, Kartikay Khandelwal, Naman Goyal, Vishrav Chaudhary, Guillaume Wenzek, Francisco Guzmán, Edouard Grave, Myle Ott, Luke Zettlemoyer, and Veselin Stoyanov. 2020. Unsupervised cross-lingual representation learning at scale. In *Proceedings of the 58th Annual Meeting of the Association for Computational Linguistics*, pages 8440–8451, Online. Association for Computational Linguistics.

Vladimir Dobrovolskii. 2021. Word-level coreference resolution. In *Proceedings of the 2021 Conference on Empirical Methods in Natural Language Processing*, pages 7670–7675, Online and Punta Cana, Dominican Republic. Association for Computational Linguistics.

Karel D'Oosterlinck, Semere Kiros Bitew, Brandon Papineau, Christopher Potts, Thomas Demeester, and Chris Develder. 2023. CAW-coref: Conjunction-aware word-level coreference resolution. In *Proceedings of The Sixth Workshop on Computational Models of Reference, Anaphora and Coreference (CRAC 2023)*, pages 8–14, Singapore. Association for Computational Linguistics.

Mandar Joshi, Danqi Chen, Yinhan Liu, Daniel S. Weld, Luke Zettlemoyer, and Omer Levy. 2020. SpanBERT: Improving pre-training by representing and predicting spans. *Transactions of the Association for Computational Linguistics*, 8:64–77.

Mandar Joshi, Omer Levy, Luke Zettlemoyer, and Daniel Weld. 2019. BERT for coreference resolution: Baselines and analysis. In *Proceedings of the 2019 Conference on Empirical Methods in Natural Language Processing and the 9th International Joint Conference on Natural Language Processing (EMNLP-IJCNLP)*, pages 5803–5808, Hong Kong, China. Association for Computational Linguistics.

Diederik P. Kingma and Jimmy Ba. 2015. Adam: A method for stochastic optimization. In *3rd International Conference on Learning Representations, ICLR 2015, San Diego, CA, USA, May 7-9, 2015, Conference Track Proceedings*.

Yuval Kirstain, Ori Ram, and Omer Levy. 2021. Coreference resolution without span representations. In *Proceedings of the 59th Annual Meeting of the Association for Computational Linguistics and the 11th International Joint Conference on Natural Language Processing (Volume 2: Short Papers)*, pages 14–19, Online. Association for Computational Linguistics.

Kenton Lee, Luheng He, Mike Lewis, and Luke Zettlemoyer. 2017. End-to-end neural coreference resolution. In *Proceedings of the 2017 Conference on Empirical Methods in Natural Language Processing*, pages 188–197, Copenhagen, Denmark. Association for Computational Linguistics.

Kenton Lee, Luheng He, and Luke Zettlemoyer. 2018. Higher-order coreference resolution with coarse-to-fine inference. In *Proceedings of the 2018 Conference of the North American Chapter of the Association for Computational Linguistics: Human Language Technologies, Volume 2 (Short Papers)*, pages 687–692, New Orleans, Louisiana. Association for Computational Linguistics.

Tianyu Liu, Yuchen Eleanor Jiang, Nicholas Monath, Ryan Cotterell, and Mrinmaya Sachan. 2022. Autoregressive structured prediction with language models. In *Findings of the Association for Computational Linguistics: EMNLP 2022*, pages 993–1005, Abu Dhabi, United Arab Emirates. Association for Computational Linguistics.

Ilya Loshchilov and Frank Hutter. 2017. SGDR: Stochastic gradient descent with warm restarts. In *International Conference on Learning Representations*.

Joakim Nivre, Marie-Catherine de Marneffe, Filip Ginter, Jan Hajič, Christopher D. Manning, Sampo Pyysalo, Sebastian Schuster, Francis Tyers, and Daniel Zeman. 2020. Universal Dependencies v2: An evergrowing multilingual treebank collection. In *Proceedings of the Twelfth Language Resources and Evaluation Conference*, pages 4034–4043, Marseille, France. European Language Resources Association.

Michal Novák, Barbora Dohnalová, Miloslav Konopík, Anna Nedoluzhko, Martin Popel, Ondřej Pražák, Jakub Sido, Milan Straka, Zdeněk Žabokrtský, and Daniel Zeman. 2024. Findings of the Third Shared Task on Multilingual Coreference Resolution. In *Proceedings of The Seventh Workshop on Computational Models of Reference, Anaphora and Coreference (CRAC 2024)*, Miami, Florida, USA. Association for Computational Linguistics.

Shon Otmazgin, Arie Cattan, and Yoav Goldberg. 2023. LingMess: Linguistically informed multi expert scorers for coreference resolution. In *Proceedings of the 17th Conference of the European Chapter of the Association for Computational Linguistics*, pages 2752–2760, Dubrovnik, Croatia. Association for Computational Linguistics.

Martin Popel, Michal Novák, Zdeněk Žabokrtský, Daniel Zeman, Anna Nedoluzhko, Kutay Acar, David Bamman, Peter Bourgonje, Silvie Cinková, Hanne Eckhoff, Gülşen Cebiroğlu Eryiğit, Jan Hajič, Christian Hardmeier, Dag Haug, Tollef Jørgensen, Andre Kåsen, Pauline Krielke, Frédéric Landragin, Ekaterina Lapshinova-Koltunski, Petter Mæhlum, M. Antònia Martí, Marie Mikulová, Anders Nøklestad, Maciej Ogrodniczuk, Lilja Øvrelid, Tuğba Pamay Arslan, Marta Recasens, Per Erik Solberg, Manfred Stede, Milan Straka, Daniel Swanson, Svetlana Toldova, Noémi Vadász, Erik Velldal, Veronika Vincze, Amir Zeldes, and Voldemaras Žitkus. 2024. Coreference in universal dependencies 1.2 (CorefUD 1.2). LINDAT/CLARIAH-CZ digital library at the Institute of Formal and Applied Linguistics (ÚFAL), Faculty of Mathematics and Physics, Charles University.

Sameer Pradhan, Alessandro Moschitti, Nianwen Xue, Hwee Tou Ng, Anders Björkelund, Olga Uryupina, Yuchen Zhang, and Zhi Zhong. 2013. Towards robust linguistic analysis using OntoNotes. In *Proceedings of the Seventeenth Conference on Computational Natural Language Learning*, pages 143–152, Sofia, Bulgaria. Association for Computational Linguistics.

Ondřej Pražák and Miloslav Konopik. 2022. End-to-end multilingual coreference resolution with mention head prediction. In *Proceedings of the CRAC 2022 Shared Task on Multilingual Coreference Resolution*, pages 23–27, Gyeongju, Republic of Korea. Association for Computational Linguistics.

Ondřej Pražák, Miloslav Konopík, and Jakub Sido. 2021. Multilingual coreference resolution with harmonized annotations. In *Proceedings of the International Conference on Recent Advances in Natural Language Processing (RANLP 2021)*, pages 1119–1123, Held Online. INCOMA Ltd.

Colin Raffel, Noam Shazeer, Adam Roberts, Katherine Lee, Sharan Narang, Michael Matena, Yanqi Zhou, Wei Li, and Peter J. Liu. 2020. Exploring the limits of transfer learning with a unified text-to-text transformer. *Journal of Machine Learning Research*, 21(140):1–67.

Noam Shazeer and Mitchell Stern. 2018. Adafactor: Adaptive Learning Rates with Sublinear Memory Cost. In *Proceedings of the 35th International Conference on Machine Learning, ICML 2018, Stockholmsmässan, Stockholm, Sweden, July 10-15, 2018*, volume 80 of *Proceedings of Machine Learning Research*, pages 4603–4611. PMLR.

Milan Straka. 2023. ÚFAL CorPipe at CRAC 2023: Larger context improves multilingual coreference resolution. In *Proceedings of the CRAC 2023 Shared Task on Multilingual Coreference Resolution*, pages 41–51, Singapore. Association for Computational Linguistics.

Milan Straka and Jana Straková. 2022. ÚFAL CorPipe at CRAC 2022: Effectivity of multilingual models for coreference resolution. In *Proceedings of the CRAC 2022 Shared Task on Multilingual Coreference Resolution*, pages 28–37, Gyeongju, Republic of Korea. Association for Computational Linguistics.

Wei Wu, Fei Wang, Arianna Yuan, Fei Wu, and Jiwei Li. 2020. CorefQA: Coreference resolution as query-based span prediction. In *Proceedings of the 58th Annual Meeting of the Association for Computational Linguistics*, pages 6953–6963, Online. Association for Computational Linguistics.

Linting Xue, Noah Constant, Adam Roberts, Mihir Kale, Rami Al-Rfou, Aditya Siddhant, Aditya Barua, and Colin Raffel. 2021. mT5: A massively multilingual pre-trained text-to-text transformer. In *Proceedings of the 2021 Conference of the North American Chapter of the Association for Computational Linguistics: Human Language Technologies*, pages 483–498, Online. Association for Computational Linguistics.

Zdeněk Žabokrtský, Miloslav Konopik, Anna Nedoluzhko, Michal Novák, Maciej Ogrodniczuk, Martin Popel, Ondrej Prazak, Jakub Sido, and Daniel Zeman. 2023. Findings of the second shared task on multilingual coreference resolution. In *Proceedings of the CRAC 2023 Shared Task on Multilingual Coreference Resolution*, pages 1–18, Singapore. Association for Computational Linguistics.

Zdeněk Žabokrtský, Miloslav Konopík, Anna Nedoluzhko, Michal Novák, Maciej Ogrodniczuk, Martin Popel, Ondřej Pražák, Jakub Sido, Daniel Zeman, and Yilun Zhu. 2022. Findings of the shared task on multilingual coreference resolution. In *Proceedings of the CRAC 2022 Shared Task on Multilingual Coreference Resolution*, pages 1–17, Gyeongju, Republic of Korea. Association for Computational Linguistics.

End-to-end Multilingual Coreference Resolution with Headword Mention Representation

Ondřej Pražák and **Miloslav Konopík**

{ondfa,konopik}@kiv.zcu.cz

Department of Computer Science and Engineering,
NTIS – New Technologies for the Information Society,
Faculty of Applied Sciences, University of West Bohemia, Technická 8, 306 14 Plzeň
Czech Republic

Abstract

This paper describes our approach to the CRAC 2024 Shared Task on Multilingual Coreference Resolution. Our model is based on an end-to-end coreference resolution system. Apart from joined multilingual training, we improved our results with headword mention representation and training large model mT5-xxl through LORA. We provide an analysis of the performance of our model. Our system ended up in 4th place. Moreover, we reached the best performance on three datasets out of 21.

1 Introduction

Coreference resolution is the task of finding language expressions that refer to the same real-world entity (antecedent) within a given text. These coreferential expressions can either originate from a single sentence or be separated by one or more sentences. In some challenging cases, it is necessary to consider the entire document to determine whether two expressions refer to the same entity accurately. This task can be divided into two subtasks. Identify entity mentions and group them together according to the real-world entity they refer to. The task of coreference resolution is closely related to anaphora resolution – see (Sukthanker et al., 2020) to compare these two tasks.

This paper describes our approach to the CRAC 2024 Shared Task on Multilingual Coreference Resolution (Novák et al., 2024), which is the third edition of this shared task. The task is based on the CorefUD dataset (Nedoluzhko et al., 2022). The CorefUD corpus, currently at version 1.2, comprises 21 different datasets across 15 languages in a harmonized scheme. Table 1 shows basic statistics of the corpus As CorefUD is meant to be the extension of Universal Dependencies for coreference annotation, all the datasets in CorefUD are treebanks. In the current version of the dataset, all dependency relations were obtained from an automatic parser. The coreference annotation is built upon the dependencies. This means that the mentions are subtrees in the dependency tree and can be represented with the head. In fact, in some of the datasets, there are non-treelet mentions – those that do not form a single subtree. But even for these non-treelet mentions, a single headword is selected. Non-tree mentions arise because some datasets were not annotated in a treebank form - the annotators were asked to find mentions as continuous spans, and the syntactic information was added during the harmonization. Notable differences exist among the datasets. One of the most prominent ones is the presence of singletons. Singletons are clusters that contain only one mention; therefore, they are not part of any coreference relation, yet they are annotated as mentions. Please see Nedoluzhko et al. (2022) or Nedoluzhko et al. (2021) for details about the dataset. The task was simplified to predict only non-singleton mentions and group them into entity clusters.

For evaluation, the CorefUD scorer[1] is provided. The primary evaluation score is the CoNLL F_1 score with head matching and singletons excluded. In the CorefUD scorer, a system mention matches a gold mention only if they share the same headword.

Participants should also predict the empty nodes for zero mentions this year. In previous years (Žabokrtský et al., 2022; Žabokrtský et al., 2023), gold empty nodes were provided. However, the organizers provide a baseline for predicting empty nodes. Due to time limitations, we focused just on coreference resolution, and we used empty nodes predicted by a baseline system.

2 Related Work

Since many of the datasets in the CorefUD collection do not contain singletons annotation, we believe that the end-to-end approach is the best

[1] https://github.com/ufal/corefud-scorer

Proceedings of the Seventh Workshop on Computational Models of Reference, Anaphora and Coreference (CRAC 2024), pages 107–113
November 15, 2024.

CorefUD dataset	Total size				
	docs	sents	words	empty	singletons
Ancient_Greek-PROIEL	19	6,475	64,111	6,283	0,0%
Ancient_Hebrew-PTNK	40	1,161	28,485	0	57.9%
Catalan-AnCora	1550	16,678	488,379	6,377	74.6%
Czech-PDT	3165	49,428	834,721	33,086	35.3%
Czech-PCEDT	2312	49,208	1,155,755	45,158	1.4%
English-GUM	150	7,408	134,474	0	75%
English-LitBank	100	8,560	210,530	0	72.8%
English-ParCorFull	19	543	10,798	0	6.1%
French-Democrat	126	13,054	284,823	0	81.8%
German-ParCorFull	19	543	10,602	0	5.8%
German-PotsdamCC	176	2,238	33,222	0	76.5%
Hungarian-KorKor	94	1,351	24,568	1,988	0.9%
Hungarian-SzegedKoref	400	8,820	123,976	4,849	7.9%
Lithuanian-LCC	100	1,714	37,014	0	11.2%
Norwegian-BokmaalNARC	346	15,742	245,515	0	89.4%
Norwegian-NynorskNARC	394	12,481	206,660	0	88.7%
Old_Church_Slavonic-PROIEL	26	6,832	61,759	6,289	0,0%
Polish-PCC	1828	35,874	538,891	864	82.6%
Russian-RuCor	181	9,035	156,636	0	2.5%
Spanish-AnCora	1635	17,662	517,258	8,111	73.4%
Turkish-ITCC	24	4,733	55,341	0	1.0%

Table 1: Dataset Statistics

choice. On the other hand, the best system in the previous year (Straka, 2023) is a two-stage model using extended BIO schema for mention identification.

Most of the end-to-end approaches are built upon Lee et al. (2017) who originally proposed to go over all possible spans and classify coreferences directly on these spans. As our model is also based on this, we will describe more details later. Many modifications of this model have been proposed mainly focusing on better text encoding (span representation), model optimization and higher-order model (Lee et al., 2018; Joshi et al., 2019; Xu and Choi, 2020; Joshi et al., 2020).

Dobrovolskii (2021) proposed to reduce mention space be selecting a single word to represent each mention. They use the syntactic head as mention representative. They perform experiments on the English OntoNotes corpus. To reconstruct the original mentions, they use a CNN-based span predictor in a subsequent step after antecedent prediction.

Hu et al. (2022) proposed low-rank adaptation as one of the most common techniques for efficient fine-tuning by reducing the number of trainable parameters with factorization. The original idea to use this in Transformer fine-tuning comes from Adapters (Houlsby et al., 2019). The schema of LORA is shown in Figure 1. We reduce the number of trainable parameters by freezing the original model and adding a small layer between all fully connected layers. The first weight matrix is initialized randomly, and the second is set to zero to preserve the original output at the initial step. By reducing the number of trainable parameters, LoRA reduces memory requirements and prevents overfitting but preserves a lot of original computational capability since weights on every layer can be changed during finetuning.

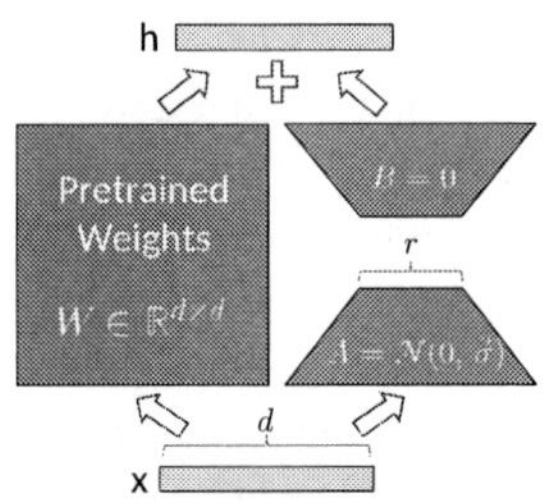

Figure 1: LoRA schema, taken from Hu et al. (2022)

Model	Pretrained params	New params
mBERT	180M	15M
XLM-R	555M	20M
mT5	5.7B	70-400M

Table 2: Number of trainable parameters of the models

3 Model

Our model builds on the official transformer-based end-to-end baseline (Pražák et al., 2021). It is based on the CRAC 2022 participating system (Pražák and Konopik, 2022) and its extension (Pražák and Konopík, 2024) with all the proposed modifications. The underlying neural end-to-end coreference resolution model was originally proposed by Lee et al. (2017). The model predicts the antecedents directly from all possible mention spans without a previous discrete decision about mentions. In the training phase, it maximizes the marginal log-likelihood of all correct antecedents:

$$J(D) = \log \prod_{i=1}^{N} \sum_{\hat{y} \in Y(i) \cap \text{GOLD}(i)} P(\hat{y}) \quad (1)$$

where GOLD(i) is the set of spans in the training data that are antecedents.

The model performs well on the OntoNotes dataset, where singletons are not annotated. We believe the model is optimal for the CorefUD dataset as well since some of the CorefUD datasets do not contain singletons. Moreover, the primary evaluation metric ignores singletons, so it does not matter that the model is not able to predict them. However, employing singletons in the model can improve mention identification capabilities of the model on the datasets where some singletons are annotated.

Here, we just describe the most significant extensions of the basic model. For a detailed description of all the extensions together with a deep analysis of their benefits, please refer to Pražák and Konopík (2024).

Employed Models We based our model on two encoders of different sizes; XLM Roberta large (Conneau et al., 2020), and mT5-xxl (Xue et al., 2021) (only the encoder part). Both models are significantly larger than the original BERT (Devlin et al., 2018) The number of parameters is provided in Table 2.

Joined Model Pretraining As you can see from Table 2, approximately 17 million parameters are trained from scratch for XLM-R and 70M for mT5 (the upper bound 400M is including adapter weights which are technically trained from scratch, but the original pretrained parameters makes them much easier to train). For smaller datasets, training so many random parameters is practically impossible. To solve this issue, we first pre-train the model on the joined dataset and then fine-tune the model for a specific language.

Heads Mention Representation As mentioned above, the official scorer uses head-match evaluation. Inspired by word-level coreference resolution (Dobrovolskii, 2021), we decided to use only headwords for mention representation. Since the mentions are considered the same if they have the same head, we do not need the span reconstruction step as in Dobrovolskii (2021). As pointed out by (Dobrovolskii, 2021), a single-word representation reduces the mention space from quadratic to linear, and the model is learning more effectively. There are also much fewer potential false-positive mentions. Moreover, we believe that for very long mentions, the standard representation (sum of the start token, end token, and attended sum of all tokens) becomes insufficient. The syntactic information should be even more beneficial in case of heads mention representation. for the model, so we use it for all the datasets.

The whole model stays practically the same, we just change the span extraction step where we consider all words in the document as potential mentions.

Singletons Some datasets in the CorefUD collection have singletons annotated, and others do not. Specifically, in CorefUD 1.2, 10 out of 21 datasets have more than 10% singletons, and 8 of these have more than 70% singletons, which is probably a sign of consistent entity annotation independent of the coreference annotation. The original model by Lee et al. (2017) completely ignores singletons during training[2]. As a result, for these eight singleton-including datasets, we discard more than 70% of training data for mention identification task. To leverage this data, Pražák and Konopík (2024) incorporated singleton modeling into the model. They modify the loss function to model mentions

[2]The loss is the sum over all correct antecedents, and since singletons have no gold antecedents, they do not affect the loss

independently of coreference relations. In this approach, we simply add a binary cross-entropy of each span being a mention to the loss function. In other words, we add another classification head for the mention classification as formalized in Equation 2. where $y_m^{(i)}$ is 1 if span i corresponds to gold mention, 0 otherwise.

In the prediction step, the mention score is evaluated only for potential singletons. If a mention has no real antecedent, we look at the mention score. If it is likely to be a mention we make it a singleton, otherwise it is not a mention at all.

Large Model For Training the large model (mT5-xxl) we suggest using LORA. We propose two variants. In the first we use LORA for both joined pretraining and fine-tuning on individual datasets. In the second variant, we use traditional training of all the parameters in the joined pretraining phase and LORA only for fine-tuning on individual datasets. We tried several different values for LORA rank (size of the adapter layer) from 8 to 128

4 Training

We trained all the models on NVIDIA A40 graphic cards using online learning (batch size 1 document). We limit the maximum sequence length to 8 segments of 512 tokens. During training, if the document is longer than 8×512 tokens, a random segment offset is sampled to take a random continuous block of 8 segments, and the rest of them are discarded. During prediction, longer documents are split into sub-documents overlapping in one segment, which is then used to merge the coreference clusters from all the sub-documents. More details can be found in Pražák and Konopík (2024). We use 80k steps for model pre-training on all the datasets and approximately 30k for fine-tuning on each dataset. Pretraining took 24 hours and fine-tuning 2-6 hours.

5 Results & Discussion

Results of several variants of our model are presented in Table 3.

The table is divided into four sections, the first two comparing the results of different encoders (XLMR Roberta large and mT5-xxl). XLMR column has two variants, one using headwords as mention representations and the other using the whole spans. mT5 column contains two variants described in Section 3, full weights updating from pretraining and LORA even for pretraining. The third section contains results when selecting the best model on dev data. It contains the version *submitted* to the shared task and the version with optimal hyperparameter setting according to Pražák and Konopík (2024). The last section describes the same settings as the third one evaluated on CorefUD 1.1 (from CRAC 2023).

When we compare the first two sections, we can see that XLM-R achieves better results for some datasets than mT5; for others, it is the opposite. Generally, we can say that XLM-R is better for smaller datasets and mT5 for larger ones. This trend would suggest that mT5 is overfitted on smaller datasets. We tried many different values of the LORA factor and all the regularization parameters, but it did not yield better results. The larger model is harder to train, and we might not find the best combination of hyperparameters.

Full joined pretraining of mT5 is better than the LORA variant for all the datasets except for *en-parcorfull*, which we consider an anomaly.

FullSpan is surprisingly better than heads-only representation on *de-parcorfull* dataset. Again, we consider this an anomaly. ParCor datasets are the smallest ones in the collection and results on these datasets are very noisy. On average, *FullSpan* is almost 3% below heads-only. It is actually better for more datasets but this is caused by a mistake. We trained the model in the configuration from Pražák and Konopík (2024), so the model is not directly comparable to *XLMR-heads* column, but it is comparable to *BEST-dev-paper24* column. We did not have enough time to rerun the experiment.

We can compare the results for individual datasets between CorefUD 1.1 and CorefUD 1.2 from the last two sections of the Table. As expected, we can observe a performance drop from 1-4% for all datasets with empty nodes. On the other hand, we can see improvement for some datasets. It is known that there were mistakes in the Turkish dataset, where the improvement is most significant. Another significant improvement is there for Lithuanian.

One more thing worth noticing. Our model is much worse for newly added ancient languages than for the rest of the datasets (compared to *CorPipe*). We believed this was caused by a bug in the submitted version where we forgot to add new languages into joined pretraining. However, after fixing this, the results are very similar. We won-

Dataset/Model	XLMR		mT5		BEST-dev		CRAC23	
	FullSpan	heads	Full	LORA	submited	paper24	Submited	paper24
ca_ancora	75.29	80.58	**82.18**	80.11	82.37	81.29	75.49	82.57
cs_pcedt	68.96	**71.13**	67.67	62.46	71.13	73.5	77.37	78.46
cs_pdt	74.72	**77.14**	74.58	69.19	77.14	77.1	76.67	80.09
cu_proiel	43.23	54.24	44.53	44.61	54.24	53.2		
de_parcorfull	**81.23**	79.44	79.9	77.83	81.61	78.34	80.45	80.25
de_potsdamcc	76.77	76.76	**79.23**	75.08	79.23	77.41	78.17	77.95
en_gum	73.72	74.36	**75.98**	71.31	75.98	75.66	73.67	76
en_litbank	66.44	71.17	**73.31**	68.04	74.47	71.29		
en_parcorfull	**76.89**	70.81	69.84	70.32	70.81	70.51	67.92	67.41
es_ancora	76.81	81.4	**81.94**	79.63	82.08	81.61	77.62	82.92
fr_democrat	66.47	**65.72**	65.41	61.95	66.57	69.31	64.47	70.35
grc_proiel	58.22	**64.54**	60.25	59.18	64.54	63.1		
hbo_ptnk	46.25	59.68	**61.83**	59.8	63.44	56.93		
hu_korkor	65.58	**70.04**	**70.01**	65.22	70.69	69.9	70.55	74.01
hu_szegedkoref	68.03	69.89	69.53	69.2	70.25	70.08	68.82	70.9
lt_lcc	**78.44**	76.68	76.3	74.46	76.3	78.99	76.41	76.91
no_bokmaalnarc	76.64	77.25	**78**	74.77	79.21	78.02	76.48	78.62
no_nynorsknarc	77.88	78.72	78.41	75.06	78.72	78.59	77.55	80.41
pl_pcc	75.04	74.88	**76.07**	73.8	76.25	75.14	75.67	76.16
ru_rucor	74.31	73.45	**74.24**	71.69	75.03	75.96	70.03	77.56
tr_itcc	55	55.07	54.9	47.26	58.35	59.77	43.9	53.72
avg	69.33	71.57	71.15	68.14	72.78	72.18	72.43	75.55

Table 3: Results

system	ca_ancora	cs_pcedt	cs_pdt	cu_proiel	de_parcorfull	de_potsdam	en_gum	en_litbank	en_parcorfull	es_ancora	fr_democrat	grc_proiel	hbo_ptnk	hu_korkor	hu_szeged	lt_lcc	no_bokmaalnarc	no_nynorsknarc	pl_pcc	ru_rucor	tr_itcc	average
CorPipe-2stage	82.22	**74.85**	**77.18**	**61.58**	69.53	71.79	**75.66**	**79.60**	68.89	**82.46**	68.16	**71.34**	**72.02**	63.17	**69.97**	**75.79**	**79.81**	**78.01**	**78.50**	**83.22**	**68.18**	73.90
CorPipe	81.02	73.71	75.84	60.72	**71.68**	71.45	74.61	79.10	**69.75**	80.98	**68.77**	68.53	70.86	60.32	68.12	75.78	79.55	77.52	77.03	83.09	59.37	72.75
CorPipe-single	80.42	72.82	74.82	57.11	61.62	67.02	74.39	78.08	58.61	79.75	67.89	66.01	67.18	60.09	67.32	75.19	78.92	76.60	75.20	81.21	53.43	70.18
Ours	**82.46**	70.82	75.80	54.97	71.40	**71.91**	70.53	74.15	55.58	81.94	62.69	61.64	61.56	**64.86**	69.26	71.97	74.51	72.07	76.34	80.47	64.49	69.97
baseline	68.32	64.06	63.83	24.51	47.21	55.65	63.19	63.54	33.08	69.58	53.62	28.76	24.60	35.14	54.51	62.00	64.96	63.70	66.24	65.83	44.05	53.16

Table 4: Results on test set.

$$J(D) = \log \prod_{i=1}^{N} \sum_{\hat{y} \in Y(i) \cap \text{GOLD}(i)} P(\hat{y}) + \underbrace{y_m^{(i)} \cdot \sigma(s_m(i)) + (1 - y_m^{(i)}) \cdot \sigma(-s_m(i))}_{\text{singletons binary cross-entropy}} \tag{2}$$

der if *CorPipe* uses any specific improvements to handle these languages better. Another possible explanation is that they were able to train large model models better, and large model handles these ancient languages with very little data available better.

5.1 Comparison To Other Systems

The comparison to other participating systems is shown in Table 4. Our system ended up in 4th place (2nd team). Surprisingly, although the winning system outperformed ours by a large margin on average, our system reached the best performance for three datasets (*german_potsdam*, *catalan*, and *hungarian-korkor*). It would be interesting to examine the differences between the two systems to find out why.

6 Conclusion

We further extended our system from CRAC 2022 and 2023 with the usage of mT5 through LORA training. We provide the analysis of different model configurations. We found out that for approximately half of the datasets, using a larger model does not help anymore. We also analyzed a drop caused by losing the gold annotation of empty nodes. Unfortunately, we did not have enough time to add zero nodes prediction into our model. Our results suggest that there is a lot of space for improvement. Our system ended up in 4th place. Moreover, we reached the best performance on three datasets out of 21.

Acknowledgements

This work has been supported by by the Ministry of Education, Youth and Sports of the Czech Republic, Grant No. SGS-2022-016 Advanced methods of data processing and analysis. Computational resources were supplied by the project "e-Infrastruktura CZ" (e-INFRA CZ LM2018140) supported by the Ministry of Education, Youth and Sports of the Czech Republic.

References

Alexis Conneau, Kartikay Khandelwal, Naman Goyal, Vishrav Chaudhary, Guillaume Wenzek, Francisco Guzmán, Édouard Grave, Myle Ott, Luke Zettlemoyer, and Veselin Stoyanov. 2020. Unsupervised cross-lingual representation learning at scale. In *Proceedings of the 58th Annual Meeting of the Association for Computational Linguistics*, pages 8440–8451.

Jacob Devlin, Ming-Wei Chang, Kenton Lee, and Kristina Toutanova. 2018. BERT: pre-training of deep bidirectional transformers for language understanding. *CoRR*, abs/1810.04805.

Vladimir Dobrovolskii. 2021. Word-level coreference resolution. In *Proceedings of the 2021 Conference on Empirical Methods in Natural Language Processing*, pages 7670–7675, Online and Punta Cana, Dominican Republic. Association for Computational Linguistics.

Neil Houlsby, Andrei Giurgiu, Stanislaw Jastrzebski, Bruna Morrone, Quentin De Laroussilhe, Andrea Gesmundo, Mona Attariyan, and Sylvain Gelly. 2019. Parameter-efficient transfer learning for nlp. In *International conference on machine learning*, pages 2790–2799. PMLR.

Edward J Hu, yelong shen, Phillip Wallis, Zeyuan Allen-Zhu, Yuanzhi Li, Shean Wang, Lu Wang, and Weizhu Chen. 2022. LoRA: Low-rank adaptation of large language models. In *International Conference on Learning Representations*.

Mandar Joshi, Danqi Chen, Yinhan Liu, Daniel S. Weld, Luke Zettlemoyer, and Omer Levy. 2020. SpanBERT: Improving pre-training by representing and predicting spans. *Transactions of the Association for Computational Linguistics*, 8:64–77.

Mandar Joshi, Omer Levy, Luke Zettlemoyer, and Daniel S Weld. 2019. Bert for coreference resolution: Baselines and analysis. In *Proceedings of the 2019 Conference on Empirical Methods in Natural Language Processing and the 9th International Joint Conference on Natural Language Processing (EMNLP-IJCNLP)*, pages 5803–5808.

Kenton Lee, Luheng He, Mike Lewis, and Luke Zettlemoyer. 2017. End-to-end neural coreference resolution. In *Proceedings of the 2017 Conference on Empirical Methods in Natural Language Processing*, pages 188–197, Copenhagen, Denmark. Association for Computational Linguistics.

Kenton Lee, Luheng He, and Luke Zettlemoyer. 2018. Higher-order coreference resolution with coarse-to-fine inference. In *Proceedings of the 2018 Conference of the North American Chapter of the Association for Computational Linguistics: Human Language Technologies, Volume 2 (Short Papers)*, pages 687–692.

Anna Nedoluzhko, Michal Novák, Martin Popel, Zdeněk Žabokrtský, Amir Zeldes, and Daniel Zeman. 2022. Corefud 1.0: Coreference meets universal dependencies. In *Proceedings of LREC*.

Anna Nedoluzhko, Michal Novák, Martin Popel, Zdeněk Žabokrtský, and Daniel Zeman. 2021. *Coreference meets Universal Dependencies – a pilot experiment on harmonizing coreference datasets for 11 languages*. ÚFAL MFF UK, Praha, Czechia.

Michal Novák, Barbora Dohnalová, Miloslav Konopík, Anna Nedoluzhko, Maciej Ogrodniczuk, Martin Popel, Ondřej Pražák, Jakub Sido, Milan Straka, Zdeněk Žabokrtský, and Daniel Zeman. 2024. Findings of the third shared task on multilingual coreference resolution. In *Proceedings of the Seventh Workshop on Computational Models of Reference, Anaphora and Coreference*, Miami, Florida. Association for Computational Linguistics.

Ondřej Pražák and Miloslav Konopik. 2022. End-to-end multilingual coreference resolution with mention head prediction. In *Proceedings of the CRAC 2022 Shared Task on Multilingual Coreference Resolution*, pages 23–27, Gyeongju, Republic of Korea. Association for Computational Linguistics.

Ondřej Pražák, Miloslav Konopík, and Jakub Sido. 2021. Multilingual coreference resolution with harmonized annotations. In *Proceedings of the International Conference on Recent Advances in Natural Language Processing (RANLP 2021)*, pages 1119–1123.

Ondřej Pražák and Miloslav Konopík. 2024. Exploring multiple strategies to improve multilingual coreference resolution in corefud. *arXiv preprint arXiv:2408.16893*.

Milan Straka. 2023. Úfal corpipe at crac 2023: Larger context improves multilingual coreference resolution. In *Proceedings of the CRAC 2023 Shared Task on Multilingual Coreference Resolution*, pages 41–51.

Rhea Sukthanker, Soujanya Poria, Erik Cambria, and Ramkumar Thirunavukarasu. 2020. Anaphora and coreference resolution: A review. *Information Fusion*, 59:139–162.

Liyan Xu and Jinho D. Choi. 2020. Revealing the myth of higher-order inference in coreference resolution. In *Proceedings of the 2020 Conference on Empirical Methods in Natural Language Processing (EMNLP)*, pages 8527–8533, Online. Association for Computational Linguistics.

Linting Xue, Noah Constant, Adam Roberts, Mihir Kale, Rami Al-Rfou, Aditya Siddhant, Aditya Barua, and Colin Raffel. 2021. mT5: A massively multilingual pre-trained text-to-text transformer. In *Proceedings of the 2021 Conference of the North American Chapter of the Association for Computational Linguistics: Human Language Technologies*, pages 483–498, Online. Association for Computational Linguistics.

Zdeněk Žabokrtský, Miloslav Konopik, Anna Nedoluzhko, Michal Novák, Maciej Ogrodniczuk, Martin Popel, Ondrej Prazak, Jakub Sido, and Daniel Zeman. 2023. Findings of the second shared task on multilingual coreference resolution. In *Proceedings of the CRAC 2023 Shared Task on Multilingual Coreference Resolution*, pages 1–18, Singapore. Association for Computational Linguistics.

Zdeněk Žabokrtský, Miloslav Konopík, Anna Nedoluzhko, Michal Novák, Maciej Ogrodniczuk, Martin Popel, Ondřej Pražák, Jakub Sido, Daniel Zeman, and Yilun Zhu. 2022. Findings of the shared task on multilingual coreference resolution. In *Proceedings of the Fifth Workshop on Computational Models of Reference, Anaphora and Coreference*, Gyeongju, Republic of Korea. Association for Computational Linguistics.

Multilingual coreference resolution as text generation

Natalia Skachkova
DFKI / Saarland Informatics Campus, Saarbrücken, Germany
natalia.skachkova@dfki.de

Abstract

This paper presents a multilingual coreference resolution system *DFKI-CorefGen* submitted for the CRAC Shared Task 2024. We cast the task as text generation and use *mT5-base* as the pre-trained model. Our system takes the sixth place out of seven in the competition. We analyze the reasons for poor performance and suggest possible improvements.

1 Introduction

Coreference resolution is an important part of many natural language processing (NLP) tasks like question answering, information extraction, text summarization, etc. CRAC 2024 focuses on multilingual coreference resolution, which is less researched than the English one. It is also more challenging than monolingual coreference resolution, as the training data typically come from different sources and may be characterized by large variability in size, domain, the definition of markables, annotation consistency, completeness and quality. Ideally, a good multilingual coreference resolution system should be able to deal with these challenges without a significant performance loss.

Currently, many state-of-the-art (multilingual) coreference resolution systems are modifications of the model first introduced by Lee et al. (2017). They are typically characterized by rather complex architectures based on pre-trained large language models and require careful data preprocessing. One needs to have not only novel ideas, but also very good programming skills and mathematical knowledge to modify such architectures. Additionally, the approach has some inherent limitations, e.g., it is tricky to use to identify discontinuous mentions or split antecedents.

On the other hand, one is always searching for easier ways to solve a task. Such possibility is offered nowadays by large language models [1] (LLMs). They are generative models, which demonstrate an excellent performance in many NLP tasks (e.g., see Zhao et al., 2023; Minaee et al., 2024; Chang et al., 2024) and are relatively easy to use for inference. However, they have their shortcomings too, the most important being a huge number of parameters, so that one needs a lot of computational resources to use them.

The aim of this work is to check if we can cast multilingual coreference resolution as a text generation task using a much smaller model, like mT5-base (Xue et al., 2021).We try to keep the task as simple as possible. No careful pre-processing is required – the input is the raw text and the output is the same text marked with coreference clusters. To summarize, our contributions are as follows.

- We investigate how multilingual coreference resolution can be represented as a purely generative end-to-end task, and discuss challenges and limitations of the approach.
- We show that mT5-base is to certain extent capable of the task, but obviously not large enough to achieve good scores and compete with the baseline.

2 Related Work

One of the seminal and most successful coreference resolution models is the one by Lee et al. (2017). It is a span-based mention-ranking model. Namely, all spans in a document are treated as potential mentions and represented as context-depending embeddings. These spans are ranked and paired with the most likely antecedent spans.

A lot of the state-of-the-art coreference resolution models, no matter multilingual or not, inherit this architecture with some modifications. E.g., it is the case for all the systems whose descriptions

[1] We use this term to refer to all models that have $\geq$ 13B parameters.

Proceedings of the Seventh Workshop on Computational Models of Reference, Anaphora and Coreference (CRAC 2024), pages 114–122
November 15, 2024.

were submitted for CRAC 2023 (Žabokrtský et al., 2023).

There also exist works casting coreference resolution as a sequence-to-sequence problem. Some early experiments are conducted by Raffel et al. (2020), who apply the T5 model to resolve ambiguous pronouns in the WNLI, WSC (Levesque et al., 2012) and DPR (Rahman and Ng, 2012) data. They focus on separate pronouns and do not build any coreference chains or clusters, as the main goal is to evaluate the model's commonsense reasoning ability. Similar experiments (often on the same data), but with LLMs and few-shot prompting are presented by Perez et al. (2021), Min et al. (2022) and Lin et al. (2022).

Some researchers cast coreference resolution as a question answering task and use LLMs to generate answers. E.g., Wu et al. (2020) generate a list of coreferent mentions, given a question about an entity, Yang et al. (2022) generate "yes/no" answers, given a mention pair, Agrawal et al. (2022) generate the most likely antecedent, given an anaphor, and Le et al. (2022) - a chain of antecedents.

Another generative coreference resolution model is presented by Bohnet et al. (2023). It is a "link-append" transition system based on mT5-xl. It is multilingual and was successfully tested on English, Arabic, Chinese, Dutch, Catalan, German, Italian and Spanish data. As input it takes an encoding of the previous sentences annotated with coreference clusters, followed by the new sentence. As output, the system produces links from mentions in the new sentence to either previously created coreference clusters or to previous singleton mentions.

Other recent sequence-to-sequence approaches are introduced, e.g., by Urbizu et al. (2020), Paolini et al. (2021), Liu et al. (2022) and Zhang et al. (2023), who focus on English and generate coreference annotation, i.e. mentions and clusters they belong to, within the given text, typically using a fine-tuned encoder-decoder model.

Our approach DFKI-CorefGen falls into the latter category, but has the following differences. First, it is multilingual. Second, we keep the pretrained model frozen, and do prefix tuning (Li and Liang, 2021) instead. Third, we process the input text incrementally and teach our model to correct clustering mistakes in the previous sentences as well. Fourth, we create training data by corrupting the coreference annotations.

3 Method

We perform multilingual mention identification [2] and coreference resolution jointly and treat the task as text generation. Thus, given a piece of text, we want to find all mentions and group them into clusters by marking them in this text with square brackets and cluster identifiers. Example 3.1 demonstrates the idea on a short text sequence from the *en_parcorfull* corpus.

Example 3.1. Gold model output
[0 [1 The victim 1] 's brother 0] , [0 Louis Galicia 0] , told ABC station KGO in San Francisco that [1 Frank 1] , previously a line cook in Boston , had landed [1 his 1] dream job as line chef at [2 San Francisco 's Sons & Daughters 2] restaurant six months ago . [3 A spokesperson for [2 Sons & Daughters 2] 3] said [2 they 2] were " shocked and devastated " by [1 his 1] death .

The approach is implemented as a prefix tuning using OpenPrompt (Ding et al., 2022) with mT5-base as the core model. We apply prefix tuning, because mT5-base is relatively small (580M parameters) and thus not designed for inference in a zero- or few-shot manner. To save computational resources, we keep mT5-base frozen and tune only the prefix of 100 randomly initialized tokens. The input for the model, as shown in Example 3.2, contains a *[TEXT]* sequence, a task tag "coreference", and a *[MASK]* token, instead of which the model is to generate the *[TEXT]* with coreference clusters. No instructions or demonstrations are given to the model.

Example 3.2. Model input
[TEXT] Task: "coreference" [MASK]

We train one model for all the languages, using the official training data only. It is done on one NVIDIA GeForce GTX TITAN X GPU with 12 GB memory for five epochs with the batch size 1, the *AdamW* optimizer, learning rate of 5e-5 and a linear schedule with warm-up.

3.1 Input data

As the input length of mT5-base is limited by 1024 sub-tokens, we have to split each document into several pieces. In addition, our initial experiments showed that the model struggles finding the correct clusters, if it receives the whole raw piece of text

[2]Discontinuous mentions are discarded. Empty tokens (zero anaphora), represented as an underscore "_" in the data, are treated like all other tokens.

as input, especially if this piece is long. We deal with this challenge as follows.

First, we limit the length of each input piece by five sentences that can have various lengths but are no longer than 512 sub-tokens. Second, the task becomes easier, if some clusters (not necessarily always correctly marked) are already identified. Therefore, we proceed with the task incrementally, i.e., we start with giving the model the very first sentence and asking to find the clusters there, then we add the second sentence and ask the model to do the same task, revising its initial predictions, and so on until the five-sentence text piece is over.

To teach our model to do that, we create input data by splitting the five-sentence pieces into overlapping sub-pieces of 1-5 sentences long and corrupting the gold annotations in them. Now, if a sub-piece consists of a single sentence only, we remove all the clusters' annotations from it, if there are any. If the sub-piece is longer, we completely remove the annotations from the very last sentence, and either keep or (partially) corrupt the annotations in the previous ones. Keeping sub-pieces with correct clusters is needed to create examples which help the model differentiate between "good" and "bad" cluster annotations. If a gold text piece does not contain any clusters at all, we keep it as it is and consider it a negative example, as the model does not need to annotate anything there at all.

Theoretically, we can create an infinite number of training examples by corrupting the gold annotations in all possible ways. However, as we are limited by time and computational resources, we want to pick out only the most useful ones. To do so, we first conduct some experiments, where our model has to deal with the raw pieces without any clusters (wrong or correct) marked in them. Based on these experiments' results, we collect the most frequent generation error types and come up with the following modifications of the gold clusters.

First, we discard the annotations of half of the clusters in the sub-piece. Second, we merge half of the clusters together. Namely, we first divide all the clusters in the sub-piece in two groups, then merge them pairwise randomly. Third, we split half of the non-singleton clusters. Each one is picked out randomly and split in two. Fourth, we mix non-singleton clusters so that the number of mentions in each cluster stays the same, but half of the mentions in them is wrong. Fifth, we violate some mentions' boundaries.

Additionally, we have to deal with all sorts of repetitions that are a problem of many generative models including mT5 (Holtzman et al., 2020, Fu et al., 2021). Our initial experiments show that mT5-base has a tendency to generate excessively the cluster markers with or without mentions inside, as well as duplicates of marked mentions. To deal with these issues, we adopt two more types of corrupted training examples.

First, we append / prepend excessive cluster identifiers to some mentions. We also insert empty ones, i.e., opening and closing brackets with indices not marking any mentions, like '[4 4]'. Second, given some randomly chosen marked mentions, we extend the original text with their duplicates. The number of duplicates typically varies from two to five.

Finally, we address two more generation problems. Namely, mT5-base tends to excessively generate either empty square brackets, or just sequences of numbers with or without square brackets. And sometimes mT5 refuses to generate any cluster markers at all. We deal with these problems as follows.

Based on the observation that the sequences of '[', ']', '[0]', '[1]', '0', '[0]' and '[1]' are among the most frequent generation errors, we create training examples by randomly inserting such sequences into gold sub-pieces. To make the model learn that it should not just copy the input text, but mark some clusters, we create additional training examples by simply removing all the gold annotations from the sub-pieces. Appendix A.3 gives examples of the main modification types discussed above.

Importantly, we noticed that it is easier for the model to perform the task, if the clusters' identifiers are consecutive, i.e., they should be assigned depending on the order in which the corresponding mentions occur. Therefore, to create each training example we always re-index all the mentions in the given sub-piece.

As a result, given one gold sub-piece, we make from one to twelve training examples, depending on the sub-piece length. Each example contains only a single modification. We first create training and development data from each official dataset. Next, we randomly sample 2,000 training and 70 development examples from the respective parts of each set, regardless of the fact that some languages, e.g., English and German, are represented by several datasets. The distribution of positive and negative examples in the data is shown in Table 1.

Data	Negative (w/o clusters)	Positive		Total
		correct	corrupted	
train	172 (0.4%)	5,220 (12.4%)	36,608 (87.2%)	42,000
dev	4 (0.3%)	173 (11.8%)	1,293 (87.9%)	1,470

Table 1: Distribution of positive and negative examples in the data

3.2 Inference

As mentioned earlier, the main idea is to process the given document incrementally, annotating clusters in each new sentence and correcting the annotations in previous context. During training DFKI-CorefGen learns to deal with sequences up to five sentences long. However, we cannot simply split each document into pieces of five (or less) sentences, because in this case it will be impossible to merge the clusters stretching across several pieces. Therefore, we process the given document using a sliding window of five sentences which moves with a step of two sentences, so that each window contains two new sentences. Because our model expects only one "raw" (i.e., unannotated) sentence, these new sentences are also processed incrementally, one by one. We re-index the clusters in each piece.

Despite having special training examples aimed at dealing with repetitions, hallucinations, or truncation of text, these errors are still very common. Therefore, after having processed a piece, we have to align the generated and gold sequences (see example in Appendix A.4). To avoid cumbersome token level sequence matching, in the future we may switch to generation of dummy tokens instead of the real ones, similarly to Urbizu et al. (2020) and Zhang et al. (2023). Finally, to get clusters for the whole document, we merge clusters found in each piece based on mentions overlap.

4 Results and discussion

DFKI-CorefGen takes the sixth place out of seven with an average 33.38 F1 score. It is far below the 53.16 F1 score achieved by the baseline (Pražák et al., 2021). The results for separate datasets are given in Appendix A.1.

To large extent, bad scores can be explained by the nature of our approach. It resolves coreference incrementally, thus, during inference it is important to (at least partially) correctly identify clusters in the very first sentence. Otherwise, the errors accumulate with each new sentence, so that there are too many of them for the model to correct. We found out that our model is not really good at this task - it achieves the F1 score of only 42.59 when applied on 1,996 single sentences sampled from the gold development data. One possible reason for that is the lack of training examples consisting of one sentence only, as our focus is on clustering and correction of previously assigned clusters in a larger context. In total we only have 1,133 (2.7%) and 33 (2.4%) training and development examples consisting of single sentences that may or may not have gold clusters.

However, we hypothesize that the main reason for such an unsatisfactory performance is that mT5-base is simply not large enough for the task. Small model size also causes difficulties in performing the task for longer inputs, and very persistent hallucinations and repetitions in the output. E.g., currently we limit the sub-piece length by five sentences, which is sub-optimal, as we loose too many clusters by doing so (see Appendix A.2).

Another important negative factor is a small training data size - due to time constraint and limited computational resources we take only 2,000 training samples from each dataset.

Finally, our current method of corrupting the gold annotations may also be sub-optimal. Further experiments are required to decide how many and which clusters are better to mix, merge or split, how many duplicates to insert, how long they should be and so on. Also, different generation errors may be typical for different datasets, languages and script systems.

5 Conclusion

In this paper we introduce a simple and purely generative end-to-end approach to multilingual coreference resolution. We show that it is capable of the task, but suffers from certain limitations, like a small size of the pre-trained model and a lack of training data, that prevent it from achieving good scores. We believe that replacing mT5-base with a LLM of much larger size can help reach better results and avoid complicated post-processing. We leave such experiments along with a proper ablation study for future work.

Acknowledgments

The research in this paper has been funded by the Horizon Europe project Fluently (grant ID 101058680).

References

Monica Agrawal, Stefan Hegselmann, Hunter Lang, Yoon Kim, and David Sontag. 2022. Large language models are few-shot clinical information extractors. In *Proceedings of the 2022 Conference on Empirical Methods in Natural Language Processing*, pages 1998–2022, Abu Dhabi, United Arab Emirates. Association for Computational Linguistics.

Bernd Bohnet, Chris Alberti, and Michael Collins. 2023. Coreference resolution through a seq2seq transition-based system. *Transactions of the Association for Computational Linguistics*, 11:212–226.

Yupeng Chang, Xu Wang, Jindong Wang, Yuan Wu, Linyi Yang, Kaijie Zhu, Hao Chen, Xiaoyuan Yi, Cunxiang Wang, Yidong Wang, et al. 2024. A survey on evaluation of large language models. *ACM Transactions on Intelligent Systems and Technology*, 15(3):1–45.

Ning Ding, Shengding Hu, Weilin Zhao, Yulin Chen, Zhiyuan Liu, Haitao Zheng, and Maosong Sun. 2022. OpenPrompt: An open-source framework for prompt-learning. In *Proceedings of the 60th Annual Meeting of the Association for Computational Linguistics: System Demonstrations*, pages 105–113, Dublin, Ireland. Association for Computational Linguistics.

Zihao Fu, Wai Lam, Anthony Man-Cho So, and Bei Shi. 2021. A theoretical analysis of the repetition problem in text generation. *Proceedings of the AAAI Conference on Artificial Intelligence*, 35(14):12848–12856.

Ari Holtzman, Jan Buys, Li Du, Maxwell Forbes, and Yejin Choi. 2020. The curious case of neural text degeneration. In *International Conference on Learning Representations*.

Nghia T. Le, Fan Bai, and Alan Ritter. 2022. Few-shot anaphora resolution in scientific protocols via mixtures of in-context experts. In *Proceedings of Conference on Empirical Methods in Natural Language Processing*.

Kenton Lee, Luheng He, Mike Lewis, and Luke Zettlemoyer. 2017. End-to-end neural coreference resolution. In *Proceedings of the 2017 Conference on Empirical Methods in Natural Language Processing*, pages 188–197, Copenhagen, Denmark. Association for Computational Linguistics.

Hector Levesque, Ernest Davis, and Leora Morgenstern. 2012. The Winograd schema challenge. In *Proceedings of the Thirteenth international conference on the principles of knowledge representation and reasoning*.

Xiang Lisa Li and Percy Liang. 2021. Prefix-tuning: Optimizing continuous prompts for generation. In *Proceedings of the 59th Annual Meeting of the Association for Computational Linguistics and the 11th International Joint Conference on Natural Language Processing (Volume 1: Long Papers)*, pages 4582–4597, Online. Association for Computational Linguistics.

Xi Victoria Lin, Todor Mihaylov, Mikel Artetxe, Tianlu Wang, Shuohui Chen, Daniel Simig, Myle Ott, Naman Goyal, Shruti Bhosale, Jingfei Du, Ramakanth Pasunuru, Sam Shleifer, Punit Singh Koura, Vishrav Chaudhary, Brian O'Horo, Jeff Wang, Luke Zettlemoyer, Zornitsa Kozareva, Mona Diab, Veselin Stoyanov, and Xian Li. 2022. Few-shot learning with multilingual generative language models. In *Proceedings of the 2022 Conference on Empirical Methods in Natural Language Processing*, pages 9019–9052, Abu Dhabi, United Arab Emirates. Association for Computational Linguistics.

Tianyu Liu, Yuchen Eleanor Jiang, Nicholas Monath, Ryan Cotterell, and Mrinmaya Sachan. 2022. Autoregressive structured prediction with language models. In *Findings of the Association for Computational Linguistics: EMNLP 2022*, pages 993–1005, Abu Dhabi, United Arab Emirates. Association for Computational Linguistics.

Sewon Min, Mike Lewis, Luke Zettlemoyer, and Hannaneh Hajishirzi. 2022. MetaICL: Learning to learn in context. In *Proceedings of the 2022 Conference of the North American Chapter of the Association for Computational Linguistics: Human Language Technologies*, pages 2791–2809, Seattle, United States. Association for Computational Linguistics.

Shervin Minaee, Tomas Mikolov, Narjes Nikzad, Meysam Chenaghlu, Richard Socher, Xavier Amatriain, and Jianfeng Gao. 2024. Large language models: A survey. *arXiv preprint arXiv:2402.06196*.

Giovanni Paolini, Ben Athiwaratkun, Jason Krone, Jie Ma, Alessandro Achille, Rishita Anubhai, Cícero Nogueira dos Santos, Bing Xiang, and Stefano Soatto. 2021. Structured prediction as translation between augmented natural languages. *ArXiv*, abs/2101.05779.

Ethan Perez, Douwe Kiela, and Kyunghyun Cho. 2021. True few-shot learning with language models. *Advances in neural information processing systems*, 34:11054–11070.

Ondřej Pražák, Miloslav Konopík, and Jakub Sido. 2021. Multilingual coreference resolution with harmonized annotations. In *Proceedings of the International Conference on Recent Advances in Natural Language Processing (RANLP 2021)*, pages 1119–1123.

Colin Raffel, Noam Shazeer, Adam Roberts, Katherine Lee, Sharan Narang, Michael Matena, Yanqi Zhou, Wei Li, and Peter J. Liu. 2020. Exploring the limits of transfer learning with a unified text-to-text transformer. *Journal of Machine Learning Research*, 21(140):1–67.

Altaf Rahman and Vincent Ng. 2012. Resolving complex cases of definite pronouns: The Winograd schema challenge. In *Proceedings of the 2012 Joint*

Conference on Empirical Methods in Natural Language Processing and Computational Natural Language Learning, pages 777–789, Jeju Island, Korea. Association for Computational Linguistics.

Milan Straka. 2023. ÚFAL CorPipe at CRAC 2023: Larger context improves multilingual coreference resolution. In *Proceedings of the CRAC 2023 Shared Task on Multilingual Coreference Resolution*, pages 41–51, Singapore. Association for Computational Linguistics.

Gorka Urbizu, Ander Soraluze, and Olatz Arregi. 2020. Sequence to sequence coreference resolution. In *Proceedings of the Third Workshop on Computational Models of Reference, Anaphora and Coreference*, pages 39–46, Barcelona, Spain (online). Association for Computational Linguistics.

Wei Wu, Fei Wang, Arianna Yuan, Fei Wu, and Jiwei Li. 2020. CorefQA: Coreference resolution as query-based span prediction. In *Proceedings of the 58th Annual Meeting of the Association for Computational Linguistics*, pages 6953–6963, Online. Association for Computational Linguistics.

Linting Xue, Noah Constant, Adam Roberts, Mihir Kale, Rami Al-Rfou, Aditya Siddhant, Aditya Barua, and Colin Raffel. 2021. mT5: A massively multilingual pre-trained text-to-text transformer. In *Proceedings of the 2021 Conference of the North American Chapter of the Association for Computational Linguistics: Human Language Technologies*, pages 483–498, Online. Association for Computational Linguistics.

Xiaohan Yang, Eduardo Peynetti, Vasco Meerman, and Chris Tanner. 2022. What GPT knows about who is who. In *Proceedings of the Third Workshop on Insights from Negative Results in NLP*, pages 75–81, Dublin, Ireland. Association for Computational Linguistics.

Zdeněk Žabokrtský, Miloslav Konopik, Anna Nedoluzhko, Michal Novák, Maciej Ogrodniczuk, Martin Popel, Ondrej Prazak, Jakub Sido, and Daniel Zeman. 2023. Findings of the second shared task on multilingual coreference resolution. In *Proceedings of the CRAC 2023 Shared Task on Multilingual Coreference Resolution*, pages 1–18, Singapore. Association for Computational Linguistics.

Wenzheng Zhang, Sam Wiseman, and Karl Stratos. 2023. Seq2seq is all you need for coreference resolution. In *Proceedings of the 2023 Conference on Empirical Methods in Natural Language Processing*, pages 11493–11504, Singapore. Association for Computational Linguistics.

Wayne Xin Zhao, Kun Zhou, Junyi Li, Tianyi Tang, Xiaolei Wang, Yupeng Hou, Yingqian Min, Beichen Zhang, Junjie Zhang, Zican Dong, et al. 2023. A survey of large language models. *arXiv preprint arXiv:2303.18223*.

A Appendix

A.1 Results

Table 2 presents official F1 scores on 21 test sets in comparison with the scores achieved by the baseline and the winning *straka-twostage* [3] model.

Data	Ours	Bsl.	Best
avg. (place)	33.38 (6)	53.16 (5)	73.90 (1)
ca_ancora	34.77	68.32	82.22
cs_pcedt	32.89	64.06	74.85
cs_pdt	30.88	63.83	77.18
cu_proiel	22.52	24.51	61.58
de_parcorfull	23.07	47.21	69.53
de_potsdamcc	45.85	55.65	71.79
en_gum	35.49	63.19	75.66
en_litbank	46.59	63.54	79.60
en_parcorfull	32.69	33.08	68.89
es_ancora	37.76	69.58	82.46
fr_democrat	36.34	53.62	68.16
grc_proiel	25.87	28.76	71.34
hbo_ptnk	37.96	24.60	72.02
hu_korkor	23.53	35.14	63.17
hu_szegedkoref	33.85	54.51	69.97
lt_lcc	42.73	62.00	75.79
no_bokmaalnarc	37.92	64.96	79.81
no_nynorsknarc	35.69	63.70	78.01
pl_pcc	27.19	66.24	78.50
ru_rucor	47.79	65.83	83.22
tr_itcc	9.65	44.05	68.18

Table 2: F1 scores on the test data.

A.2 Input length impact

As our approach struggles with cluster assignment in longer text sequences, we limit the input length by five sentences up to 512 sub-tokens in total. This leads to the following problems. First, long distance coreference cannot be recovered. Second, certain clusters get split into two or more clusters. Third, the number of singletons grows. To see how many clusters get lost due to such document splitting, we perform an experiment, where we first split the gold data into pieces keeping all the annotations, and then merge them back trying to restore the clusters. Table 3 shows the results for eight development datasets out of 21 official ones. The numbers clearly indicate that even the perfect system will be able to achieve only 84.58 F1 score on average, if its input is limited by five sentences.

[3]It is an updated version of the model presented in Straka (2023)

Data	w sngl.	w/o sngl.
avg.	84.58	82.89
ca_ancora	89.29	90.97
en_gum	89.34	81.67
hbo_ptnk	91.77	82.72
hu_korkor	86.07	86.86
lt_lcc	83.63	86.68
pl_pcc	92.77	85.86
ru_rucor	73.38	76.73
tr_itcc	70.40	71.63

Table 3: F1 scores on the gold development data with and without singleton clusters.

One of the obvious solutions to the problem would be to use a larger pre-trained model that is capable of processing longer inputs. Also, it is important to set the number of sub-tokens as the main constraint, and not the number of sentences, as sentences can be very short in some datasets.

A.3 Data augmentation

The examples below illustrate how we modify the gold coreference annotations in order to create our training data. The gold annotation examples are taken from the *en_gum* corpus.
Gold annotations: *Thus , [0 the time [1 it 1] takes 0] and [2 the ways of visually exploring [3 an artwork 3] 2] can inform about [4 [3 its 3] relevance 4] , [5 interestingness 5] , and even [6 [3 its 3] aesthetic appeal 6] . [7 This paper 7] describes [8 a collaborative pilot project 8] focusing on [9 a unique collection of [10 [11 17th Century 11] [12 Zurbarán 12] paintings 10] 9] . [9 The [13 Jacob 13] cycle at [14 [15 Auckland 15] Castle 14] 9] is [9 the only [16 UK 16] example of [17 a continental collection preserved in situ in [18 purpose - built surroundings 18] 17] 9] .*

Example A.1. Discarding clusters
Thus , the time [0 it 0] takes and the ways of visually exploring [1 an artwork 1] can inform about [2 [1 its 1] relevance 2] , [3 interestingness 3] , and even [1 its 1] aesthetic appeal .

Example A.2. Merging clusters
Thus , [0 the time [1 it 1] takes 0] and [0 the ways of visually exploring [3 an artwork 3] 0] can inform about [1 [3 its 3] relevance 1] , [5 interestingness 5] , and even [3 [3 its 3] aesthetic appeal 3] .

Example A.3. Splitting clusters
Thus , [0 the time [1 it 1] takes 0] and [2 the ways of visually exploring [3 an artwork 3] 2] can inform

about [4 [7 its 7] relevance 4] , [5 interestingness 5] , and even [6 [7 its 7] aesthetic appeal 6] .

Example A.4. Mixing clusters
Thus , [0 the time [1 it 1] takes 0] and [2 the ways of visually exploring [9 an artwork 9] 2] can inform about [4 [9 its 9] relevance 4] , [5 interestingness 5] , and even [6 [9 its 9] aesthetic appeal 6] . [7 This paper 7] describes [8 a collaborative pilot project 8] focusing on [3 a unique collection of [10 [11 17th Century 11] [12 Zurbarán 12] paintings 10] 3] . [3 The [13 Jacob 13] cycle at [14 [15 Auckland 15] Castle 14] 3] is [3 the only [16 UK 16] example of [17 a continental collection preserved in situ in [18 purpose - built surroundings 18] 17] 3] .

Example A.5. Inserting lonely cluster IDs
Thus , [0 the [0 0] time [1 it 1] 1] [0 0] takes 0] and [0 0] [2 the ways of visually exploring [3 an artwork [3 3] 3] 2] 2] [3 3] can inform about [4 [3 its 3] [3 3] relevance 4] 4] , [5 [2 2] interestingness 5] , and even [6 [4 [3 its 3] [4 4] aesthetic appeal 6] .

Example A.6. Inserting repetitions
Thus , [0 the time [1 it 1] [1 it 1] [1 it 1] takes 0] and [2 the ways of visually exploring [3 an artwork 3] 2] can inform about [4 [3 its 3] [3 its 3] relevance 4] , [5 interestingness 5] , and even [6 [3 its 3] [3 its 3] [3 its 3] [3 its 3] [3 its 3] aesthetic appeal 6] .

Example A.7. Violating mention boundaries
Thus , [0 [1 the time it 1] takes and [2 0] the ways of [3 visually exploring an artwork 3] 2] can inform about [4 [3 its 3] relevance [5 4] , interestingness 5] , and even [6 [3 its 3] aesthetic appeal 6] . This paper describes a collaborative pilot project focusing on a unique collection of 17th Century Zurbarán paintings .

Additionally, we modify original coreference annotations in short text sequences (containing up to three sentences) inserting empty brackets.
Gold: *[0 Aesthetic Appreciation 0] and [1 Spanish Art 1] : [2 Insights from [3 [4 Eye 4] - Tracking 3] 2]*

Example A.8. Adding empty brackets
[0 Aesthetic Appreciation [0] and [1 Spanish Art 1] : Insights from Eye - Tracking

A.4 Alignment

A generated sequence with cluster identifiers may differ a lot from the original string. It can contain hallucinated tokens, unnecessary repetitions, or be truncated. Such problems are especially frequent when smaller models like *mT5-base* are used. In such cases it is impossible to extract the correct mention indices, even if certain mentions were correctly identified and clustered. To solve this problem, we try to transform the generated text into the gold one, keeping the cluster indices.

We use the *difflib* library for this task. The algorithm splits the generated string into parts and suggests one of the four actions, namely *'insert'*, *'delete'*, *'replace'* and *'equal'*, to be performed for each part. If *'delete'* or *'replace'* actions are chosen, we follow the commands, but keep all the cluster identifiers, no matter wrong or correct. We show how a generated text can be aligned with the gold one below. Example A.9 illustrates the steps of the sequence matcher from *difflib*.

Generated text: *Thus , [0 [1 the time it 1] takes and [2 0] the ways of [3 visually exploring an artwork 3] 2] can inform about [4 [3 its 3] relevance [5 4] relevance [5 4] relevance [5 4] relevance [5 4] relevance [5 4]*

Gold text: *Thus , the time it takes and the ways of visually exploring an artwork can inform about its relevance , interestingness , and even its aesthetic appeal .*

Example A.9. Alignment

equal	*"Thus ," → "Thus ,"*
delete	*"[0 [1" → ""*
equal	*"the time it" → "the time it"*
delete	*"1]" → ""*
equal	*"takes and" → "takes and"*
delete	*"[2 0]" → ""*
equal	*"the ways of" → "the ways of"*
delete	*"[3" → ""*
equal	*"visually exploring an artwork" → "visually exploring an artwork"*
delete	*"3] 2]" → ""*
equal	*"can inform about" → "can inform about"*
delete	*"[4 [3" → ""*
equal	*"its" → "its"*
delete	*"3]" → ""*
equal	*"relevance" → "relevance"*
replace	*"[5 4] relevance [5 4] relevance [5 4] relevance [5 4] relevance [5 4]" → ", interestingness , and even its aesthetic appeal ."*

Aligned result: *Thus , [0 [1 the time it 1] takes and [2 0] the ways of [3 visually exploring an artwork*

3] 2] can inform about [4 [3 its 3] relevance [5 4] [5 4] [5 4] [5 4] [5 4] , interestingness , and even its aesthetic appeal .

Note that the aligned text above contains some excessive cluster identifiers, and certain mention boundaries are wrong. We discard all the opening brackets that cannot be properly closed later during the post-processing.

Author Index